Vinyl F

Vinyl Freak

**Love Letters
to a Dying
Medium**

**John
Corbett**

DUKE UNIVERSITY PRESS *Durham + London* 2017

Cover designed by Matt Tauch. Text designed
by Amy Ruth Buchanan. Typeset in Minion Pro
by Westchester Publishing Services.

Library of Congress Cataloging-in-Publication Data
Names: Corbett, John, [date] author.
Title: Vinyl freak : love letters to a dying medium /
John Corbett.
Description: Durham : Duke University Press, 2017. |
Description based on print version record and CIP data
provided by publisher; resource not viewed.
Identifiers:
LCCN 2016048113 (print)
LCCN 2016045049 (ebook)
ISBN 9780822373155 (ebook)
ISBN 9780822363507 (hardcover : alk. paper)
ISBN 9780822363668 (pbk. : alk. paper)
Subjects: LCSH: Sound recordings—Collectors and
collecting—United States. | Sound recordings—Reviews. |
Jazz—Discography.
Classification: LCC ML1055 (print) | LCC ML1055.C74 2017
(ebook) | DDC 780.26/6—dc23
LC record available at https://lccn.loc.gov/2016048113

COVER ART: Mauricio Kagel, *Towards a Higher
Low-Fidelity*, 1970. Courtesy of the Mauricio Kagel
Estate. FRONTISPIECE: Drawing by Michael Jackson,
2000 (original logo for the *DownBeat* magazine Vinyl
Freak column).

DUKE UNIVERSITY PRESS GRATEFULLY ACKNOWLEDGES
THE SUPPORT OF THE GLOBALIZATION AND THE ARTIST
PROJECT OF THE DUKE UNIVERSITY CENTER FOR
INTERNATIONAL STUDIES, WHICH PROVIDED FUNDS
TOWARD THE PRODUCTION OF THIS BOOK.

My roots are in my record player.
—Evan Parker

Before gas came along, if you traded in whale
blubber, you were the richest man on earth.
Then gas came along and you'd be stuck with
your whale blubber. Sorry mate—history's moving along. Recorded music equals whale blubber.
Eventually, something else will replace it.
—Brian Eno

Contents

Track Three / Freak, Not Snob

Column Two / 2004–2006

Track Four / Brand New Secondhand: Record Collector Subcultures   113

Column Three / 2006–2012

/ **Formation of a Freak**

A Day in the Life of a Dinosaur was my first taste of vinyl. I was three. I remember listening to it, holding the bright red gatefold sleeve, studying the cartoon reptile, my special friend who multiple times a day would crawl into my ears. Soon thereafter I was given a *Batman & Robin* LP, my first encounter with Sun Ra, who worked as a session musician on the recording. I was a bit young to see the Arkestra in the mid-1960s, but because of records I could listen to the uncredited band playing the Batman theme, probably planting a seed that would be harvested forty years later. What did I know? I was just out of diapers.

I loved my records, even if I was rough on them. My parents tried to show me how to care for them, and I took their instruction to heart as best a drooling, uncoordinated little kid can, avoiding contact with the grooves, holding them between two flattened hands, learning to flip them by making a fulcrum in each palm, sliding them in and out of the inner sleeve, always putting it back in with the opening at the top so that the outer sleeve keeps the disc from slipping out. Habits that are now second nature.

At five I was listening to a Peter Rabbit record that had a big impact. Peter expresses confusion about why he sometimes misbehaves, singing: "Why do I do it, what can it be . . . ?" The way he phrased it, I heard "do it" as one word. "What does *doyt* mean?" I asked my mother. She tried to explain that it was two words, but I was adamant. If I relax my rational brain, I still wonder what he meant. When I trace my interest in sound poetry, I think this is its origin.

My folks had diverse taste in records, nothing too strange but some jazz, classical, folk, and pretty early on Beatles records. Babysitters were impressed at that. Maybe most interesting to me was an LP by Flanders & Swann, a

British comedy team. I learned to recite the routines by heart, listening to them repeatedly. Snippets made their way into daily life, a gag from the track about a dinner party at a cannibal's house transformed into a little premeal mantra: "A chorus of yums ran round the table—roast leg of insurance salesman!" I can hear my father reciting this punch line incessantly.

Comedy records were especially formative. My mom's brother, Uncle Tim, turned me on to George Carlin, total linguistics revelation, probably why I am a writer. Neighborhood friends played Richard Pryor, another epiphany, and Monty Python's Flying Circus. On the latter, a slip groove—two grooves running in parallel so that any play might equally get one or the other—completely astonished me and brought my attention directly to the technology of the record album and its status as an object. Like any kid growing up when I did, Cheech & Chong were essential; later on Steve Martin assumed the position of a nerdy high priest with his hilarious first LP. An early girlfriend, when I was about thirteen, played Firesign Theater for me. The side-long track "The Further Adventures of Nick Danger, Third Eye" became a talisman, with submerged drug and sex references that I didn't fully understand for decades, all secreted within a self-referential narrative that set me up to read Donald Barthelme and John Barth.

I recall vividly my first experience purchasing records. It was at the mall, of course, right next to the Spencer Gifts, where I bought my velvet black light poster of a swooping owl and felt the inexplicable draw of a pet rock. I had enough money saved to purchase two LPs. After much consideration, I narrowed it down to Elton John's *Greatest Hits* and *Honey* by the Ohio Players. My best friend, Scooter Johns, and I loved Elton, so the music was the motivating force in that case, but with the Ohio Players, while I dug the record's hit "Love Rollercoaster," I must confess ulterior motives for buying the record, which sported a soft-core cover of a beautiful nude woman drizzling herself with honey. Already, it was not only the music that attracted me to vinyl but the whole package. The cover was a vehicle for other kinds of information and imagery, a springboard for fantasy. Also, I was an adolescent. I took sexy stuff anywhere I could find it. I remember the electric feeling that came with putting the record on the counter and giving the clerk some cash. It was a jolt that I came to crave, perhaps some kind of sublimated sexual thing. In any case, it never went away.

By this time I was already a seasoned collector. I was born with the genetic collecting disposition. I collected butterflies, chloroforming them and pinning them to mounts, and I was good at capturing very rare ones. I also collected live animals, mostly amphibians and reptiles. Uncle Tim bought me some stamps, and I got the philatelary bug, collected them seriously for a while; I was drawn to weirder specimens, like some beautiful triangular ones from Albania that were rarer if they had been canceled, a flip on the normal search for mint uncanceled ones. I managed to get a copy of the first stamp, the British Penny Black, and I invested in a bunch of sheets of the world's first self-adhesive stamp, thinking it would be valuable one day and not realizing that the glue backing was acidic and would burn through to the front. Next in the queue were baseball cards. I distinguished myself from my classmates by seeking older cards, buying weird black-and-white ones from the '30s and the tall, thin tobacco cards from even earlier. I would show them off, and my friends would scoff, holding out the dozen contemporary copies of a Hank Aaron card that they had extracted from hundreds of bubblegum packages. Again, the weirder and more arcane objects were fascinating to me. What my buddies did, I figured, was not collecting. It was *amassing*. A collector must hunt, and to hunt you have to have elusive prey. Anyone could amass, but it took something more to collect.

Record collecting started with those first two LPs and was always inextricably linked with a kind of connoisseurship, looking for new experiences in music, adding to my understanding of the world by way of sound. I eventually grew to see myself as a record collector, and by 1976, when I left Philadelphia, the town where I'd started the collection, I had already begun shopping at used record shops, acquiring such essential releases as the debut LPs by Starz and Dust (the latter sporting a Frank Frazzetta painting that caught my numbskull eye), Ted Nugent's *Cat Scratch Fever*, and several Pink Floyd releases, which were considered so weird in my circle of friends that I might well have been listening to musique concrète or field recordings of frogs. Good thing they didn't know about my small collection of . . . frog pond records. I remember the feeling of ill ease going into the used record shop, the wooden bins full of things I didn't recognize, acres of jazz records, classical avant-garde, bluegrass and hillbilly and rockabilly and surf. These terms I could not yet decipher. Deeply meaningful labels that meant nothing yet. It felt the same as walking into an R-rated film, recognizing that there was a parallel universe of significance as yet unyielding of its secrets, a mute realm that was nonetheless uncontrollably seductive. I bought things indiscriminately, experimentally, sometimes foolishly, often led by the cover. Other times I researched like a hound, mapping webs of association, connecting the dots, plotting musical genealogies like I was charting a family tree.

The more immersed I grew, the more I discovered that the universe of records was one of exploration. I wrote the essay for my college application about how records had made me interested in world culture. It was true, if by world culture you mean the streets of 1970s London, but most of all records made me interested in more records. When I went away to school, I took my complete collection, totaling eight hundred LPs. Somehow, by the end of school, I had managed to push that to four thousand. How I did so on my nonexistent college kid budget is a mystery. But record fiends are just like junkies; they'd rather get a fix than eat or see a movie. Or pay their phone bill. I was studying film, so going to movies was covered, and I ate at the cafeteria, so hey, let them turn off the electricity. I get all the power I need from my new Cecil Taylor box set!

The bulk of my identity as a collector was done forming by the time I had my first full-time job. The primary excitement I felt at those initial paychecks, naturally, was because they meant I could buy more records. And the collection bulged helplessly in my twenties, through canceled credit cards and innumerable domestic battles, with new musician friends whose passion was as fierce as mine, and finally until I decided that I'd probably acquired enough, or better that I'd devoted enough time to building the collection, and I all but stopped adding to it. That's where I am now, a collector who's only barely collecting. Now and then, I buy for other folks, a different kind of vicarious thrill. Whenever I feel the urge to add to my own pile, I go into the basement and pretend it's a record shop. Truthfully, I have never been in a store that good. That's a nice feeling. I smile and hit the stacks, pulling out things I've forgotten that I have, sometimes realizing I've got a duplicate copy of this or that, putting it aside to trade, refiling the stray records, admiring them and then taking a few upstairs to the stereo to do what they were made to do.

"News of My Death, Greatly Exaggerated," Quoth the Record

Love letters. That's what the Vinyl Freak entries were. Passionate, intimate, probing little parries. For twelve years, from 2000 to 2012, I wrote magazine columns that were missives to a mistress or a missus, dedicated to the most beloved. Compiling them for this book was like unearthing a box of scented envelopes long ago sealed with kisses and hidden away.

Love letters to a dying medium. When I first imagined the column, vinyl's days were numbered. That was part of the plan—to write about a medium that was moribund. Inspired in part by former *DownBeat* editor Art Lange's Rara Avis column of twenty years earlier, which had invited critics to conjure the "rare birds" of their collection, Vinyl Freak was meant as a personal challenge to awaken in myself the critic as connoisseur rather than solely as judge and jury, sending me deep into my collection to retrieve an inspiring and fascinating object, just the way I would if I was listening at home with friends.

For a trade magazine like *DownBeat*, embracing Vinyl Freak was a very uncommercial gesture. In my mind—and in many of the e-mail responses I received during its run—this made it that much more powerful and surprising. To write about music that was not readily available to the consumer, to celebrate a record that was difficult or impossible to find, this was counterintuitive for a consumer periodical. I meant for it to spark curiosity, to tweak the little connoisseur that is latent in all cultural consumers, to charge up the competitive mechanism that drives cultural debate, to get listeners thinking about all that music that had recently become unavailable to them, and to urge them to think: that seems worthwhile, why can't *I* hear it? Maybe in all that jealous froth, I supposed, they would also wonder about how history gets told and who gets to tell it—the column's ulterior motive.

Toward the end of the column's existence comes a new twist: the patient begins to make a miraculous recovery. Vinyl is reborn, and the meaning of our enterprise is transformed. Rather suddenly a column on vinyl records is the hippest thing in the world; all the magazines are doing it. And the simple Vinyl Freak premise—covering music that has not made the transition from vinyl to digital—can be seen as irrelevant because vinyl reissues of out-of-print vinyl are now common, sometimes in lieu of CD or MP3 altogether.

Your lover was sick unto death but now has recovered. The forlorn letters remain. What do they tell you about yourself? About the nature of your love? About the object of your affection? And why *these* particular records? They're not the most rare, by and large, and they're not always an artist's crowning achievement. But they represent something rich—each one multilayered in itself, in its relationship to an oeuvre, in its existence as part of a moment, and in its potential to transcend that moment. Enough so to make me want to write about it.

At this point, there is nearly full remission. Vinyl's resurgence is going strong, although the question of what music is and is not obtainable remains on the table. Plenty of the LPs and singles that I covered have been reissued in the meantime, but many of those were released on small labels that have not kept them in print, hence they are again difficult to find. On the other hand, you can readily dig up lots of out-of-print material online. The lost and found of musical subcultures is as active as ever, though it's a little more tangled. To determine what's discarded and what's retained or rediscovered in a world awash in reissue compilations and YouTube posts is in itself a job deserving a detective.

Following the logic of successive technologies—the very same life cycle that vinyl's renewed health and well-being seem to be thwarting—it's the discs that are on their way out. Compact disc is the dying medium. But I will not be composing love letters to CDs. Ours has been a pragmatic relationship, not a romance. Looking back with dewy eyes upon the LP, single, ten-inch, and shellac, those love letters refer to a time when, weak limbed and short of breath, vinyl was but a ghost. Dead man walking. As they sometimes say of things when they pass, it was *history*. But it hadn't vanished altogether; it had just retreated into places like used record shops, college radio stations, and people's personal collections, where it gave witness to a time when records ruled the earth. And in those dark places it lurked, waiting to be rediscovered. No doubt we'll still have to chase the music—an apparition in whatever material form it manifests—deep into the woods of the future, to make sure it is not forgotten.

/////

When I first proposed writing a regular column about vinyl records for *DownBeat* magazine, I could never have predicted the fate of the medium. At the time, CDs were still the primary way that music changed hands, with all sorts of downloadable possibilities in the brewing luminous. But the little world of music has since embraced the vinyl medium with a ferocity that even I, a committed LP collector of more than thirty-five years, find surprising. This resurgence is, in part, fueled by a fashion for nearly obsolete technology, the same impetus that has made '70s-style boom boxes and cumbersome earmuff-like headphones once again tenable. I initially realized how hip used records had become when I discovered that major clothing stores in New York were hiring buyers and selling LPs alongside their duds. Like all things fashionable, this wave of intense interest will come and go. But in the case of vinyl LPs, I have the feeling that it's more than just a fad; it is in part a resurgence caused by the special character of the medium itself. More on that in a minute.

In the initial period of decline for vinyl, which started with the advent of the compact disc in the mid-1980s, consumers witnessed the progressive demateralization of music. First, there were CDs, with their artwork shrinky-dinked down from twelve inches to just over five, and much of the information that would have been spread over the sleeve buried in a microscopic liner booklet. From there, the road to complete object-less-ness has been swift and, it would have seemed, decisive. The heir to the Walkman, the iPod, has allowed listeners to cart around entire libraries in a tiny, digital case. What would have taken an entire basement to house now occupies an infinitesimally wee chip; each single track requires virtually no space, and for all intents and purposes it has no material presence. It exists as sound, not as stuff. For those who see music as an exclusively auditory experience, this is no doubt a sort of ultimate confirmation.

I don't see it that way. My proclivity has always been toward material culture. Not that I'm opposed to downloading, streaming, iPods, and the like. I'm not. I use them all, to one degree or another. But when it comes to the full-on experience, the sound of music has most often been accompanied by some object-ness, something concrete through which the music arrives and into which the power of the music can be projected. What's been interesting is to see a rise in the number of pressing plants, lowering the difficulty for young people wanting to produce their own vinyl. Students of mine have experimented with portable lathes, making their own one-of-a-kind record art objects; meanwhile, specialists are willing to manufacture really strange vinyl oddities, like locked-groove LPs or grooves that stretch out in a straight line rather than in a coil on a disc. The manufacture of record players has risen as well, making cheap players available alongside the ultra-high-end audiophile machines that continued to be accessible all along.

The notion behind the Vinyl Freak column was based on the assumption of a waning medium. I sought out records that had been out of print and had never made it onto CD, and even today I find plenty of great, terrible examples, music that has slipped through the cracks, possibly into the dustbin of history. I continue to be fascinated by the way that music history is written and rewritten through the gatekeeping mechanism of in-print-ness. But reports of the death of the record album turned out to be premature, and with the revival I found plenty of new releases to delight in and write about. It helped complicate the column in, I think, an interesting way, keeping it from being a nostalgia trip by an old fart record fan. I am surely that, but I also appreciate the fact that there are really wonderful developments in record production, like the option to press heavier—180- or 200-gram—vinyl, various creative new strategies for packaging, and a higher ratio of small-batch, limited edition vinyl releases, which might have been prohibitively expensive to produce in an earlier era. Who says you can't teach an elderly medium new tricks?

As I've said, it can be objected that the question of whether an LP has made the transition to CD is moot. What's the use of asking whether records have been issued on disc when CDs themselves are on their way out, bemoaned and reviled by many for their impersonal regurgitation of data, the way they scratch, the way their clip-in hubs and jewel case plastic hinges tend to break, their unbecoming looks, their cumbersomeness and inelegance. Fair enough, but the fact is that making that transition from vinyl to disc has been almost essential in getting the music into the digital domain. Reviewing the fate of the music in all the columns I wrote, only one of the LPs had jumped from vinyl to download without passing through CD. This is how histories are now tacitly written; neglected material goes more distantly into obscurity, deeper into the vaults, further from the gates of the digital archive, virtually inaudible, having failed to move from one medium to another.

In Greece, they bury you twice. First you are entombed for a year, then your bones are excavated and examined. If everything is going as expected, you are put back into the ground for eternity. Music that hasn't made it to CD gets the Greek treatment. Except rather than being exhumed it's just repeatedly buried.

/////

In the late 1990s, on a Goethe-Institut fellowship, I visited several German radio stations, exploring their libraries of original tapes of free jazz, improvised, experimental, and electronic music. I'd heard through the grapevine that, like archives of all sorts, these treasure troves of musical pleasures were being faced with possible extinction due to space shortages, that some tapes were already being discarded. Fearing the worst, I thought I'd see what was there and if there was anything irreplaceable try to intervene. What I found was that these German radio productions, which have been quite well stewarded and for the most part have not fallen victim to downsizing, provide an incredible, otherwise inaccessible portal into developments in progressive music during the 1960s and 1970s, a period of rapid growth and rabid development. They cover not only European music but American and Japanese music as well and could perhaps help us see the milieu in a much richer and more exciting way than the official commercial and underground records released during the same epoch.

Electrified by the trip, I began to think about ways to make the material available to a wider public. My other sources of inspiration at the time were the New York Review Books series, which has published an impressive spectrum of out-of-print marvels, and the Criterion Collection series of films, with its impeccable style, great documentation, and always engaging extras. These companies helped an inveterate material-culture vulture see the world anew, confirming my long-held belief that there's a wider, more diverse range of works that should be available than what passes for the basic canon of world culture. Expand the books and movies and music that make up that canon, and in turn you may revisit the mainstream with refreshed senses and a keener understanding of what was possible and what possibilities were explored.

In my own case, what grew out of this was a project: the Unheard Music Series. Over the course of the same decade as Vinyl Freak, roughly the aughts, I worked diligently to reissue key records that had fallen out of print—we started with Peter Brötzmann's monumental *Nipples* and Joe McPhee's free funk masterwork *Nation Time*—and to issue tapes that had, for one reason or another, never been released, like Guillermo Gregorio's beguiling Fluxus-like recordings from Buenos Aires in the 1960s. The Unheard Music Series produced something like seventy releases, including a couple of Sun Ra DVDs and a book of Brötzmann's artwork. Along the way, I was careful not to cross the series and the column, and I refrained from writing about things when I thought I had a chance of reissuing them. Conflict of interest is a reality; I had no desire to publicize my own productions under cover of reportage. Better anyway, I reasoned, to try to interest others in taking up the gauntlet and reissuing some of the great unheard themselves.

Happily, that often seems to have come to pass. Looking back at these selected installments of Vinyl Freak, it's gratifying to know how many of them are now in fact available on CD, as downloads or streamable files, or, in the most hilarious twist of fate, having passed through those media, once again available as newly reissued LPs. (In a few cases, a decade after the column entry and still un-reissued, I have gone ahead and done it myself.) *Nation Time* just got the full treatment. Produced in a small quantity in 1972, out of print for several decades, almost lost to history, finally reissued on CD, then an elaborate box set I issued on Corbett vs. Dempsey (the successor to UMS), it was selected for British funk compilations, suddenly became a sought-out rarity on vinyl for deejays, and is now reissued on vinyl to satisfy the newly fomented demand.

If vinyl's dead, long may it die.

/////

Nine explanations for the vinyl revival:

1. *Music as physical object.* Records are the stuff of music. People love their stuff. I think that recorded music basically begs to be accompanied by something physical and visual. Many listeners long to have something to hold and look at and read, to assuage the weird, fleeting feeling produced by recorded music, which is by its nature unanchored in anything material. LPs have enjoyed a haptic history, chapter upon chapter of tactility—the weight, texture, and surface as well as more obvious design features. Of course, other media offer their version of this, their own ontological existences, but nothing quite so perfectly salves the recorded music rash the way that vinyl does. Are MP3 "collectors" really collectors? As Sacha Baron Cohen's character Bruno says: *Ich don't think so.*

2. *Material collectability*. As physical objects, records are an ideal format for being collected. Tall and thin, lots of surface area seen one direction and almost invisible seen from ninety degrees, able to be shelved and scanned by spine, LPS are a librarian's dream, fitting together into an archive like extraskinny children's books. Yet they are substantive objects, their packaging part of their identity, quite unlike the CD and its wan little jewel case, which is like a permanent plastic coffin, or the MP3, which sometimes tries vainly to associate images with songs—downloadable covers, liner notes, and so forth, video projects like Beyoncé's *Beyoncé*. These images are always accessed via the screen, so they are virtual, not material, ephemeral, not solid. The record collector's technique: hands poised as if typing, fingertips resting on the first LPS, flipping them forward, eventually anchoring the meat of the palm on the closest ones while moving on toward row's end; an inquiry appears, one is extracted, examined, then replaced, and the beat goes on. CD design imitates LP design. Anything good about a nicely packaged disc, except for its name-sake compactness (from a storage standpoint, an undeniable asset), is typically an echo of classic LP packaging, from the double-disc gatefold to the inner sleeve. The most attractive CDS are the ones that make no bones about being HO-scale albums. The real reason that LPS are superior objects for collecting and displaying is simple—they're bigger. The covers have more surface area. Early in the compact disc era, the Willem Breuker Kollektief issued a CD packaged in an LP sleeve; the cover image depicted a comet that had landed on earth and cracked open to reveal the CD inside, a new medium that had arrived from outer space, still reliant on its antecedent to allow it to nestle together with the other long players. On LP covers more text is possible and it's not necessary for the words to shrink down so microscopically as to be indecipherable. Twelve inches square is a more interesting scale for images, plain and simple. And without the distorting jewel case, there's nothing between the image and the viewer. Like the difference between a drawing that's glazed and one that's loose—you see so much more.

3. *LPS are built to be displayed*. Collectors enjoy nothing more than exhibiting their collections, and record albums are designed to be shown off. Think of the common format of the gatefold sleeve, which can be opened halfway to allow the record to stand upright—little cardboard soldiers from Flatland. Concurrent with the vinyl revival, a range of standard LP frames has been developed in order to hang the cover on the wall, for continual viewing. Growing up, I liked to put my copy of Emerson, Lake & Palmer's (quite dreadful) LP *Pictures at an Exhibition* up . . . you get it, like a painting. Pure genius. At any respectable record store a "now playing" station displays the LP that's rotating on the turntable.

4. Running length. They're shorter. Which may seem like a setback, but seems to fit better into most people's daily schedule.

5. A-sides and B-sides. It always makes me chuckle to see a CD with A- and B-sides listed, even though there are none. The drama of vinyl, in part, is an echo of theater's standard use of the intermission. Something happens. Then a break to reflect, shake it off. Something else happens. Great LPs and even exceptional singles make hay with this fundamental aspect of vinyl, which entails the exposure of one face of the platter while the other side is hidden, then vice versa. There are always two sides to the story.

6. Nostalgia. Whatever format, recordings are time machines. Instant mnemonics. They're prone to dredge up memories, so they can easily generate surplus nostalgia. There's a raw sense of past romance in the revival of ye-olde-vinyl. It may be not only a genuine pang for something lost, a hazy longing for bygone experiences by former LP users who want to return to simpler, predigital ways when records were records, but also a projected nostalgia, adopted by younger folks, perhaps on behalf of their parents or aunts and uncles or adopted as a desire formulated upon seeing vinyl in movies like *Diner* or *High Fidelity*, reading about it in hipster music magazines, or seeing records strewn about a photo spread in a fashion rag. In 2016, vinyl records are automatically nostalgic, as are cassette tapes, which have also beaten great odds in being successfully revived. Eight-tracks must not be far behind.

7. Vinyl is a fad. There's a trendy quality to the revival. A new association between records and reproduction workwear, midcentury furniture and gold rush–era cocktail recipes. Like all those style campaigns, this too will expire. The shallowest among us, who use records as accessories for hipster cred, who are collecting vinyl because they think it makes them look cool, will eventually find another music object with which to associate. What percentage of the new school is made up of these pretenders? Very hard to tell, but I suspect it's neither a majority nor statistically insignificant.

8. Records are magical; CDs are scientific. Compact discs (and all their digital kinfolk) approach music like a very complex math problem to be solved by a number-crunching computer. We may not know how it works, but we're confident that the proper equations will be applied and the code will be read. That vinyl records are capable of producing music is harder to believe and understand, but the transformation of matter into sound is accomplished in public, on the stage of the turntable, where the needle is applied and . . . presto . . . music comes out.

9. Surface noise's changing connotations. Once abjured by record fans, representing vinyl in its mistreated state, vinyl's inevitable noises—scratches, pops, crackle, groove wear, and so on—now have another association: the real. As with a good pair of denim jeans or a leather bag, wear is not all bad. Many audio programs come equipped with surface noise that can be overlaid onto pristine sounds, giving them instant grit. A vinyl record is surprisingly resilient. When vinyl gets lightly scratched, up to a point it acquires a patina, a haze of clicks and pops. When digital media is damaged, the result is catastrophic: it becomes unplayable.

Philly Joe Jones, *Philly Joe Jones*
(French Vogue, 1969)

Flipping through new arrivals at Chicago's Jazz Record Mart, I'd already passed this LP before I realized it might be worth singling out. The cover is mundane enough to miss; I'd mistaken it for a foreign compilation of some sort, a collection of Philly Joe Jones classics repackaged for a French audience. But enough was weird about it, like the lovely little set of Vogue logos in the upper-right corner as colorful as a general's medals, to make me do a double take. And I'm glad I did, for not only is it an original session and an almost unknown Philly Joe record, it comes from a remarkable moment in the drummer's career.

After a two-year residence in England, Jones relocated to France in 1969, where he shocked fans who had come to know him through his trendsetting work with the first Miles Davis Quintet by experimenting with free jazz. In December of that year, for instance, he recorded with saxophonists Archie Shepp and Anthony Braxton.

Earlier in '69, Jones waxed this Vogue date. It appears to have been a project of pianist Jef Gilson, who is credited with composing and arranging all but one of the tracks. Already solidly established as a key Parisian mainstream player, leader of a successful septet in the early '60s, Gilson made some strong New Thing–oriented records later in that decade, including the recently reissued *New Call from France* (MPS, 1966), which featured tenor saxophonist Jean-Louis Chautemps. With a very enjoyable burr to his tone, Chautemps is here as well, part of a variable group that also features two trombones, cello, and rhythm section.

In his liner notes, Gilson proclaims that Jones has "arrived to reconcile traditional jazz and free jazz." This record leans more toward the former, with some moderately adventurous soloing over straight-ahead time—adroitly steered by Jones—plowing through Gilson's quirky, angular tunes. But what makes this a vinyl freak's jackpot is a single track titled "Spontaneous Expression." It's Jones's solo, stretching out over ten unaccompanied minutes—casual but absolutely killer. He starts on brushes, explores the toms with mallets, leads into his hotshot sticks finale with a long, loving press-roll. Of course, Baby Dodds, Kenny Clarke, Papa Joe Jones, and others had predated this, and Jones himself had recorded a solo in '59 ("Tribal Message" on Riverside's *Drums around the World*). Milford Graves, Andrew Cyrille, and others were making solo drum concerts commonplace in free music. But to hear Jones play at length like this is a scrumptious, rare treat indeed—the tastiest vinyl snack I've had in months.

[June 2000]

POSTSCRIPT 2016: *Sixteen years later, the first Vinyl Freak entry is still out of print and has never been available on CD. Happy hunting. Sad to say that you won't be able to do so at Jazz Record Mart, which bit the dust in February of this year. Thanks to Bob Koester for sixty-plus years of service. So much for the durability of bricks and mortar.*

Paul Gonsalves, *Cookin'*
(Argo, 1957)

One of the things I like most about LPs is the way they absorb history. By that I don't mean only the history of the music, but also the history of each record as an object; records are repositories of music's material culture. CDs seem much less historically palpable than LPs. Collectable CDs? Maybe, but not for me.

This Paul Gonsalves record has had an interesting history. It was given to me by a friend in Mississippi who has a tremendous collection primarily focused on trombone jazz. An acquaintance of his decided to dump a small, but choice, collection of '50s and '60s vinyl, and this was among the items he sold. Thing is, the fellow had bought all those records when they first came out, played them once to tape them, then filed them away and never played them again. The story made my freakish heart go pitter-pat, particularly when I landed on this nice, fat Argo package, with a great Le Roy Winbush design, looking just the way it did when it was bought four decades earlier.

The music on *Cookin'* has a pretty interesting history, too. Recorded on Argo's home turf in Chicago when Ellington was playing at the Blue Note, this was the first Gonsalves made under his own name, one year after his twenty-seven-chorus sensation at Newport, and it was clearly designed to capitalize on and in part try to re-create the ambience of this historic event. The opener, one of three simple blowing tunes penned by the tenor saxophonist, is tellingly titled "Festival," and it features Gonsalves in Newport mode: riffing, repeating, snaking, building tension, wending a series of increasingly extended lines.

The group is a scaled-down version of the Newport Ellington band, with Jimmy Woode on bass and Sam Woodyard on drums. Clark Terry offers some splendid trumpet and is credited with writing (or cowriting) the remaining six pieces. His "Impeccable" is an excellent ballad vehicle for Gonsalves. *Cookin'* was part of a brief Argo series called "Daddy-O Presents . . . ," and Terry's "Daddy-O's Patio" refers to Chicago disc-jockey Daddy-O Daylie.

Over the course of three months in '57, Argo recorded this LP by Gonsalves, and ones led by Terry and Woode. It says something about how confusing the reissue market is these days that the tracks from *Cookin'* were in fact reissued a few years ago as part of a CD under Terry's name, *Daylight Express*, which buried the original LP titles in discographical fine print and didn't reproduce the great Gonsalves cover anywhere. Hence, technically, the

LP jacket remains out of print, and the Woode LP from these sessions still languishes in the vinyl graveyard.

[August 2000]

POSTSCRIPT 2016: *In 2007, the Fresh Sounds label re-reissued* Cookin' *together with the associated recordings previously issued under Terry's and Woode's names. They nearly excavated the original cover but for some reason updated it, which is too bad because it was absolutely perfect in its original incarnation. I had a chance to meet its designer, Le Roy Winbush, before he died at ninety-one in 2007; Winbush presented a two-hour slideshow on his life's work at the School of the Art Institute of Chicago, cycling through the window displays he'd made for Goldblatt's department store in the late '40s, the first such work done by an African American, and his work at Ebony's art department, also recounting early days painting murals for jazz shows on the front of the Regal Theater. By the way, in this review I fail to mention the incredible and eccentric contribution of pianist Willie Jones, an underappreciated figure on the Chicago scene who managed to play dense clusters and made them work in a mainstream context.*

Takashi Furuya with the Freshmen, *Fanky Drivin'*
(Teichiku, 1960)

Lost records are ciphers, archaeological relics with meanings scrambled by time. Finding an obscure LP—or an LP obscure to me—provides incentive to learn and an admission that conventional histories are built by leaving some things out as much as by including other things. The slag heaps of material culture are fascinating repositories; at least they offer a broader spectrum of color to the accepted history, and at best they can change a whole historical paradigm.

Pawing through a used bookshop that also stocks some records, I found this unusual goodie. Its spectacularly weird front cover first attracted me, particularly the constellation of five needlepoint images of women—or rather three women and two apparent attempts at Greek mythological figures—all awkwardly rendered, cartoonish, and nearly pornographic in overemphasis of T&A. Rocking chair pillows for a perv grandpa. Then I noticed the askew title: *Fanky Drivin'*. No doubt a phonetic mistranslation of "funky" and the requisite hipster apostrophe that only a non–English speaker would choose.

I found a liner text in Japanese, a few English titles in parentheses, a price (1,500 yen), and a nice photo of a five-piece modern jazz band in action. In the snapshot, the alto saxophonist adjusts his neck strap while the trumpeter solos; a name appears on the bass drum: "TOM." Now, this is fun. I've got lots of clues to work with—the Freshmen's repertoire includes some standards, a version of Miles Davis's "Dig," and what seem to be original tunes, like "Arrow after Dark"—but there's much I don't understand.

In the store, the clerk and I sampled the record: hard bop / soul-jazz, very solid, particularly strong alto sax; the first cut, only listed in Japanese, has an Asian-sounding intro, and there's a version of the exotica classic "Taboo." Someone, perhaps the leader, sings in English on "I'll See You in My Dreams" and "You Don't Know What Love Is." And what appears to be an original—"Loose, Lousy Blues"—has an effective slow grind. Studiously American sounding, the record has enough personality and Orientalist quirks to make it really interesting.

Now, maybe the leader is as familiar to you as "Sleepy" Matsumoto, but I must confess that I'd never heard of Takashi Furuya. Or his bandmates: trumpeter Koaru Inami, pianist Zenshow Otsuka, bassist Hirokazu Okumura, and drummer Tom Naohara. I contacted Kiyoshi Koyama, former editor of *Swing Journal* and *DownBeat*'s man in Japan, and he graciously filled in some of the missing details. Furuya is one of the top alto saxophonists in Japanese jazz, second in this period only to Sadao Watanabe. *Fanky Drivin'* was the Freshmen's debut, recorded in September 1960, never reissued on CD; the band lasted sixteen years before splitting up. Now sixty-four years old and still active (he released a CD on the King label recorded in New York in '95 with Kenny Barron), Furuya lives in Osaka, where he and the Freshmen held a regular gig at a club called Arrow. Turns out the Asian-sounding piece was a jazz arrangement of a folk tune "Jogashima No Ame" ("Rain over Jogashima").

[November 2000]

POSTSCRIPT 2016: *Finally reissued as a CD on the Japanese Think! label in 2006, together with another LP from the same session (Minyou Shuu), Fanky Drivin' was simultaneously made available as a vinyl reissue. For very serious freaks.*

Carsten Meinert Kvartet, *To You*
(Spectator Records, 1968)

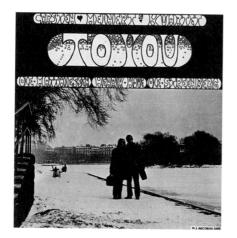

A few months ago, Roger Bergner from the Swedish Jazz Archive sent me tapes of some Scandinavian music he thought I might find interesting. Included was a 1968 quartet record by Carsten Meinert, a Danish tenor saxophonist whom I believe is still active.

I should preface this with an admission: I've got a problem with Coltrane. Or rather with Trane copycats. The '70s were so full of slavish imitations and less-close approximations of the Coltrane concept that I find the practice hard to stomach. My first impression of the LP was negative for just that reason—no bones about it, this is straight-up Coltrane Quartet music. Hell, the record starts with "Naima," Ole Mattheissen throws down wide block chords just like Tyner, and Ole Streenberg's cymbal splashes are studiously Elvin. So I listened once, then put *To You* aside in favor of more original music.

But weeks later, on the way to the airport to pick up my pal and fellow record-nut Mats Gustafsson, I put the cassette in my car stereo and began to really dig it. First, I noticed that Meinert's tone is really not precisely Trane. Throaty, brusque, with a hoarseness that might call comparison to Pharoah Sanders as much as Trane, the Dane's playing integrates a few voices. On the other hand, where other ensembles are bent on adapting the Coltrane sound to their own thing, these Copenhagenites are flamboyant in their emulation. A year after Trane's death, here is where the idea of tribute or memorial turns into wholesale facsimile. Something about that forthrightness appealed to me.

With his composite sound, Meinert *does* have a bead on Coltrane's multi-note pileups. But you can hear his provenance. Like other Trane-influenced tenors from Scandinavia, such as Nils Sandström, Bosse Wärmell, Borje Fredriksson, Gilbert Holström, and Juhani Aaltonen, he's part of a specific subculture: the Nordic take on Trane.

Gustafsson—who was coming to Chicago for a gig—is an interesting case; a young Swedish saxophonist and serious student of sax history, he's made a personal vow never to perform Coltrane. (I know he's broken that vow, too; with the trio Gush he once played "Afro-Blue," tsk-tsk!) Mats and I always exchange LP goodies, and in a startling coincidence this time he'd brought me a copy of the very same extremely rare Meinert Quartet record I'd been listening to.

It's got a homespun cover, hand lettered by one "Clovis Gauguin," with a photo of Meinert and adoring gal strolling along a frozen river. The debut (only?) release on the minuscule Spectator Records, it's a record I've grown quite fond of, accepting all its imitative foibles. There's "One for Alice," obviously aimed at Trane's widow, Meinert's "Blues to Someone" (reference to the "Blues To . . ." series on *Coltrane Plays the Blues*), a post–"Favorite Things"–style waltz titled "Dansevise," and the very Sanders-esque "Before Sunrise." The record's only real stain is the title track, a poppy bit of fluff with stupid changes and an insipid melody. But like Coltrane impersonators, ill-advised crossover attempts were also rampant in '68.

[February 2001]

POSTSCRIPT 2016: *I was delighted when Meinert himself wrote to me after this column ran, even more when early in 2015 Frederiksberg Records reissued it with period photographs and fresh liner notes on CD and LP.*

Melvin Jackson, *Funky Skull*
(Limelight, 1969)

There are a few ways that rare jazz vinyl circulates these days. Collectors, of course, hoard and swap and sell and buy the goods; eBay is a magnet for febrile discaholics. Then there are straight-up music fans who don't fetishize the LPs as objects, but treasure them exclusively for the precious sounds encoded in their grooves. Somewhere in between—half collector and half music lover—there's a shadowy character who seeks out the hard-to-find sounds for delectable samples he or she can use in hip-hop or as material for dance mixes.

Any of the vinyl freaks in the last category would be well served by finding Melvin Jackson's elusive 1969 record *Funky Skull*, a unique blend of hardcore funk jollies and Chicagoan vanguard oddness. The record's abiding gimmick is that Jackson plays upright bass with effects—very, very extensive effects. He's listed in the credits on "acoustic string bass with Maestro G-2 filter box for guitar, Boomerang, Echo-Plex and Ampeg amplifier" (endorsement complete!), and on various tracks he unabashedly features himself sawing

MELVIN JACKSON · FUNKY SKULL

away, some zany sonic treatment hovering over his bass like a cloud. It's unyieldingly stupid—like Jackson's motto on the back of the record: "I heard it! I dug it! I did it!"—and yet somehow fantastic at the same time.

Two of the cuts, "Bold and Black" and "Cold Duck Time," were penned by saxophonist Eddie Harris, who was not averse to strange and sometimes gimmicky recordings. "Cold Duck Time" is a Staxish R&B piece with wacky bass, and on this and the similar title track Jackson used a band with guitarists Phil Upchurch and Pete Cosey, and drummer Morris Jennings holding down the stone groove. "Everybody Loves My Baby" is a sparse bossa with arco wah bass, a Jackson specialty. On the remaining six tracks, the ensemble is especially noteworthy, loaded with future AACM all-stars and drummer Billy Hart. Roscoe Mitchell's bass sax riff buoys a jam called "Funky Doo," and Mitchell takes a harsh alto solo on "Say What," a nutty way-out bass blues on which Jodie Christian adds some very Sun Ra–like organ.

"Bold and Black" is a gritty, spaced-out funk number, with a terrific Lester Bowie trumpet solo (sometimes twining with Leo Smith), replete with scrumptious slurs and a send-off kiss. It's reminiscent of the great grooving Art Ensemble tracks of the early '70s, like "Theme de Yoyo," from *Les Stances a Sophie* and their outstanding record with French chanteuse Brigitte Fontaine, *Comme a la Radio*. Jackson gets busy with his looping Echo-Plex on "Dance of the Dervish," psychedelic haunted-house singing courtesy of the Sound of Feeling Voices. The longest track comes at record's ends, "Silver Cycles," a Jackson original. Here the group makes a simple bed for Jackson to layer sheets of echo on; in the end his bass is humming like an Afrocentric Fripp & Eno.

There are enough solid breaks and off-kilter funk bits on this to fuel a Bomb Squad revival. Word has it that *Funky Skull* will in fact be reissued soon on LP only (in fact I tried to license it for reissue on CD, unsuccessfully), keeping it exclusively in the realm of the Vinyl Freak.

[May 2001]

POSTSCRIPT 2016: *During its relatively short run as a label, Dusty Groove, the music emporium that happens to reside underneath (and act as landlord for) my art gallery in Chicago, reissued this warped classic on* CD *in 2007. It's now rather rare even on* CD. *Come to think of it, I think I bought* Funky Skull *at Dusty in the first place. Watch the record spin: what goes around comes around.*

Gloria Coleman Quartet featuring Pola Roberts, *Soul Sisters*
(Impulse!, 1963)

Ah, the silt of history covers all sorts of things. Many great forgotten records are forgotten because they were pressed up in small batches on tiny labels and hardly anybody ever had a chance to hear them in the first place. But being on a bigger label by no means assures great ones of being remembered—it's easy for special little recordings to get lost, passed over repeatedly in the megacorp milk-the-cash-cow mentality. Some of the niftiest music in the world still languishes in the jazz industry's main vaults.

Hard to believe, with its superheavy cover, that anyone could overlook *Soul Sisters*, but alas, every time I see a new batch of Impulse! CD reissues, I'm disappointed not to find this wonderful funky diamond among them. Recorded by Rudy van Gelder in '63, after the group had apparently been working for some time at a club in New York called Branker's, it's a minor masterpiece of soul-jazz. Not to mention the gravity-defying architectural wonder that is Pola Roberts's beehive!

Leader Gloria Coleman was a stellar B-3 player—there were not many woman organists at that time, Shirley Scott and Trudy Pitts excepted—and she penned five of the six tunes on the LP, all of them blues-based swingers. On "Hey Sonny Redd" she tweaks the requisite one-note organ routine, adding little details to the drone; and throughout the record her driving pedal work means you have to force yourself to remember there's no bassist. Coleman's featured partner Roberts is a very hip drummer, understated but full of pep. She doesn't bowl things over like Joe Dukes, but she percolates underneath, stirring the soul with an easy ride, subtle snare bursts exploding like kernels in a Jiffy Pop popper.

Soul guitar kingpin Grant Green and saxophonist Leo Wright (thankfully fluteless on this date) round out the foursome. "Melba's Minor," dedicated to Melba Liston, has a saxophoneless A section in which, as liner notician Stanley Dance put it, "one can imagine Grant Green on the steppes with his balalaika." That stretches the bounds of poetic license, methinks, but perhaps . . . It is a strangely Russian, soundtrack-like theme, in any case. Coleman takes a great solo, with nice dissonances and some more single-note shenanigans. Written for then recently deceased saxist Ike Quebec, "Que Baby" is a very groovy up-tempo groove, a nice way to kick the LP off, while "Funky Bob" is a slow grind blues concocted by Green for producer Bob Thiele, with a chewy alto solo and ultra-laid-back guitar. Composition-ally, "My Lady's Waltz" (dedicated to Coleman's daughter with husband, sax-ophonist George Coleman) is the record's apex, a really funky tune in 3/4.

Pssst . . . hey GRP! Soul-jazz is back, baby. The polite tap on the shoulder should remind the folks who control the Impulse! archives of their li'l trea-sure, and maybe *Soul Sisters* can find the ready audience for which it's been waiting the last thirty-eight years.

[July 2001]

POSTSCRIPT 2016: *A few years after this column ran, European Verve reissued* Soul Sisters *in a limited edition, now long gone to consumers. The Impulse! label had been through the ringer, as Universal Music Group, which acquired PolyGram in 1998 (parent company for GRP, which had managed Universal's jazz offerings, hence my "psst"), the company that in turn owned Impulse!, bought EMI, which owned Blue Note, hence consolidating two of the titanic forces in '60s recorded jazz. Somewhere in this turbulent sea, the modest little organ group may continue to be too small a fish for the big trawlers to notice.*

Elmo Hope Ensemble, *Sounds from Rikers Island*
(Audio Fidelity, 1963)

Such a gorgeously designed cover, such tasty tracks. This elusive little one took me years to track down. When I did, it was waiting for me at a fine record store in Munich, Bird's Nest Music, for the agreeable price of forty-five deutsche marks. The recording itself has been reissued once on LP—though even the reissue is rare enough that I've never seen it—and it is reputedly now available on CD in Japan. But for the non-Japanese market, it's been totally unavailable for decades, which is a damned shame.

Tenor saxophonist John Gilmore only made a smattering of recordings away from the Sun Ra Arkestra. A few of these are still super-rare, including his 1970 record co-led with trumpeter Dizzy Reece, *From In to Out*, a bootleg of his British TV appearance as a member of Art Blakey's Jazz Messengers in 1965, and this wonderful outing with pianist Elmo Hope. *Sounds from Rikers Island* is primo Gilmore, recorded in August 1963 in the time just after he'd transplanted with Ra and crew from Chicago to

New York (in 1961). It came at the beginning of a highly active period in his playing—between July '62 and May '67 he also recorded with Blakey, Freddie Hubbard, McCoy Tyner, Paul Bley, Andrew Hill, Pete LaRoca, and, of course, the Arkestra—and his playing was arguably at its most expansive and captivating.

Fellow Arkestra member Ronnie Boykins plays along on bass, adding his impeccable, propulsive time and woody sound, and Philly Joe Jones sits at the kit. On one ballad, "Monique," it's straight quartet, with Hope manning the piano and Gilmore featured front and center. Gilmore also assumes the spotlight on a killing version of "A Night in Tunisia," where he hooks up dramatically with Hope's dry, always intriguing piano. Earl Coleman's rich voice makes a cameo on "It Shouldn't Happen to a Dream," recalling some of the chewy Sun Ra ballads crooned by Clyde Williams; it sounds like a cross between Billie Holiday and Billy Eckstine.

A loose concept record, the LP focuses on incarceration (hence the tile) and drug use, an implicit reference to Hope's own troubles at that time. Nat Hentoff writes a detailed treatise on the superiority of rehabilitation over punishment in the liner text, and many of the tracks refer in one way or another to drug use—"Ecstasy" and "Trippin'" most obviously. The former features short solos by some lesser-known horn men, Lawrence Jackson's blunt trumpet and Freddie Douglas's anachronistic alto.

"One for Joe" is a feature for Jones, and he makes the very best of it on Hope's great tune. In fact, *Rikers Island* is an excellent showcase for Hope's writing—he's scandalously overlooked as a composer and could by rights be considered an off-center bop great alongside Thelonious Monk and

Herbie Nichols. He digs into his pieces "Kevin" and "Three Silver Quarters" in pared-down trio format, making a case for this argument.

The last track on the LP sports another vocal cameo, this time by Marcelle Daniels, who does a Babs Gonzales–like vocalese version of "Groovin' High," replete with the darkly comic lyric: "This is the story of, this is the glory of . . . *dope!*"

[September 2001]

POSTSCRIPT 2016: *The intrepid Spanish label Fresh Sounds reprinted* Sounds from Rikers Island *in 2004.*

Chris McGregor's Brotherhood of Breath, *Brotherhood*
(RCA, 1972)

In the geography of out-of-print jazz records, South Africa unfortunately ranks quite high. Wonder why, for instance, Columbia hasn't reissued the Dollar Brand debut, *Duke Ellington Presents Dollar Brand*? That one's certainly ripe by now. There are only a handful of CDs currently available by relatively prolific pianist and bandleader Chris McGregor, including a handful of beauts on Ogun Records, as well as a glorious 1972 radio performance, recently issued as *Traveling Somewhere* by Cuneiform.

After going expat, many South African musicians moved around a fair amount, releasing records in various ports of call. Perhaps that accounts for the dismal track record we have of their activities. As for McGregor records that remain to be reissued, there is a batch of real ultrararities. A few copies of a test pressing cut for Polydor in the late '60s are floating around: one side of the LP is a tough piano trio of McGregor, bassist Barre Phillips, and drummer Louis Moholo, the other an unkempt but fascinating septet featuring the same rhythm section plus saxophonists Dudu Pukwana, Evan Parker, and John Surman and trumpeter Mongezi Feza. Only slightly less obscure is a Polydor album that did see the light of day, *Very Urgent.*

But the record I concentrate on here is the second one he made with the Brotherhood of Breath, *Brotherhood*, cut for British RCA and issued in '72. McGregor, like many of his South African bandmates, was living in London in this period. The band is twelve-strong, a mix of South African and British musicians, with lesser-known trombonists Malcolm Griffiths and Nick Evans, a trumpet section of Feza, Harry Beckett, and Marc Charig, saxophonists Pukwana, Mike Osborne, Alan Skidmore, and Gary Windo, powerful bassist Harry Miller, and Moholo behind the kit.

The LP kicks off with "Nick Tete," an infectious Pukwana-penned number with horn sections arranged antiphonally, deftly blending Basie and kwela. Pukwana takes an extensive, agitated alto solo over rolling rhythm and layering riffs. McGregor's "Joyful Noise" is a stunning piano feature, beginning with open playing, piano out front, sparring with Moholo's extremely light but powerful snare. Big, sophisticated, orchestrated, Ellingtonian phrases emerge gradually as backdrops for the pianist's action, which is, in the end, unfortunately cut short by a fade.

Side two commences with Osborne's punchy "Think of Someone," the alto man playing a searing solo followed by Evans's full-throated trombone spot over horn interjections calibrated to build intensity. This track also fades out abruptly after the recap of the head. A final medley starts with the leader's "Do It," an ostinato-based tune much like "MRA" from the band's first record—completely intoxicating, with shifting riffs, driving groove, and a spitfire solo by Feza, fragments of Don Cherry falling all around the boisterous party like a burst balloon. Wildman Windo eventually joins, screeching along evilly. This segues directly into Windo's short "Funky Boots March," a fittingly potent, effervescent nightcap, closing one of the great out-of-reach LPs.

[November 2001]

POSTSCRIPT 2016: *I was wrong about the Dollar Brand debut, as a* DownBeat *reader kindly informed me in a letter: it had been reissued in 1997. However, there were still many unplumbed South African grooves in 2001, some of which have since been . . . er, plumbed.* Brotherhood *was finally reissued in 2007 on Fledg'ling, a label otherwise dedicated to British folk and folk-rock; the same company also reprinted the Brotherhood's glorious 1971 debut, essential listening, and a never-released trio session, also recorded by legendary producer Joe Boyd, who had also included McGregor on Nick Drake's* Bryter Later. *Acetate copies of the trio session, together with a plosive pre-Brotherhood septet later released as* Up to Earth, *had been floating around Europe for years; Fledg'ling has also reissued the latter, bless them.*

Morris Grants Presents J.U.N.K.

(Argo, early 1960s)

Jazz and comedy are uncomfortable bed-fellows. But like sex and religion, music is something that people believe in passionately, so there'll always be some wiseacre taking cheap shots at someone else's musical article of faith.

There are in fact a few relatively rare—though not especially prized—jazz comedy records. Take *Out of My Head*, a set of monologues issued on Riverside in the early '60s by "famed *DownBeat* humorist" George Crater, a character played by comedian Ed Sherman. It's definitely a period piece, mildly funny, delivered in a Lenny Bruce–like nasal drone featuring routines about his new Miles Davis windup doll (dressed in a fine Italian suit) and Charles Mingus windup doll (which punches critics).

I've got a fave Bob Dorough LP that should probably be classified as a comedy record—*The Medieval Jazz Quartet (Plus Three)*, released on Classic Editions sometime in the late '50s, with Paul Motian on drums, George Duvivier on bass, Al Schackman on guitar, and a foursome of various-sized recorders, playing plainchant-meets-jazz arrangements of standards. And then there are the Jonathan and Darlene Edwards records, including the great Columbia LP *The Piano Artistry of Jonathan Edwards*, on which Darlene is depicted gazing adoringly at the two hands on the keyboard, both of which, on close inspection, turn out to be right hands.

The LP I most treasure when it comes to this comic jazz realm is an obscure little satirical item from Argo, issued in the early '60s. The acronym of the title, *J.U.N.K.*—an obvious reference to J.A.T.P.—stands for Jazz University's New Kicks, and it's subtitled: "The album they tried to suppress." The essay on the back is by Ira Morris, "America's Foremost Liner-Note Writer." Of the bogus testimonials on the back, I'm fondest of a line by one Sidney Clean of the Department of Sanitation: "I fully expect the *J.U.N.K.* album to become a collector's item."

The music is a hodgepodge of parodies, all of them attributed to known musicians, most of them for some reason renamed "Morris." Morris Brewbeck with

Sol Desman, Miles Morris with Can-E-Ball Naturally, Morris Ferguson. There's one by Gene Blooper (a "Krupa" joke) and Merry Julligan with Bet Taker. In truth, most of them are terrible facsimiles, bearing little resemblance to their razzed referents. That in itself is enough to make it a pretty funny record. The piece by Thelonious Plunk ("'Round Lunchtime") isn't totally un-Monk, and there's something familiar about the sweet sound of Morris Garner.

But the real showstopper is a hysterical spoof of the Ornette Coleman Quartet. The announcer introduces: "Once every generation, a new leader . . ." He's interrupted by a squealing alto sax, then some audience cheers copped from a Hitler rally. "Please, let me introduce him!" More cheering. "All right," he relents. "The new king—Ornette Morris!" Thus begins "Creative Love, However" (what a title!), attributed to O.M. with Mon Cherie on trumpet, replete with a fantastic, leaden Charlie Haden and damned sharp Ornette spoof, playing a vicious rewrite of "Lonely Woman."

If every good parody betrays a secret love of the thing it makes fun of, then these anonymous pranksters must have studied O.C. more intimately than any of the other musicians they roasted.

[January 2002]

POSTSCRIPT 2016: *A few months after publishing this column, I got a very sweet letter with a cassette tape from Jordan Ramin, brother of composer/arranger Sid Ramin and the secret brains behind J.U.N.K. I followed up with a phone call, and we spent an afternoon discussing his many adventures and misadventures in film and music, which included another jazz parody record,* The Worst of Errol Morris, *an Errol Garner spoof that he recorded at Columbia Records, the studio of Garner's label. He was banned from the studio and earned the wrath of many radio and record execs, as well as Garner, who didn't find his playful poke funny. That LP was issued on Ramin's own Thunderbird label, which also put out various novelty singles, including "Around the World," a song calculated to capitalize on the success of the film* Around the World in 80 Days, *produced by his good friend Mike Todd (then husband of Elizabeth Taylor), and "Ho Ho Rock and Roll," an extremely weird jump blues augmented with looped (and loopy) recordings of a laughing man. (On the inner label, the genre is listed as "Ho-Ho's with Orchestra.") In the same period as the Argo record, Ramin also worked on* Scent of Mystery, *a Smell-O-Vision film with an original soundtrack of his own devising. The cassette in the package contained all these recordings, of which he was very proud. Ramin died in 2012, and his archives were saved from a dumpster by Bruce Baryla. A good Samaritan of vinyl history. Needless to say, most of Ramin's offbeat efforts remain unreissued.*

Tom Stewart, *Sextette / Quintette*

(ABC-Paramount, 1956)

When I first saw Tom Stewart's lone LP in the impressive collection of Ken Pickering, artistic director of the Vancouver Jazz Festival, I put it at the top of my want list. With its gorgeous, thick cover, old-style tip-on with glossy front and matte back, issued in ABC-Paramount's first batch of jazz sides in '56, this record would eventually take its place in a relatively short stack of LPs from the label in my library. Aside from the front photo of Stewart, pensive with his tenor horn in his lap, one sideman's name grabbed my attention: Steve Lacy.

Real freaks know that Lacy's discography is one of the great challenges in jazz record collecting—acquiring all his LPs is like climbing Kilimanjaro, and if you pile them up they might give the mountain a run for its money. Among Lacy's scarcest are the "progressive Dixieland" session with trumpeter Dick Sutton on the Jaguar ten-inch *Jazz-Idiom*; the vital trio from '66, *Disposability*; the wonderful solo on Chant du Monde, *Points*; a cache of impossibly hard-to-find Japanese LPs like the Morgue solo *Torments*; and various ventures on Horo, America, or Adelphi.

With Lacy as bait, the whole Stewart record turns out to be quite a treat. Six tracks feature a five-piece band, with Dave McKenna on piano, Whitey Mitchell on bass, and Al Levitt on drums, while the remaining four tracks expand the group to include Herbie Mann (on alto flute and tenor sax), subbing Joe Puma's guitar for McKenna and in a few cases swapping Bill Bradley for Levitt. Recorded in New York, the music consists of lightly swinging West Coast versions of standards, with economical soloing and fairly inventive arrangements. Stewart's playing deserves mention, not only because he plays one of the least frequently sighted brass instruments in jazz but because he plays it so sweetly, with a deep purr. On "Let's Get Lost," his tenor horn has a lilt that many trombonists would envy. I've no idea what happened to Stewart—judging by this album he could have done well in the commercial circuit of the late '50s.

Although the CD almost completely superseded the LP more than a decade ago, a small cadre of vinyl purists persist, among them several good jazz labels. The San Francisco–based outfit 4 Men with Beards, for instance, has issued two classic creative jazz LPs licensed from Atlantic: the Art Ensemble of Chicago's 1972 live recording *Baptizum* and guitarist Sonny Sharrock's 1968 record *Black Woman*. The vinyl itself is notably well made with 180-gram stock. Stellar sound quality is strikingly evident on Sharrock's solo acoustic slide blues cut "Blind Willie." The LPs come with all the original artwork and new liner notes; the AEC issue includes a lengthy recollection of the concert by John Sinclair, who organized the festival at which it took place. 4 Men with Beards is less fussy when it comes to the visuals, though, and the reproductions of cover photos are dark and murky.

[February 2002]

POSTSCRIPT 2016: *Fresh Sound and its sister label Lonehill have both reissued the Stewart, the former on a compilation, The Early Years 1954–56, the latter on a Whitey Mitchell comp. I'm not positive how legitimate these reissues are or whether they're pirated. Most of 4 Men with Beards' vinyl activity has revolved around soul, folk, and rock, and they've done an outstanding job reissuing gems by Captain Beefheart, Allen Toussaint, and Funkadelic, but these two early forays into jazz did not lead to more, and they are both now out of print and impossible to find. They were early into the pool with the LP revival and seem to know how to swim.*

Kenny Graham and His Satellites, *Moondog and Suncat Suites*
(MGM, 1956)

Pathways to unknown worlds. More than anything else, that's what record collecting is to me. Sure, I've got a want list of things I desire in any decent shop. But that's more like piecing together a puzzle: find the right store, pay the right price, you've got the goods. I'm much more interested in music I don't know about yet, LPs waiting for me to remember them, and with them a new avenue of investigation.

Some years ago I drove to Rockford, Illinois, to visit Toad Hall, a hot spot for 78-rpm collectors. I didn't find much, but one unusual LP stole my attention, and

I bought it after haggling over the price. The nice Miró painting on the cover, the band's name—Kenny Graham and His Satellites—and the fact that it was a jazz record on MGM, something relatively unusual, attracted me. A quick perusal of the notes explained that one side's worth of the music featured Graham's arrangements of pieces by '50s New York outsider Moondog. I was hooked.

Turns out, Graham was one of the most original figures in British bop. The tenor saxophonist, composer, and bandleader was born in London in 1924, and he cut his teeth in bands led by Nat Gonella, Ambrose and Jack Parnell, Nat Temple, and Jiver Hutchinson. In 1950, he formed his own group, the Afro-Cubists. Five of their tracks from '51, recorded for the Esquire label, were reissued on the four-disc *Bebop in Britain* box, and these already hint at Graham's fascinating mind. Listening to Graham's unusual reworking of "Over the Rainbow," the group sounds more like the midsized bands Sun Ra would front five years later in terms of a pronounced futuristic aspect and a mounting interest in exoticism.

In July '56, Graham allowed the latter to come to full flower on *Moondog and Suncat Suites*. The "Moondog Suite" is made up of nine short tracks, five of them under fifty seconds, all of them garishly arranged rhythm studies with virtually no improvising or jazz feel. In addition to Graham's tenor and flute, the band includes pianist Stan Tracey playing vibes, cello, marimba, celeste, and very little piano. Danny Moss's bass clarinet is prominent in the arrangements, and the two drum kits and tympani are manned by Don Lawson and Phil Seaman.

Moondog made two records for Prestige—also in '56—but they were issued *after* Graham's LP; Graham was apparently inspired by private tapes that circulated quite widely in jazz circles, which explains why some of the pieces on his record aren't on either of Moondog's. Graham extracts a folksy, atmospheric, often pseudo-Polynesian feel from Moondog's naive-sounding sketches, pitting time signatures against one another and dressing simple ostinati in flamboyant combinations of timbre. A singer named Yolanda intones wordlessly on "Lullabye," calling to mind Sun Ra's earliest space scats or the less piercing registers of Yma Sumac. "Suncat Suite" is Graham's companion piece for the Moondog arrangements, and his compositions are longer, less rhythmically compulsive, but just as kitschily touristic. "Sunrise," for instance, is overtly Orientalist, with a chopsticks-like motif. "Sunday" is in fact a telling bit of exotica: over a gloomy, tolling bell, its melody is so close to Eden Ahbez's "Nature Boy" as to seem like an intentional comment.

[March 2002]

POSTSCRIPT 2016: *Graham's* Moondog and Suncat Suites *was reissued on CD by Trunk Records in 2010.*

John Coltrane, *Cosmic Music*
(Coltrane Records, 1968)

With all the recent issues and reissues, it's a wonder that there's any of John Coltrane's known oeuvre that hasn't been released on CD. But then some music is in for a very bumpy ride when it sets off down reissue road, and the session from February 2, 1966, that produced *Cosmic Music*, released posthumously two years later, has certainly seen some of the most potholed side streets in Coltrane's discography. In 1972 it was reissued on LP by Impulse!, new bass and piano parts dubbed over the originals plus added organ and vibraphone. (This version has apparently been reissued on disc in Japan, though I've never seen or heard a copy of the CD; the two tracks led by the pianist have been reissued domestically.)

But the superior version is definitely the first, available now only as a very rare LP. Alice Coltrane produced the record and chose to mingle the tracks by her late husband with some fine music from 1968 by her trio and a quartet with Pharoah Sanders. The cover image was from a sketch by Trane; a nice photo of him worshiping at a Japanese temple adorned the back. It seemed a loving tribute to the great musician's memory.

So it's hard to say why she soon thereafter felt compelled to mess with the music—and she really didn't hold back a bit, completely changing her piano parts and dubbing Charlie Haden in place of Jimmy Garrison. What a weird gig that must have been for Haden, altering classic music; imagine someone overdubbing his bass parts on Ornette's recordings— unthinkable. The strange thing is that Garrison's original bass playing jibed perfectly with the rest of the music (Was this a contractual issue or an aesthetic one?), and Alice's piano work was not atypical. So why the adjustment? Judging by the explanation on a Michael Cuscuna–produced 1978 release that included another piece from the same session, similarly overdubbed in '72, it seems possible that those overdubs might have been on the master tape (gads, one hopes not!), in which case the vinyl might well be the only way one could ever hope to hear the music in its initial, historically undistorted form.

The two Trane pieces on *Cosmic Music* actually come from a rather sparsely documented phase in Coltrane's late development, just a few months after McCoy Tyner and Elvin Jones had left the fold. The first cut, "Manifestation," which doesn't appear on any subsequent issues, abruptly joins the band midflight, Trane blowing hard, luminescent tenor, dovetailing with Sanders on skittish piccolo (and also some tenor). They drop out during a lengthy piano solo, then rejoin Rashied Ali's blazing drums, augmented by Ray Appleton's shakers—beautiful energy music, as Coltrane knew how to craft it. The second track is a bluesy Alice-led number on which Sanders gives a valuable lesson on varieties of articulation.

Side two contains another expressionist Trane track, "Reverend King." The saxophonist asks his wife to begin, gently beckoning: "Alice. . . ." Then he chants quietly, revving up the modal meditational engine. The piece's explosive apex contains some gloriously ecstatic bass clarinet—another underdocumented facet of Trane's recorded history—and more joyous group interaction by the full ensemble. The LP's final cut jumps off with a snippet of Coltrane's voice reciting a mantra on peace, love, and perfection in all things, seguing directly into a swirling piano trio piece, sans Sanders.

[April 2002]

POSTSCRIPT 2016: *Surprisingly, the original* Cosmic Music *has still never been reissued.*

André Hodeir, *Jazz et Jazz: Jazz Experiments*
(Philips, 1963)

Triple Play Stereo: Pop + Jazz = Swing
(Audio Fidelity, 1962)

Bill Russo Orchestra, *Stereophony*
(FM, 1963)

The first stereo LPs hit the shelves in 1958, preceded by a few years by mass-produced reel-to-reel tapes. It took some time for consumers to catch up with the new technology, to collect the necessary hardware to play the vanguard software. Jazz and stereo demonstration were label-mates from the start.

By the early '60s, the stereo hi-fi fad had turned into music industry standard, and musicians and producers were thinking about creative ways to mix the two, sometimes taking them far beyond the nearly universal practice of making stereo recordings. People began composing and arranging for stereo, the way you would compose or arrange for a big band. As a nice precursor, if you can find it, search out French pianist, critic, and composer André Hodeir's *Jazz et Jazz*, collected in '63 along with various other film soundtrack scores (some of which appeared last year on a CD reissue in Universal/Gitanes's Jazz in Paris series) on a Philips LP. This three-minute piece mixes jazz and musique concrète with astonishing facility—a swinging rhythm section sparked by Martial Solal's piano is met by all sorts of tape effects, from horns and drums turned backward to speed variation, electronic filtration, and stereo ping-ponging. *Jazz et Jazz* is a little gem of musical studio experimentation and an example of jazz composed specifically in relation to audiotape technology.

The diligent discoholic will find a reference to another stereo-specific jazz outing buried in Eric Dolphy's dicography. Producer Tom Wilson supervised a strange project in 1962 for Audio Fidelity spotlighting the magic of stereo. Benny Golson was called in to arrange a set of ten jazz standards, and in April of that year he took a modest little group into the studio to play them: Dolphy on alto saxophone, Wayne Shorter on tenor, Grachan Moncur III and/or Curtis Fuller on trombone, Bill Hardman and/or Freddie Hubbard on trumpet, Bill Evans on piano, Ron Carter on bass, and Charlie Persip on drums. On two selections, Paul Chambers and Jimmy Cobb subbed on bass and drums. Later that month, a group of string, flute, brass, and saxophone players was assembled, and that ensemble recorded Golson's arrangements of the original pop songs on which the jazz standards were based, playing along with the original recording, multitracked at exactly the same tempo. The result: *Triple Play Stereo: Pop + Jazz = Swing*. The wizardry of audio technology means that, according to the hilarious cover notes (with graphs and instructions!), by virtue of the balance knob a home listener can achieve "by means of increasing or decreasing the relative volume of the Left or Right channels, a continuously variable transition from all-Pop to all-Jazz music."

The effect is, of course, ridiculous. At best, it's perhaps an easy way to demonstrate the principle of chord changes to someone who knows nothing about modern jazz. But if you pot your preamp all the way to the right, all-jazz, there's an incredible lost session with some completely electrifying, angular Dolphy (who solos on five tracks) and gorgeous Shorter (on four) and Evans (three). In spite of the zany concept, it's a classic recording, a must for any deep Dolphy fan.

Our final showpiece in this vein is *Stereophony*, issued on United Artists' sister label FM in 1963, with compositions by bandleader Bill Russo and a British orchestra. This project was conceived and arranged specifically to relate the sectionality of big-band jazz to the spatial effects of stereo. The pieces are excellent, high-contrast, often oddly structured in a Russoan manner. My copy of the vinyl is the most valuable version, which ironically makes it impossible to appreciate the dazzling stereo effects. That's because it's mono.

[May 2002]

POSTSCRIPT 2016: *A Chilean label called Jazz Beat reissued the* Triple Play Stereo *album as* Just Jazz! *Is it a bootleg? Not sure. The Russo record remains undigitized.*

George Davis Sextet, various acetates
(no label, 1949)

This month's column comes in the form of a puzzler: Can anyone tell me who George Davis is?

The question dates back a couple of years to a trip I made to a little shop called Record Dugout on Chicago's South Side. On this day I found little of interest in the LPs but noticed a few intriguing 78s out on a table, including a brown Ma Rainey on Paramount. I'm not such a shellac hound—arguably an even more dedicated and freakish crew than we straight vinyl freaks—but I'm interested

in recorded music in general and am willing to bend my compulsion. So I put the Rainey and a few others aside and made my way to the 78s.

Leafing through the clunky discs, I ran into a cluster of acetates with handwritten labels. It's always interesting to hear what music or speech personalized records bear. Three of the records were credited to the George Davis Sextet, five more simply listed George Davis along with a recording date of April 3, 1949—a nice detail. My first impression was that these must be amateur Dixieland recordings based on the way they looked, the date, and that there were plenty of groups around then playing that music for kicks. The store owner explained that the records had recently been brought in by a woman who said they were by her dad; the owner had reluctantly bought them, figuring they'd be difficult to sell, but he didn't have any follow-up information on her. I negotiated a price and took them home.

Later that evening, I put one of the heavy, extremely brittle discs onto my phonograph. Surprise, it's not Dixieland, it's bebop! And very good bop. Now my interest was totally piqued. Unfortunately, one of the Sextet discs was broken beyond playability, and another had a hairline crack, but it played OK. The Sextet sides list full personnel, which might have been a good thing except quirkily they include first name and last initial only: "Tenor + alto—Tom G., trumpet—Lee R., trombone—Jack R., guitar—Ross R., drums—Sid S., bass—Don N., scat—Marsha S." These are all hep coed bop vocal pieces, neatly arranged in early Lambert, Hendricks, and Ross mode by one "Santy R" (*DownBeat's* Dave Zaworski points out this is probably saxophonist and mouthpiece mogul Santy Runyon). One of them is a tribute to Joe DiMaggio, the other three wordless, swimming in "oobli-ahs" and "doobli-ohs." And the playing on all of them is first-rate, with a driving rhythm section and especially strong saxophone work by George Davis and Tom G.

But the coolest tracks are the nine other ones (one of the five is one-sided), which are from a date at which Davis and his band pretended to be making a recording in front of a live audience. "Well, well, 1 a.m. and people still awake," Davis says at the beginning of the first disk. "If you're awake you know this is the George Davis Sextet. If you're not awake, you soon will be." With the exception of one missing pair of sides, this seems to be a complete session, and they feature booting, supercharged R&B sax on Nellie Lutcher's "I'm Gone," several original boppers including the niftily titled "Scapula," and versions of "Lover" and "Body and Soul." Nobody seems to know who Davis or any of his comrades are. I've asked a huge number of folks, scrolled through microfilm looking at nightclub ads, even called the Chicago American Federation of Musicians, who didn't have a George Davis in their files. So, does anyone recognize Sid S. or Lee R.? Or, better yet, Mr. Davis, the mystery man?

[June 2002]

POSTSCRIPT 2016: *Davis turns out to have had an interesting but short career in Chicago, one that I documented when we issued these shellacs on Corbett vs. Dempsey in 2014. The vocal works, in fact, were actually by Charlie Ventura—a surprise that the phone app Shazam helped me uncover. Don't know why Davis, who was probably quite angry at Ventura at the time for having stolen his vocalist, chose to pretend these tracks were by him. Very strange, but I suspect we will never know. My brief notes from the CD, which we titled* Scapula: *"Alto and tenor saxophonist George Davis is an enigmatic figure, best known for leading the band in which Jackie & Roy met. Young singer Jackie Cain encountered pianist Roy Krall in the mid '40s, playing together under Davis at a club on the south side of Chicago called Jump Town. As the George Davis Quartet, they cut two 78-rpm records for Aristocrat that followed Davis into obscurity. In 1948/49, Jackie & Roy went on to work with Charlie Ventura. At the same time, Davis cut a group of acetate sides with an unnamed band, music that was rediscovered a few years ago. Awkwardly announced as if there was an audience, these privately recorded bop and R&B sides are pure Chicago jazz, hot, swinging, and bristling with attitude."*

A Mount Rushmore of '60s guitar innovators would of course include familiar
faces—John McLaughlin, Sonny Sharrock, Derek Bailey, Jimi Hendrix—and
maybe the lesser-known Japanese great
Masayuki "Jojo" Takayanaki. One visage
that probably wouldn't be sculpted in
stone, even though it should, is that of
Staffan Harde.

Trouble is, Harde only made a single commercially released recording,
and that on the minuscule imprint of a
Swedish jazz collective. Which is to say
it didn't put Staffan Harde on the side of a mountain—or even really on the
map. But anyone lucky enough to encounter Harde's lone eponymous LP is in
for a delightful shock. Fans of Bostonian plectrist Joe Morris, among whom I
certainly stand, will find in this music a particularly startling premonition of
the new directions Morris has taken guitar since the '80s.

Like Morris, Harde prefers unprocessed sound, the clear ringing tone of
the guitar itself, lightly amplified, with a modest, natural-sounding reverb.
Unlike some, he doesn't avoid treble, but deals with it as another aspect of
the guitar's sound. Harde most often plays single-note lines, but here's where
his genius starts—his harmonic and melodic sense is completely his own, a
highly chromatic marvel. The first of two solo pieces on the record, "Substance I," sounds an incredible amount like one of Morris's solos—complex,
snaking lines with driving rhythms and subtly molten phrasing, closing with
an unusual and brilliant herky-jerky staccato section articulated in a way that
sounds like he's pumping the volume pedal, though he's not. "Substance II,"
recorded in 1968 (the rest of the tracks were recorded three years later), is
even more personal, unlike anything I've heard before, based on mutations of
folk melodies including "Santa Lucia" (which has special resonance in Swedish
culture), forcing strange and fascinating harmonizations through a funhouse
of chordal variations. It's utterly unique.

The LP features other musicians too, all Swedes and all immersed in adventurous interactive jazz. "Incitement," a duet with bassist Lars-Urban Helje,

is a dark, brooding track; Harde is extremely inventive, lightning quick, with an attack sometimes reminiscent of Jim Hall's pinpoint sound. Helje walks at different tempi, setting the backdrop for intimate action. Drummer Bengt Berger, retroactively the big name on the LP, joins with some light swinging kit and vivid hand percussion on two quartet tracks, "Bigaroon" and "Electrification," where pianist Lars Sjosten does a tremendous job of complementing Harde's lines without getting tangled up in them. "Cordial L," a trio without drums, is another ultrarelaxed showcase for Harde's beautiful guitar. His playing in the group contexts recalls Billy Bauer's work in the 1949 improvisations with Lennie Tristano—oblique lines motivated by a strong linear logic but not governed by a unitary tonal principle. Indeed, Tristano's linearity and sense of counterpoint leave fingerprints all over the outing.

Rumor has it that Harde gave up music and now lives in southern Sweden, working in a bakery. But to get a taste of his earlier confections, freaks had better get hunting for this important and delectable rarity.

Joe Morris Responds

Years ago a writer told John Coltrane that Sun Ra claimed to have done everything credited to Coltrane first. Coltrane replied "He probably did." John Corbett claims that a Swedish guitarist I never heard of before, Staffan Harde, "sounds an incredible amount" like me before I did. The similarity is described as "particularly startling" and a "delightful shock."

Back when I started to play my way (1973) there were dozens of guitarists working off of the same influences like Coltrane, Cecil Taylor, Eric Dolphy, Lennie Tristano, Ornette Coleman, and Anthony Braxton. Like me, they were inspired by groundbreaking guitarists like Tal Farlow, Jimmy Raney, Billy Bauer, Jim Hall, Barry Galbraith, Attila Zoller, Joe Diorio, Jay Berliner, and Sal Salvador to explore new harmonic and melodic possibilities. No doubt Harde was one of them, too. Michael Gregory Jackson, James Emery, and Bern Nix are three more. Every year I hear of others.

It's strange though that Corbett would declare that Harde, whose sole recording contains a couple of tracks that sound like me, belongs alongside Jimi Hendrix, John McLaughlin, Derek Bailey, all of whom created extensive bodies of work. Considering the huge effort made by so many guitarists to sound like themselves in open and shifting tonalities, giving all that credit to one guy who no one outside of Sweden has ever heard is absurd.

Joe Morris, New York

John Corbett Responds to Joe Morris's Response

I completely agree with Joe's clarification and he's right to call me on my overstatement. There were a great many musicians grappling with the same issues at that time. At one level, Staffan Harde was one of the pack. I hear Harde as something of an anomaly, rather more extreme, perhaps eccentric and out-of-step with the prevailing fashions, but he didn't arrive *deus ex machina*. He was part, however remote, of a community of thought. Furthermore, I did not mean to imply that Joe's concept came from or is adequately summarized in these few shreds of Harde's music—Joe has spent decades developing and changing his music in a way, at least in terms of recordings, that we cannot claim for Harde.

I mentioned being startled and experiencing "shock" only because I've not heard anyone at all close to Morris's sound before, so encountering someone who was dealing with similar—not identical—solutions was especially unexpected. That should suggest how unique and personal Joe's music is, in that it hasn't really reminded me of anybody else's before.

One implication, however, that I disagree with is the suggestion that the fact that somebody is well known should in any way impact whether we attribute him or her credit. Who cares whether anyone outside of Sweden has heard Harde? We should be hungry to hear things we haven't heard, open to the idea that something (even something historical) might surprise us. That's the subtext of this column. Icons sometimes deserve their iconic status, but on the other hand sometimes great musical thinkers don't get their due. Or people create one incredible record, then fall off into making trivial fluff. Should we think less of that one record? As for the necessity of extensiveness of an artist's body of work, I can definitely think of some figures who are better documented than their music merits, and, conversely, wouldn't it be interesting to hear that one fabled Buddy Bolden cylinder?

[August–October 2002]

POSTSCRIPT 2016: *After years of research and consideration, working with Mats Gustafsson and in conjunction with the Harde family, I finally reissued* Staffan Harde *on Corbett vs. Dempsey this year. We've discovered ample previously unreleased material—music he recorded on reel-to-reel tapes that he sold or gave away as unique objects—to issue a follow-up if it is well received. Meanwhile, still no sign of the Buddy B.*

Art Pepper, *Chile Pepper*
(CP Records, 1956)

Sometimes, it's very difficult to figure out the exact flight path of a given recording. Take this fine session by Art Pepper, recorded in Hollywood in August 1956. Pepper's alto saxophone is alone out front, with the Marty Paich Quartet supporting, Buddy Clark on bass, and Frank Capp on drums. Perhaps, for instance, you might pick up a copy of the CP Records (short for Charlie Parker) issue of this music, as I did, drawn by the irresistible force of its utterly grotesque cover image—the genius handiwork of one Howard Goldstein—which features a bowl of chili con carne on a checked tablecloth, with two flies busily supping from the side of the bowl. The design is so foul as to be fascinating, and it boggles the mind that this could have seemed marketable to anyone.

But what's at least as interesting, though you'd find nary a shred of evidence on the record itself, is that the CP issue of this is actually a cut-rate reissue of an earlier release of exactly the same music, published on Tampa Records under the title *Abstract Art*. That edition actually sported an abstract painting on the cover, and yes, for those sticklers out there, it's been reissued on CD, so technically this music's been released in digital form. Nevertheless, if you don't have a copy of the CP version, you're really missing a prime piece of weird jazz hi-fi culture, not only because of the front cover—which also spells out the title in peppers—but the whole (if you'll pardon the wordplay) enchilada.

For instance, the CP motto on the upper-right corner of the back cover: "Dedicated to Jazz thru Sound." Hmmm, now how else would you access jazz? (In the late '50s, United Artists had a more sensible, and very funny, motto: "Music for the Talented Listener.") A vague reference in *Chile Pepper*'s liner notes to the "turmoil of the American Musical Scene" seems directed at the fearful menace of free jazz, suggesting that this reissue came something like five years after the initial recording. The notes go on to promise "a cheerful bit of musical sanity" on *Chile Pepper*. They also mention that the record is good "if you want some pick-me-up music without the severe intrusion of the music itself." A most strange guarantee and a real disservice to the actual sounds in the LP's grooves, which repay close attention perfectly well.

While the name Marty Paich doesn't always perk up my ears, in this case he's playing extremely well, attentive and inventive, and even contributes a couple of nice tunes. Pepper plays gorgeously, as he often did then, perked up on whatever he was ingesting. You can't make too much of the toss-off liner notes, uncredited (for good reason), but they do say something about the perceived selling points of certain music, like sweetness, prettiness, and loveliness—all terms taken from the notes.

My favorite artifact on this strange bargain-basement reprint, however, is located on the inner label of the record, in the position usually reserved for words asserting the superior fidelity—"full-frequency stereo" and other such more or less meaningless euphemisms. Here, CP proudly, with an exclamation point, proclaims: "MONO-PACT!" Sad, but they just don't make quality mumbo jumbo like that anymore, do they?

[September 2002]

POSTSCRIPT 2016: *Two months after this entry, a* CD *version of* Chile Pepper *arrived on the market, sporting a benign redesign with an anachronistic photo of A.P. and lots of extra tracks. But where's the carne?*

Jack Wilson, *The Jazz Organs*
(Vault Records, 1964)

To the extent that he's known at all, Jack Wilson is thought of as a fine pianist and onetime musical director for Dinah Washington, but in September 1964, he made an excellent outing playing organ. The session was novel not simply for that, but for the rest of its instrumentation, which revolved around the unusual idea of a front line consisting of two organs. On most of the LP, the second organist is Henry Cain, while on two tracks one Ghenghis Kyle is employed (gotta be a pseudonym, but who is it really?). It's an Indiana-centric date, too, with Wilson having grown up in Fort Wayne and Cain and bassist Leroy Vinnegar hailing from Indianapolis. All three, at that point, had settled in Los Angeles, where the session took place. Strangely, although Wilson released other records on the Atlantic label—including the outstanding reissued trio session with Vinnegar and Philly Joe Jones, *The Two Sides of Jack Wilson*, and a great quartet LP with vibist

THE JAZZ ORGANS
VAULT RECORDS
MY FAVORITE THINGS · BLUES 'N BOOGIE · LONELY AVENUE
STREET SCENE · ONE MINT JULEP · CAIN'S ABEL · FOR CARL
JACK WILSON

Roy Ayers—*The Jazz Organs* came out on Atlantic subsidiary Vault Records. It's adorned with a smart, simple, sans serif Woody Woodward cover design, and the recording itself sounds terrific.

Things start off with the one throwaway cut on the record, "My Favorite Things," obviously trying to cop a contact high off Coltrane's Atlantic success four years prior. But from there things take wing, a smoking version of "One Mint Julep" rollicking into Vinnegar's easy-swinging number "For Carl," a groovy tune likely dedicated to Carl Perkins, the pianist and long-term Vinnegar associate who'd died in '58. Guitarist Gene Edwards takes the requisite Wes Montgomery–like solo, maybe offering a sly nod back at Indianapolis. "Lonely Avenue" is a chunking blues, mojo juice aplenty, on which Wilson chooses a particularly nice setting for his little unaccompanied cadenza.

The second side begins with the misty ballad "Street Scene," which finds Wilson's organ emotive, but not simpering. He swells, his lines pulse with vibrato, and on this track and the version of Dizzy Gillespie's "Blues 'n Boogie," he's supported by Philly Joe, instead of drummer Donald Bailey, who plays elsewhere. As is the modus on *The Jazz Organs*, the two keyboards always stay clear of each other, never getting their hooves tangled as has so often happened in multiple-organ pileups over the ensuing years. That's abundantly clear on "Cain's Abel," an up burner with a more modern hard-bop organ sound, slick and funky, spotlight on Vinnegar's sprinting bass and a thrilling Wilson/Cain chase chorus climax.

According to the Lord discography there were two unreleased tracks, "Spontaneous Blues" and "Juicy," waxed at the same studio date. Time's come for someone to reissue the historic two-organ session in full. Double our pleasure, double our fun.

[December 2002]

POSTSCRIPT 2016: *Jack Wilson died in 2007. The Jazz Organs was digitally remastered in 2011 by a company called the Essential Media Group. They offer it as an on-demand CD-R. At least it's available.*

In some ways, following a boom ten years earlier, the middle of the '80s was a particularly inhospitable time to make an independent creative jazz LP in New York City. For one thing, the neocons were clamping down on outcat outlets, spreading their message of reawakened values and decrying exploration as hoodwinkery. At the same time, the new compact disc technology was poised to take over the market. Smaller purveyors of vinyl, like the wee O.T.C. label (that's "Of the Cosmos"), fell into the chasm, their productions now more or less a lost cause, eventually relinquished to some warehouse cemetery. But some folks do still have turntables, so records such as trombonist Craig Harris's ambitious septet outing *Tributes* aren't completely gone with the wind.

From Dave Holland's opening 7/4 bass ostinato on "High Life" to the closing didjeridoo moans of "Underground Journey," *Tributes* is of its time—it's in the extremely good company of early '80s projects by David Murray, Henry Threadgill, Edward Wilkerson Jr., and Julius Hemphill. Writers (at least the ones paying attention) of the period were fond of proclaiming a new epoch of orchestration and arrangement. Harris was (and still is) a very good arranger. A member of Sun Ra's Arkestra on and off for nearly a decade, ending a couple of years before this date, he's well acquainted with the methods of making a little band sound big. His charts are thick, warm, playful, lyrical, and bluesy; he backs soloists with urgent riffs, opts for shorter solos rather than epic statements, calls for powerful swing time and revels in the ensemble sound. (In other words, he does everything the neocons said his ilk weren't doing.) The tender "Lorna," a midtempo ballad, is a radiant showcase for his own trombone, and "D.A.S.H." is likewise sweet as a ripe honeydew.

With Billy Higgins and the Art Ensemble of Chicago's Don Moye sharing drum duties, Holland on bass, and a saxless horn section of fellow Arkestran Vincent Chancey on French horn, Olu Dara on cornet, Junior Vega on trumpet, and Harris on trombone, the music can't help but have a second-line element; indeed, Higgins and Moye (what an unlikely, but perfectly matched pair) lend a buoyancy to the proceedings that would make a supercharged marching band envious. Dara contributes a little harmonica and African trumpet, foreshadowing his more recent emphasis on multi-instrumentalism, but he's also a sensational cornet player, as demonstrated here. On "24 Days an Hour," Harris uses two devices he might have copped from Ra: word inversion and the anthemic chant.

"Underground Journey" is the LP's meditative number, Moye's balaphon and Dara's African trumpet floating spacily over the didjeridoo pedal. "High Life" is punchy, with an Afro-pop feel, rolling snare work by Higgins, sharp soloing by Vega (where's he these days?) and Harris, and a biting dollop of massed brass in the staccato theme. Harris's trademark 'bone-scream appears on "Same Places, New Faces," peaking his solo as the track is urgently propelled from elegant, multidimensional opening theme to the swirling out-head by Holland, who is customarily wonderful on the whole record.

At this point, it's even hard to find many of the major label creative music releases from the same period—how about those incredible Threadgill Sextett LPs, or Hemphill's essential *Dogon A.D.*—so the offerings of a tiny label like this are tough to locate. But if you can scrounge one up and you're a fan of that sort of sound, *Tributes* will make you one satisfied freak.

[February 2003]

POSTSCRIPT 2016: *Neither* Tributes *nor the other O.T.C. release, bassist Sirone's* Artistry *(the design for which was the inspiration for the debut LP by the group* Tortoise*), has been reissued in any form.*

Quintet Moderne, *The Strange and the Commonplace*
(Po Torch, 1989)

The medium shapes the message. Bebop proclaimed: now's the time. But what of bebop time? It is, in no insignificant way, the same time as swing and early jazz. Two-and-a-half minute pieces. The 78-rpm single, two sides, an era of mentally strung together "Part 1" and—halt, lift, turn it over—"Part 2"; or, rarely, more lengthy side-to-side relay races. Wire recordings, the then-emergent technology of magnetic tape, and the equally fallible storage system of personal recollection, have allowed us to understand other things about the bebop era— that it wasn't entirely an epoch of conciseness, terse solos, the furious crunch of trying to cram a gigabyte of musical data onto a shellac pancake. Fascinating late-'40s recordings by Charlie Ventura and Bill Harris, with epic solos, show how different the live practice of bebop could be from its record-bound self-conception.

A common image of a given music derives from its recordings, from the limitations and opportunities of its medium, and it's arguable that jazz has proven particularly responsive to shifts in the prevalent mode of representation. The revolutionary change instigated by the long-playing record offers a link between seemingly incongruous musics: hard bop and freely improvised music are both babies of the LP generation.

THE STRANGE AND THE COMMONPLACE   QUINTET MODERNE

The CD offered the next significant leap in recorded music's hang time, in terms of consumer technology. Possible length of uncut musical endeavors is longer than an hour; recently, it's extended an additional twenty minutes. For the information pack rat, that's a real boon. Reissues can supplement an original package with so much additional material that they often don't worry about the quality of the alternates. But do we need four or five virtually identical takes of three tracks on Kenny Burrell's *Guitar Forms*? It's inelegant and undermines the producer's careful work, which is to isolate one especially beautiful take from among more common ones.

Which takes us to this month's Vinyl Freak entry, from the Po Torch label. Founded by percussionists Paul Lovens and Paul Lytton in 1977, Po Torch has continued as a vinyl-only outlet. Issuing at the pace of a little less than a record per year, Lovens (who now runs the label himself) has kept the full catalog in print. All of them are superb, gorgeously packaged and pressed, expertly selected highlights of spontaneous music by European musicians, and one of them, *Weavers*, by Lovens, trombonist Gunter Christmann, and bassist Maarten Altena, is probably my favorite improvised record from the '70s.

But *The Strange and the Commonplace* is something even more refined. Waxed in '89, it's the coda at the end of a full set. It consists of less than three and a half minutes of sound, the run-off groove longer than the music. The B-side is smooth and grooveless. This release abides by a pre-LP standard, suggesting what might happen if we were forced to single out a single's worth of music from a longer blow. It better be good to justify such drastic editorial

measures. And it is—a breathless, sublime moment. Violinist Phil Wachsmann loops a little plucked figure, Lovens joining on delicate, sympathetic
gong, bassist Teppo Hautaaho and saxophonist Harri Sjostrom virtually inaudible. Our hero: trombonist Paul Rutherford, who lofts an incandescent
melody tinged slightly with melancholy. Who says free music doesn't allow
for loveliness? Or for that matter, that it has to go on forever?

Po Torch can be contacted and its albums ordered through the mail: P.O.
Box 1005, D-5100, Aachen, Germany.

[March 2003]

POSTSCRIPT 2016: *Po Torch ceased issuing music years ago, but Lovens has not
released any of the LPS on CD, nor has he licensed any of the music, including*
The Strange and the Commonplace. *I know. I've tried.*

A. K. Salim, *Afro-Soul / Drum Orgy*
(Prestige, 1965)

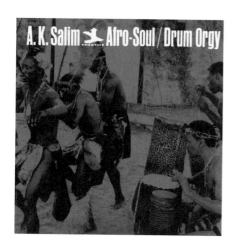

Are you ready to get your freak on? I
speak of orgies—drum orgies, the mass-
ing of Afro-Cuban rhythms into ecstatic
waves of lap-dancing percussion. Afro-
Latin jazz was rife with these mildly
offensive stereotypes at one time, but
then we're referring to a period in which
"to swing" optionally meant something
different from what it primarily does
now. (In most households . . .) A half
century ago, the orgiastic connotations
of the drum ensemble (think simultane-
ous contiguous multiple pulses: an orgy)
were enough to lead to *Erotica: The Rhythms of Love* (Fax Records), in which a
grunting Afro-Cuban percussionist is augmented by the intimate sounds of a
copulatin' couple. Tasteful, eh? In more polite jazz circles, Art Blakey hosted
the first so-named event, the two volumes of *Orgy in Rhythm* recorded for
Blue Note in 1957. By the mid-'60s, the sex party was a tired, but not completely spent, metaphor.

The idea for composer, conductor, arranger, and onetime bopper A. K.
Salim's *Afro-Soul / Drum Orgy* reportedly came from producer Ozzie

Cadena. Get a bunch of percussionists together, play some African patterns without rehearsals or prearranged charts, throw a few howling horns on top, and zip, you've got a cheaply made but hot record. Put a few gyrating Zulus on the cover, and you're guaranteed to sell a few copies. Out of just this sort of half-baked, ridiculously shallow concept came a very interesting LP, one that Fantasy should consider dredging from their seemingly inexhaustible shelves, an unusually successful instance of exotica grafted with free jazz.

On Salim's record there's more than a passing connection to Sun Ra, who was hosting many percussion-intensive parties of his own in New York during the early '60s. It turns out that this session's percussionists were hired at the suggestion of drummer Willie Bobo, with whom John Gilmore played a celebrated jam session (the one that so thrilled Coltrane). The horn section—if you can call it a section—includes Yusef Lateef, who played with Ra in the late '40s (when Lateef was still known as Bill Evans and Ra was Sonny Blount), as well as Ra's long-standing baritonist, Pat Patrick. Trumpeter Johnny Coles provides the brass timbres with surprising adaptability. The only African musician on the record is percussionist Philemon Hou, a genuine Zulu who contributes striking balaphon. The rest of the percussionists are Latin musicians, including Julio Callazo (who spot-arranged some of the rhythms), Osvaldo Martinez, Marcelino Valdes, Juan Cadaviejo, and William Correa. Whatever role Salim had must have been relatively reduced, but the result is a loose, sweaty percussion backdrop, implicitly modal, for horn solos. On the up-tempo "Afrika," we're offered a rare listen to Patrick on alto, and his solo is as fiery and penetrating as a burning spear. Lateef follows with more tensile, even boppish lines leading to an ecstatic eruption.

"Kumuamkia Mzulu (Salute to a Zulu)" features a skimpy melodic idea, horns gravitating around a few notes, Lateef glissing on an ocarina-like flute; the track fades out midstep, begging the question whether there's more in the can. For the touristic exotic track, turn to "Ngomba Ya Tembo (Elephant Dance)," with scrapers and airy flutes. Lateef's back on tenor with a vengeance on "Pepo Za Safari (Trade Winds)," sporting huge multiphonics and wonderfully fuzzy articulation, like a drunk man slurring his speech, but saying something significant.

[May 2003]

POSTSCRIPT 2016: *Still no sign of Drum Orgy, but Pat Patrick's almost mythically rare Sound Advice was reissued by Art Yard, as both a CD and an LP. The latter is packaged with a beautiful hand-silkscreened cover.*

Tristan Meinecke, home recordings

(1939–1943)

This month, think of me as the Acetate Freak. Before World War II, when people wanted to record themselves, they might have done so directly onto disc. These old home records might be one- or two-sided; twelve, ten, or the quickly obsolete five inches in diameter; and they tend to hold up better than many magnetic tapes.

Recently, I've auditioned some acetates from the early '40s documenting the music of important Chicago painter Tristan Meinecke. These recordings offer proud testimonial to the way that jazz was presumed to be the most relevant music in virtually all arts communities. Indeed, Meinecke's story shows how fuzzy the borders between the visual arts and jazz were, and how strong the allure of improvisation was to a modern-minded artist. Looking back, Meinecke calls himself "a latecomer to jazz." He first learned about it around 1928, when he was twelve. At the time, growing up in the suburbs of Ann

Tristan Meinecke in his studio, 1939 (courtesy the Estate of Tristan Meinecke)

Arbor, Michigan, he'd listen to Cab Calloway on the radio. In '32, he moved to Ann Arbor, and at nineteen he got a clarinet. He taught himself to blow while sick in bed, then took a few lessons from the leader of the Michigan band from whom he learned basic fingerings. Eventually he got tired of the instruction and committed to teach himself by ear.

In Ann Arbor, Meinecke met Harvey Brown, the guitar-playing brother of Chicago alto saxophonist Boyce Brown. They jammed regularly, drinking gin and raising a ruckus. Together with his drumming / trumpet-playing brother Phil, seven years his junior, Meinecke canvassed the small black section of town for unwanted jazz and blues 78s, collecting shellacs by Ma Rainey, Bessie Smith, Louis Armstrong, King Oliver, and various members of Chicago's Austin High Gang. Meinecke aspired to play like Johnny Dodds, Mezz Mezzrow, and Pee Wee Russell. But where Russell was a massive clarinetist who was also a very good painter, Meinecke probably could have gone either way. He's a visionary visual artist and a natural musician—that he never practiced the clarinet is hard to fathom listening to the slinky sound and bottomless trove of melodic ideas on these acetates.

All of them were recorded in Ann Arbor, before the Meinecke brothers relocated to Chicago in '43. The earliest is a five-inch from '39, with Phil on drums, "Tom" on guitar, and Jim Bridges on terrific trumpet. One from '40 was recorded live with a band of professional musicians at the exclusive Barton Hill Country Club. There are some music-minus-one-style recordings featuring a lithe Phil on trumpet and Tristan's confident clarinet. A bouncy version of "Coquette" from two years later is backed by a grinding blues, as is a roughly recorded version of "Sheik of Araby." A five-inch from '42 spotlights Phil's Bix-like trumpet, duetting with Tristan on brushes and snare.

In the Windy City, Meinecke found lots of opportunities to play. Earl Hines's clarinetist Darnell Howard, with whom Meinecke and his wife, Lorraine (television's Angel Casey), were friends, gave him a new mouthpiece. Years later, after Phil had tragically taken his own life, Tristan worked out intriguing pieces for solo piano and electric piano, highly chromatic things he referred to as "atonal compositions," as well as forays into musique concrète. These early '60s tape recordings seem distant from the legacy of his hot jazz days until you listen to the short extra track on one of the '43 acetates: there's Tristan, alone on piano, testing out an advanced harmonic idea, presaging his own subsequent investigations.

[June 2003]

POSTSCRIPT 2015: *Tristan Meinecke died in 2004, Angel Casey in 2007. They had a long life together, including many jazz-era romps that were wilder and more lascivious than you might expect. A year before Tristan passed, the couple invited my wife, Terri, and me over for breakfast. We had pancakes. I admired the sculpture Tristan made of Baby Dodds, for which the drummer had posed when they were acquaintances in the '40s. During a lull in conversation, Tristan looked at his octogenarian wife and said: "It's too bad we're so damned old, or we could have an orgy!" I expected the demure Casey to be scandalized. "Oh, Tris," she said. "Now you know that's the kind of statement that can lead from one thing to another!"*

The Chico Hamilton Quintet, *Sweet Smell of Success*
(Decca, 1957)

Some of the most engaging jazz records might well be filed in a section other than the one marked "jazz." While the movie soundtrack genre is packed with lots of marginal and largely unlistenable dross, it also happens to be home to a hidden enclave of wonderful jazz recordings. What's more, the very fact of it being a soundtrack seems to have a liberating effect on composers and musicians, removing some of the format conventions that can, when done to death, become so tedious, and offering a blank slate for the jazz conceptualist.

Spinning around on the Vinyl Freak's plate this month is just such a platter, the soundtrack to *Sweet Smell of Success*. In fact, it's one of two such soundtracks; the other orchestral score for the film was composed by Elmer Bernstein and issued on a separate LP, also on Decca. The terrific 1957 film revolves around Burt Lancaster's megalomaniacal newspaper columnist J. J. Hunsecker and Tony Curtis as an unctuous agent, and it actually features the Chico Hamilton Quintet quite prominently, playing in the nightclub scenes and even acting a bit. The jazz tunes, composed by cellist Fred Katz and drummer Hamilton, crop up in various places, both as part of the narrative and alongside Bernstein on the soundtrack proper.

Side one of the Hamilton record includes seven original themes from the film recorded in the studio as basically straight jazz numbers. They're great, not so unlike the Hamilton Quintet dates of the day, with the drummer sure and tasteful behind Katz's cello, Carson Smith's bass, John Pisano's guitar, and the multiple horns of Paul Horn, who handles alto sax, flute, and clarinet. The standout track is "Susan" (alternately titled "The Sage"), a stately, quasi-classical vehicle. Other tracks display impish humor ("Chick to Chico"), a West Coast sophistication ("Night Beat"), and sometimes a noirish aura of torn-curtain sensuality ("Goodbye Baby"). On "Sidney's Theme," Hamilton shows off some sincerely hot rimshots.

One spin of this side would already have been enough to make me glad I'd obtained the vinyl item up in Milwaukee at an exquisite little shop called Lotus Land, but it's side two that really sets this puppy apart. Here we find Hamilton, Katz, and Co. engaging in what amounts to a full side of freely improvised music. On the cover, claims are made that it's a "Concerto of Themes from Soundtrack to 'Sweet Smell of Success,'" but that's misleading, since as far as I can tell, any thematic material seems to have been generated on the spot. The liner notes call it a "composition in free concerto form," exclaiming that "not even a sketched arrangement was made for this recording." I'd heard that some of the Hamilton groups played spontaneous music, even in studio sessions, and the practice is not historically unprecedented (check out Tristano's landmark cool-free pieces from '49), but I believe that this might be the earliest instance of a side-long recording—nearly twenty minutes uncut, one track—of free music.

Of course, the piece is open within rather narrow limits. Episodic, the improvising tends to center around patterns (bass and drum ostinati, predominantly) with a strong overarching tonality anchoring the linear instruments. Nevertheless the playing enjoys a much looser feel and sometimes moves through much more dissonant passages than you'd expect if the music had been prearranged. A translucent moment in the middle of the piece features guitar harmonics and triangle over walking bass. Maybe not for *Sweet Smell of Success*, but, retroactively applied, side two would make a sensational soundtrack for something.

[July 2003]

POSTSCRIPT 2016: *Él Records, a subsidiary of Cherry Red, reissued the Chico Hamilton soundtrack in 2008, bundled together with Elmer Bernstein's orchestral score.*

Lehn-Strid, *Here There*
(Fylkingen, 2003)

Klapper-Küchen, *Irregular*
(Fylkingen, 2003)

If the LP and twelve-inch single are experiencing something of a minor renaissance—due in no small part to DJ culture—there's one format that never really went away: the seven-inch single. Once the prime vehicle of jukeboxes and mainstay of Top 40, the seven-inch persists largely because of its centrality to punk and post-punk circles, where it's beloved for its terseness (no album-length jams here), its portability, and its cheapness to produce and consume. In the '70s, the picture-sleeve single became the standard, and for underground musics it has remained a viable medium ever since.

Dutch pianist Misha Mengelberg once told me that he thought high-energy free jazz was a music for seven-inch singles: it's exciting, but it often goes on much too long; better to hear it for a little while only, a few minutes at a time, like a single. That's not a bad formula, and it could be extended to other forms of improvised music on record, too. In fact, the potency of the seven-inch for free music seems to be coming into its own of late. There are still plants pressing singles—some places are making much heavier, better-quality ones, with far better sound (though 45-rpm singles already sound great, since they're moving so fast and spreading the data across so much space rather than cramming it on, like on a 33⅓-rpm)—and people continue to invent novel ways to package them.

Swedish saxophonist Mats Gustafsson, for instance, has made a three-record set, seven-inch, called *Trees and Truths* (Olaf Bright Editions, 2003), consisting of solo sax improvisations and packaged in a beautifully spare embossed heavy cardboard box, hand-signed and numbered in a limited edition of three hundred. More art object than commercial release.

A little more down-and-dirtily packaged are two other Swedish productions from the Stockholm record label and experimental music institution called Fylkingen, the fifth and sixth of their newly instituted seven-inch series. Composed of freely improvised duets, both are recent recordings featuring one Swede paired with one non-Swede. On *Here There*, drummer Raymond Strid plays brilliant ashcan school percussion in tandem with German analog synthesizer player Thomas Lehn, one of the greatest electronic improvisers currently in business. The music is explosive, sudden, disquieting clamor and very sensitively executed in two six-minute bursts.

Saxophonist Martin Küchen and Danish/Czech multi-instrumentalist Martin Klapper conspire on *Irregular* for a more overtly playful, sometimes even wacky outing, with lots of space, hyperbolic sounds, amplified noises, and collage fragments. Both records have been exquisitely mastered, so the fidelity is outstanding and the musical interplay comes through loud and clear. And they're pressed on such thick vinyl you could probably stop a bullet with one of them. (Unless, of course, the shooter hit the spindle-hole bull's-eye. Ouch! The most feared death for a vinyl freak.)

[September 2003]

Bill Leslie, *Diggin' the Chicks*
(Argo, 1962)

Thornel Schwartz with Bill Leslie, *Soul Cookin'*
(Argo, 1962)

Ah, the inevitable apostrophe in soul-jazz, totem of hipness, guarantor of grease. From the vaults of Chicago's Argo label, a huge backlog of great groove, here are two lesser-known pearls featuring the dynamic duo of guitarist Thornel Schwartz and tenor saxophonist Bill Leslie. Both waxed in '62, these LPS are, in fact, quite different from each other—one features a high-power acoustic New York rhythm section, the other a down-and-dirty organ group.

Diggin' the Chicks gives the clearest picture of Leslie's rather warm, fuzzy sound. The unusual program, centered on glorious gals, includes Leadbelly's "Goodnight Irene," a nice folk-jazz adaptation, as well as Earl Hines's "Rosetta," a showcase for Leslie's tenor. "Madge" is a down-the-barrel blues (propelled by Art Taylor's swingful drumming), "Margie" is another straight

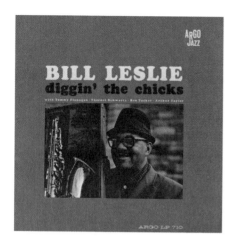

changes piece, and "I've Got a Date with an Angel" gives pianist Tommy Flanagan a chance to stretch. Leslie's approach is well attuned to ballads, as he shows on a silky "Angel Eyes," but his version of Ornette Coleman's "Lonely Woman" is a hilarious misunderstanding, his saxello lending the garbled piece a helium falsetto. It's funny to hear mainstreamers trying to get their heads around Ornette in the early '60s.

Schwartz is front man on *Soul Cookin'*, and the band might be accused of burning, not just cooking. Organist Lawrence Olds makes a rare appearance here (hmmm, wonder if he could be related to Larry Young?), and Jerome Thomas holds down the kit. The guitarist's sound is incisive, with Wes Montgomery–like octaves and soulful licks. On this date, the producer ladled a bit more echo on Leslie than necessary, but he still sounds good. A bossa number, "Brazil," is least interesting, while an unusually long take on the blues waltz "You Won't Let Me Go" provides plenty of thrills, with Olds (Young) adding pert organ. The capper is a short, zany "Theme from Mutiny on the Bounty," with Leslie forcing some hard harmonics out of his pacifist saxophone.

[October 2003]

POSTSCRIPT 2016: *Bill Leslie died in 2003. Neither of these worthy Argo releases has been released on* CD.

Tony Scott and His Buddies, *Gypsy*

(Signature, 1959)

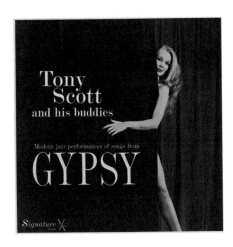

The indignities great jazz has sometimes had to suffer. But that's one thing jazz has been especially good at: fitting profundities into goofy places. Like, for instance, the cover to this 1959 LP by clarinetist Tony Scott, which features a trite, *Playboy*-esque girlie-shot that turns the Jules Styne–Stephen Sondheim Broadway musical *Gypsy* into a pretext for pulp paperback come-on. Together with the cut-rate-looking logo for Signature records, it appears prepackaged for the discount bin.

But slip that sucker out of the cover, and it's a whole new ballgame. First of all, the music is beautifully recorded, everything clear and mixed perfectly, with a remarkably natural sound (in spite of garbacious vinyl). From the unaccompanied opening clarinet on "I Had a Dream," tinged with the slight melancholy of a blueblood Tzigane, this is no economy-class ride—purely first-class. The band? Likewise. Heavyweights: Mundell Lowe on guitar, Jimmy Garrison on bass, and Pete LaRoca on drums. Given this crew, the awful cover begins to seem even that much more ridiculous.

Scott's playing in this period is remarkable, and unduly overlooked in retrospect. His clarinet sings with a marked, at times unusually big, vibrato, but the sound is round and full, and what he's playing is almost always melodically interesting. On a quietly rocking version of "Little Lamb," his vibrato is nearly Bechet; Scott perks it up on a second, more boisterous version, on which he draws unimagined energy from the sweet little lullaby, LaRoca adding Elvin Jones–ish triplets.

Throughout, Lowe is crisp and tasty, comping or taking a short solo here and there. "Cow Song" features Garrison in the lead role, sans clarinet, which offers a nice, unexpected opportunity to hear the future Coltrane comrade. The bassist plays a duet with Scott at the opening of "Together Wherever," matching the clarinetist's highly imaginative phrasing with instant counterpoint. The record's centerpiece is a fabulous take on "Everything's Coming Up Roses," on which Scott breaks the main line into little dollops of notes, then bursts into a joyous solo, heart in full song. LaRoca plays like his life depends on it.

There's ample Broadway-style belting from Scott on "Rose's Tune," and he makes the most of stop-time breaks on "Some People," uncorking some memorable, fast runs. Scott's modernistic arrangement shows that "Small World" has untapped potential as a jazz vehicle.

What's particularly pleasing about this LP is how forward the clarinet is in a period that saw too few clarinet-only front lines. We all know how neglected the instrument was during bop's reign, even more so when hard bop hit town. But there were stalwarts, like Scott, who kept the flame burning. He made a number of wonderful records in this period, recorded for a hodgepodge of labels (Brunswick, RCA Victor, Coral, Signature, ABC-Paramount, Secco, Perfect) before waxing his better-known Verve releases. Same year as *Gypsy*, he made a fascinating session, co-led by trombonist Jimmy Knepper, called *Free Blown Jazz* (Carlton), and there's a Fresh Sound two-CD set that shouldn't be missed. It compiles his sessions with pianist Bill Evans.

For this one, however, you'll have to scour the flea markets looking for the record with the ugliest cover you can find.

[November 2003]

POSTSCRIPT 2016: *A limited-edition Japanese reissue of* Gypsy *appeared on* CD *in 2011, replete with the horrendous original design.*

Herbie Mann, *Great Ideas of Western Mann*
(Riverside, 1957)

Bass clarinet was one of the great doubler's instruments in early jazz. It was a prominent part of the tonal palette in novelty bands and in cartoon music, but as a leader's tool it took quite a long time to come into its own. Buster Bailey and Harry Carney played it, and in later contexts John Gilmore and, of course, Eric Dolphy did, but always as a second horn, never without the possible switcheroo to another sound color. A few years back, Koch reissued a rare and fascinating Buddy DeFranco record called *Blues Bag*, which almost exclusively features DeFranco's bass clarinet (he plays clarinet on one track), recorded in 1964 and originally released on Vee Jay. I'd thought this was the first full-fledged bass clarinet LP in jazz. But a lucky vinyl find once again proved me wrong.

Strange to find this anomalous 1957 LP, released on Riverside, with erstwhile clarinetist, then flutist, then bass clarinetist, then flutist again, forever, Herbie Mann leading an entire session on nothing but the long black wooden horn. It was clearly seen, by its producers and musicians alike, as a stunt, almost an impossible one, but this little item appears at the cusp of the big breakout of new timbres and instrumentations in jazz in the '60s. In that sense it looks forward to players like David Murray or Ken Vandermark, who don't think twice about using the bass clarinet on the front line.

The other gimmick on this date was a West-meets-East concept, with East Coaster Mann matching wits with the West Coast rhythm team of Mel Lewis on drums, Buddy Clark on bass, with Jimmy Rowles on piano and trumpeter Jack Sheldon on some tracks. The amalgamation comes up with a laid-back but perky set of six numbers, Lewis swinging wonderfully, Clark on juicy and totally Los Angeles bass, and Rowles playing some economical and inventive piano. It's nasty to say, but to these ears it's a treat to encounter a Mann record with no flute on it—I must admit that I've passed over many possibly good LPs by Mann just to avoid the flute.

Mann's approach to bass clarinet is unusual from today's point of view. He tends to lurk down in the lower and middle registers, with none of the altissimo outbursts so common in today's playing styles; he's like a baritone crooner grooving on the deep cavernous sound of his own voice. This lowdown reveling seems to limit the expressive range of the horn, however, and it's safe to say this isn't the first really great bass clarinet record, even if it is a fascinating one. To compensate for some of the oddness of the low clarinet, many of the heads are arranged with trumpet unisons, which makes a sort of third timbre out of the combination.

The program includes one original, Mann's "A Stella Performance," along with the stuttering Miles Davis tune "The Theme," Tadd Dameron's "Lady Bird," which sounds especially glorious on bass clarinet, and Cole Porter's "Get Out of Town." A version of "Is It True What They Say about Dixie?" points in the direction of bass clarinet's history in novelty bands, although the melody has a bit of Ornette Coleman about it, too. On the ballad "A Handful of Stars," you can begin to hear Mann really find his legs on the instrument, and he buries himself in the tune in a way he doesn't elsewhere on this unique outing.

[December 2003]

POSTSCRIPT 2016: *Once again, Fresh Sound digitized this record, issuing it on* CD *in 2008.*

TRACK THREE / **Freak, Not Snob**

As advertised, I am an equal opportunity ear-filler.

Give me music via LP, single, shellac, cylinder, cassette, reel-to-reel, DAT, radio, boom box, iPod, or MP3. I refuse no medium. Preferential treatment is awarded to hearing music in live performance, without mediation. As far as formats go, I have my playback hierarchy, but I am a freak, not a snob. Audiophilic concerns are always secondary; the focus for me is on obtaining the content. I want music any way I can get it.

Years ago I produced a CD of some previously unknown tapes of Sun Ra's Arkestra and caught flak from a few such snobs who complained that they could hear distortion. It's true, there was noise; the producer who recorded it in 1959 didn't have complete command of the equipment and set the input too high. He did have the good sense to make the recording, however. The tapes were compromised, this was the only way the music was going to be issued, and it could not be conserved, so the question was: Make it available or bury it because it had a minor flaw? Sometimes I am amazed at the squeamishness (and bitchiness) of the listening public. Me? Like I said, I'm a freak, so a little burr on the top end didn't put me off. It just added patina.

Debates over the innate qualities of various playback media are, from my perspective, mostly a distraction. I have listened to the best arguments in favor of analog. As a guest lecturer in one of my classes, Steve Albini made the strongest and most fervent statement I've heard, explaining how compromised digital recording and reproduction were, drawing graphs to highlight the way that error correction introduced unwanted artifacts into the music, demonstrating the meaning of the word "dithering," and recalling the fact that CDs have a limited shelf-life, degenerating via oxidation, while the earliest records, if stored properly, sound exactly the way they did when they were made.

I'm pretty convinced. All in all, records are best. But I'm also a floozy. So what if I like the sound of vinyl better, enjoy the way it's packaged better, and am certain that it will be around when the final human breath is breathed, providing a wellspring of entertainment for the postapocalyptic cockroaches? That doesn't keep me from listening to CDs or, even more heretical, to MP3s. Truth is, though, that MP3s sound terrible, comparatively speaking, and the only reasons anyone would use them are that (1) they don't really understand that there's an alternative; (2) they find them irresistibly convenient. They are very convenient, no doubt. Ever tried playing vinyl on an airplane? As you walk down the street? In the gym? I listen to the CD player in my car perhaps most of all, followed by my iPod, then dedicated listening at the stereo at home.

If I need to listen to very quiet classical music, I'm sorry, but I prefer CD to vinyl. The constant chatter about vinyl being "warmer" and more natural than digital overlooks the record's more obvious drawbacks, which are the fact that no matter what condition the LP is in and what kind of snazzy system you're playing it on, it will always have an audible noise floor. It's the undeniable residue of the violent way that sound is made on a record—a needle is drawn kicking and scraping across a grooved surface. You can muffle the cry of the vinyl, but it will never hush up completely.

So be it. If the only way I could get a great recording of quiet music were on a scratchy old 45, it wouldn't stop me. But I'm also happy to oblige the music if it needs more pristine presentation. And if that's possible. Measure what is available against what is desirable, and find the optimal balance. If you keep yourself open in terms of playback devices, you're more likely to come out with the right stuff to hear.

I remember meeting someone once who claimed to have the best stereo system I would ever hear. Blowhards rarely have the goods. I've encountered more impressive gear by any standards many times. But what was particularly galling was that this fellow wanted to show the system off by playing Madonna. I asked what else he had to listen to—no particular problem with Ms. Ciccone, but any showroom salesman will tell you that you've got to have multiple styles on hand, to appeal to every sensibility. This guy had about ten audiophile LPs, all of them mainstream and highly produced. His system was steroidal, as was his paltry selection of music. I had to tell him I wasn't wowed.

One of the unsung joys of recorded music is its portability. I was enthused to get my first automobile, not because I didn't have to walk or take the bus all the time, but because it had a stereo. This meant listening to the music, *my* music, in different places, with new backgrounds, in unfamiliar contexts. That VW bug was fueled on cassette tapes. So were the early journeys I made to Europe (and road trips in the States). I lugged boxes of cassettes with me everywhere. That's a burden I don't miss. For the last twenty years, I have made mix CDs for annual trips up to Lake Superior with my wife, Terri, and we now have all sorts of associations between the soundtrack and the changing landscape. These pleasures are all possible in spite of the existence of vinyl; to enjoy them you have to go with the flow and let any record collector snobbery melt away.

If we're tallying the good points of each medium, as mentioned earlier, one of vinyl's strong suits is its limited running time. Like any greedy consumer, I can get jonesed about a CD jammed with eighty-plus minutes of music, but in terms of really listening, the twenty-ish-minute constraint per side is a positive attribute. That's about an ideal chunk. You can take the time to turn the LP over as an intermission or as an opportunity to change up what you're listening to. Again, it's dependent on context; there are long trips where I like to have shuffle choose for me endlessly, and there are parties where it's fun to bring a box of mixed singles and take turns with other folks spinning for three minutes a pop. There's also music that lasts longer than an LP side. Sometimes that break can be a buzzkill, and in those cases—think of longer symphonic works, extended minimalist drone, or epic free jazz—CD may be the best option. I'll admit, though, that it's harder and harder to find more than an hour in my schedule to listen uninterruptedly these days. Attending concerts of live music offers a good excuse to pay attention at length, silencing all the demanding devices and meditating on what you hear in an unbroken way.

I have a relatively good stereo setup. By audiophile standards, it's decent. It sounds great, but my turntable doesn't look like a glass building from the city of the future, and I have not dominated the living room with giant, towering speakers. I like to comfortably cohabitate with my music, not be its guest or servant. When the record collection started to feel like it was taking over, I put it in the (clean, dry) basement. I've got a hundred LPs upstairs at any given time, don't need more than that; the library is right downstairs if I desire a freshened selection. Once I tried to construct a database of the vinyl. I made it to the "G" section of jazz LPs and gave up. It was too daunting, and with each entry I felt myself wanting to include more details than artist and title—full personnel, recording date, date of issue, label, condition. After a while, the task just seemed futile. Anything I needed to cross-reference, I'm confident that my brain (and an Internet search) will help me out.

I haven't seen definitive demographics, but I'd bet that hunting records today is a wealthier person's sport. I doubt that the record revival has been as democratic as vinyl once was. They're much more expensive now, and even though you can find a budget turntable if you look for it, the equipment is more of a boutique item than something you'd pick up at Best Buy. House-holds everywhere used to have records. The bluegrass guitarist Doc Watson told me about growing up in the hollers of Deep Gap, North Carolina, where they were equally excited by 78s of the Carter Family and Memphis Minnie. Records were a legitimate way of expressing fascination with alien cultures. Inspired by records of New Thing jazz from New York, Impulse! LPs by Archie Shepp and Roswell Rudd, a cadre of weirdos in Novosibirsk, Siberia, made up their own bizarre music as a response. Records have been the catalyst for a global game of telephone, a chain of tangential interpretations and creative misunderstandings.

Music continues to function in a similar way, but when records were the primary medium, it was somehow different. They were precious, were hard to find, required diligence, and that made owning them special. Acquiring them meant more than forking over the money; you had to search for them, and that completely changed their status in the world of things. For anybody living outside a major city, being interested in nonmainstream stuff is much easier today. Get on the Internet and order what you want if you've got the funds or download it however you can if you don't. It's a giant grab bag of music. That's great. But the special quality that finding records once had isn't quite there in the same way anymore. Is that a net loss? I'm not sure. Some-thing's lost, something's gained.

If they came up with a medium that had everything I like about vinyl and more, I'd switch. But it's still around, and I marvel at its longevity. They're manufacturing 78-rpm shellacs again, for goodness sake. Against all odds, in spite of authoritative predictions, and in the face of an industry that wanted otherwise, vinyl is on the rise in our day and age. Out in the world, lurking almost everywhere, there are hungry freaks, daddy, with fingers primed to flick LPs toward them, scanning covers as they search for their next great score. Dig on, fellow freaks.

/////

My appreciation for the specific qualities of different media was sharpened by twenty years in college radio. As a rosy-cheeked freshman rocking Brown University's massive AM radio empire, my first deejay rig was basically like driving a truck—in a business office cubicle the turntable was fixed to the ground like a bathroom sink; a gear shift changed the speed, and a foot pedal on/off switch allowed for free hand mobility. With equipment that had been in use since the 1940s and was retired the following year, this broadcast juggernaut forwent the airwaves, instead pumping the jams via hardwired network that linked all the dorms' radiators. Let's say the audience was handpicked.

The following semester I joined the FM jazz staff, which meant late nights on a fifty-thousand-watt station that covered most of New England. Completely different story, audience-wise, though we did everything we could to drive them away. While the daytime programming was more mainstream, shaping young broadcast professionals and helping to establish the new category of alternative rock, WBRU's *Jazz after Hours* was a petri dish of experimentation, and we wee jockeys were indulged with little editorial oversight. My first slots were during the graveyard shift, 3:00 to 6:00 a.m. Made no never mind to me, as I'd be up anyway, and probably listening to records.

The activity of cueing a record, something that deejays come to take for granted and which I mastered in those first years, really puts the programmer in touch with the materiality of the medium. It requires facility at visually locating the start of a track, knowing how far backward to roll it, knowing when to hit "start" to leave the desired amount of room between cuts, doing a very quick fade-up to avoid hearing the record get up to speed, knowing how to fade up and down simultaneously to create a seamless cross-fade. Learning to listen to records backward is a rite of passage. I recall a moment as a twelve-year-old when the search for hidden messages in reverse tracks became suddenly and inexplicably urgent; my friends and I dismantled a belt-driven turntable in order to comb the collection for any secrets, starting with the Beatles, where we strained to make something out of nothing like Victorians looking for spirits in photographs. Electric Light Orchestra obliged us most startlingly, however, when we sent a track upstream and heard, loud and clear: "The music is reversible but time is not! Turn back, turn back."

Some key aspects of vinyl that became immediately evident when playing them on the radio: (1) they can skip, which is embarrassing to a broadcaster, especially if there's nothing on the other table; (2) a twenty-minute John Coltrane side makes a nice stretch to read a biology textbook or party with your guests; (3) seven-inch singles require constant attention, choosing and cueing and choosing and cueing, making such antics impossible; (4) on vinyl, starting points are chosen by random access, meaning you can drop the needle wherever you want to sample the music, rather than relying on preset cue points; (5) when a side is done, the needle moves briskly through the run-off groove and then skips, so if the deejay has fallen asleep or isn't paying attention, he doesn't get dead silence but an annoying repeated thump that will incite hostile phone calls even at the break of dawn.

I recorded these shows onto cassette tapes, listening back to them incessantly when driving. For me, a long-standing symbiotic relationship was forged between my radio show and my car. I could basically program my drive time, using cassettes to do what LPs have such trouble doing, namely, dealing with bumps in the road. Reviewing the shows, I evaluated them critically, learning from them and then applying that newfound knowledge to the real-time process in the studio. My understanding of the art of improvisation, the value of timing and inflection, continuity and contrast, the construction of a dramatic arc or the willful rejection of that narrative device—all these things received on-the-job training at WBRU. One especially ambitious night, after I had marshaled all available forces, played three turntables and two cassette machines at the same time, and collaged together improvised music and soul and electronic music and spoken word, my friend and the station's jazz director, Russell Fine, called me and gently reminded me that it was a jazz show. As I said, we were indulged. But there were limits.

By the time I had a show at WHPK in Chicago in 1987, compact discs had added another possible source medium to the radiophonic work. At this station, my pal Ben Portis and I took the notion of creative programming further, naming our show *Radio Dada*. My first year in grad school, I wrote "Radio Dada Manifesto," which was later published in *Radiotext(e)*, edited by Neil Strauss. Audacity upon audacity: we not only played vinyl, disc, and cassette, used the microphone for recitation as well as announcement, but we invited musicians to participate live in studio or by remote. Improvisers Davey Williams and LaDonna Smith joined us for a memorable evening, as did the group Shrimp Boat, and *Radio Dada* hosted a workshop with sound artist Gregory Whitehead called "True Bugs in Chicago," involving every imaginable kind of broadcast mediation, particularly the on-air telephone. The pinnacle of my experience on *Radio Dada* was a radiophonic collage with saxophonist Mats Gustafsson, released as a CD called *Sticky Tongues and Kitchen Knives*.

A year after starting *Radio Dada*, I began doing a jazz show at Northwestern University, where I was studying in the radio/TV/film department. In this context, my jollies already being expressed on the city's South Side, I enjoyed more conventional programming, moving between CDs, LPs, cassettes, live interviews (phone or studio), and the occasional in-studio performance. My favorite in that first season was the Flying Luttenbachers, with Hal Russell and Chad Organ on saxophones and Weasel Walter on drums. At the end of the session, live on the air, a frantic Walter smashed a glass jar he'd been using for tuned percussion, sending shards all over the records in the station's vast library.

My second year, the school invested a huge amount in a makeover for the station, which gave us a very nice little performance studio. I made use of those facilities to record off-air a few times, including separate sessions with bassists Peter Kowald and Barry Guy. And I recall listening back to a DAT of Gustafsson's solo Steve Lacy dedication *Windows* in that studio together with Lacy, who commented delightedly on each track. For a minute, DAT seemed like a viable medium, too, vying for attention with the others. Terri Kapsalis (text), Ken Vandermark (saxophones, clarinets), and I (turntables, records, CDs, cassettes) had a short-lived trio called Wounded Jukebox; we recorded direct to DAT in that studio.

Immersed in such a fertile multimedia environment, fully engaged with each recording and playback medium on its own terms, I had little opportunity to be a vinyl snob. An image returns: Gustafsson and I are in headphones; he is on sopranino sax, blowing into the talkback microphone, while I play a CD and two LPs, woozily changing the speed of the vinyl on one table and needle-dropping the other; a portable cassette machine documents Mats's sounds at close range, then is snapped into the house system and plays him back at himself; all the while, a DAT machine records the broadcast for posterity. Each medium has its own powers, merits that need to be teased out, exploited, sometimes provoked and pushed. As a listener and as an occasional medium massager, I learned from college radio how to respect each button, screen, stylus, and knob for what it is. In those polymorphous environs I came of age.

Afreaka!, *Demon Fuzz*
(Janus, 1970)

Now for a short meander off school property into the beyond: this rarity is one of the most enigmatic LPs in my collection. First of all, there's the confrontational cover photo—a buff naked black male torso in a colorful ski mask, conjuring all sorts of potentially terrorizing and/or kinky connotations. On the rear cover, the same figure is turned three-quarters to reveal a scar on his bare back.

The imagery is opaque and difficult to read in the parlance of record covers, which normally at least tells you something about what genre the music might be. In this case, the cover might fit the front of a Wu-Tang Clan CD or some serious neo-funk record of recent vintage, but *Demon Fuzz* is—as best I can chart it—a strange progressive rock record by what is described in the dim-witted liner notes as "an English coloured group." As Willie Nelson says, the words don't fit the picture.

Other points of reference: Lee Morgan's composition "Afreaka," recorded two years prior, perhaps the origin of the group's name. A Google search uncovers little but a bevy of gay African websites, maybe imbricating the record in a subculture's network of significations. Listening to the odd music, I find this unlikely. But it's definitely an identity-politics brain teaser, a charged bundle of signs begging to be decoded.

With "Past Present and Future," the program begins with W. Raphael Joseph's heavily distorted guitar ("demon fuzz," no doubt), which sounds like it might lead into Metallica; the out-of-tempo intro leads into an anthemic horn theme over swinging drums, which get increasingly funky (nice organ solo, too) until an abrupt change to a chugging 4/4, jazz-rock horn charts, yet more tempo shifting, and an electrifying trombone solo by Clarance Brooms Crosdale, deceleration until standing still, over and out.

Other pieces feature the vocals of Smokey Adams, who conjures Traffic-era Steve Winwood with his sweet, light singing. The rhythm team of drummer Steven Jonn and bassist Sleepy Jack Joseph deftly shifts gears throughout the multisectioned proceedings. On "Another Country," the song takes an unexpected detour into a modal vamp, allowing a Middle Eastern–hued tenor saxophone solo by Paddy Corea. Even the record's one throwaway track, "Hymn to Mother Earth," which skirts too close to Moody Blues heavy-handedness, has some enjoyably crooked moments.

The horn section sometimes sounds like Blood Sweat & Tears filtered through Brotherhood of Breath—tight but nicely off in an African way. Sax and trombone work contrapuntally with Ray Rhoden's organ on "Mercy," Jonn's malleted toms bursting into another jazz romp for Crosdale's pliable 'bone. It's enough to make me wonder if these were actually African musicians based in London, like South African saxophonist Dudu Pukwana, who also made some great, unreissued fusion records with his group Agassai. Anybody want to help a freak decipher this mysterious Afreaka!?

[January 2004]

Contemporary Sound Series
(Mainstream, 1960s)

What's at stake in the practice of vinyl freakery is more than just fetishism and collectability; it involves a concept of viable history. What gets to be part of the active historical archive, and what gets left out? Not only the oddball, eccentric items get deleted from the "in print" category, but other, certifiably canonical recordings are sometimes the casualty of format changes.

One of the most significant bodies of contemporary classical recordings has been unavailable for decades now, apparently due to a legal battle over rights, and it seems plausible by now that the music will never be reissued, which is a terrible loss (except for the vinyl-friendly). In the early 1960s, American composer Earle Brown served as A&R director for a monumental group of recordings first (briefly) issued on the Time label, then licensed by Mainstream. It couldn't be more ironic than the fact that these potent offerings from the

forward ranks of the avant-garde appear on a label with the name "mainstream," but that's the perversity of labeling. Mainstream's catalog included jazz and a variety of hi-fi demonstration records, many of them kitschy beyond compare. But they all came packaged in thick, glossy, gatefold covers, not unlike first-generation Impulse! releases, and the vinyl itself was outstanding.

Brown's "Contemporary Sound Series," which amounted to around twenty LPs, included music by American, European, South American, and Japanese composers, performed by the absolute top specialists in the music. One of the LPs is dedicated to flute music and features Severino Gazzelloni, the virtuoso flautist to whom Eric Dolphy dedicated his memorable piece on *Out to Lunch!*.

Another classic from the series splits an LP between Mauricio Kagel's "Transition II," for piano, percussion, and two bands of magnetic tape, and two pieces by Karlheinz Stockhausen, "Zyklus" and "Refrain." The performers include pianists David Tudor, Aloys and Bernhard Kontarsky, and the stupendous German percussionist Christoph Caskel. Another record is a showcase for the voice of Cathy Berberian, with pieces by Sylvano Bussotti, Luciano Berio (with e. e. cummings), and John Cage.

Indeed, Cage and the so-called New York School are featured prominently in the series, which makes sense given Brown's central role in that movement. Another split LP features Cage's important 1960 composition "Cartridge Music" and Christian Wolff's "Duo for Violinist and Pianist."

The single record that stands out from the series sports a lovely cover painting by Franz Kline and features music by Brown himself and Morton Feldman. This LP includes some completely astonishing music from Brown's "mobile composition" period, in which his pieces had fixed parts with indeterminate relationships, so they could change each time they were performed, not unlike Alexander Calder's mobiles. Feldman's four "Durations" are likewise treated to indispensable performances, exacting but passionate studies of what the same compositional material can yield given different parameters of performance.

[February 2004]

POSTSCRIPT 2016: *Starting in 2009, the German Wergo label has resolved the legal wrinkles and reissued the complete Mainstream Contemporary Sound Series as a string of three-CD anthologies.*

Beaver Harris / Don Pullen 360-Degree Experience, *A Well-Kept Secret*
(Shemp Records, 1984)

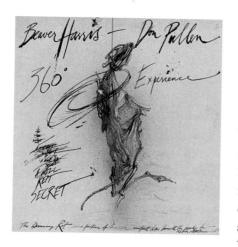

Producer and *Saturday Night Live*'s musical overlord Hal Willner created a string of boundary-pushing, eclectic collections in the '80s, including glorious concoctions that celebrated Nino Rota, Thelonious Monk, Charles Mingus, and Kurt Weill. Along the way, he also produced this appropriately titled Beaver Harris / Don Pullen LP, issued—to the best of my research—as the only release on a label called Shemp, the logo for which features a wicked little headshot of said Stooge. With its Ralph Steadman cover and fantabulous music, it's a wonder this record was allowed to drift off into total obscurity, but I rarely even see it mentioned anymore. One source claims it was issued in '84 on Hannibal, presumably on CD, but I've found nothing further to confirm this, and I'm relatively sure it's only ever been on vinyl.

The 360-Degree Experience is, in fact, a much older project of drummer Beaver Harris, who sought to integrate the entire spectrum of jazz styles rather than leave them to their inevitable Balkanization. Formed in 1968, the 360-Degree Experience was initially co-led by Harris and pianist Dave Burrell. Its debut release, which was at the time, in '74, issued under Harris's name, included bassists Jimmy Garrison and Ron Carter, singer Maxine Sullivan, trumpeter Doc Cheatham, Burrell, trombonist Marshall Brown, and steel drummer Francis Haynes, among others. Titled *From Ragtime to No Time* and self-issued on 360 Records, it too remains unreissued.

By the time of *A Well-Kept Secret*, in the early '80s, the group was being jointly fronted by Harris and pianist Don Pullen, and for this studio recording it featured baritone saxophonist Hamiet Bluiett, tenor saxophonist Ricky Ford, and bassist Buster Williams. Haynes appears on steel drums.

Harris's seventeen-plus-minute piece "Goree" is the album's centerpiece, an amalgam of styles that drives home the integrative point without resorting to dry polemics. In the middle, a swelling crescendo finds piano, tenor, and steel drums churning around in the same repeating patterns, before an elegantly arranged, African-sounding horn section (featuring an expanded group with Candido on percussion and Sharon Freeman, Willie Ruff, Bill Warnick, and Greg Williams on French horn) ushers in Pullen's patented clustery, slashing solo and finally an unaccompanied statement from the drum kit. The drummer's "Newcomer" pulls some heartstrings, a luxurious midtempo ballad.

Pullen's tunes are a special treat. "From the Land of the Pharaohs" is a blistering up-tempo number that spotlights the excruciated horns, including a squealing stop-time duet (something straight from the Marshall Allen / Pat Patrick book) and extended solos over adrenaline-primed rhythm section.

But for my money, the LP's best moment is "Double Arc Jake," a Pullen-penned composition that seems at points like it's going to completely jump off the lovely melodic track into a protracted spasm of energy; just when it's about to lose itself, the tune snaps back into its calypsoid celebration. Pullen was terrific at the tension-and-release game, and in his solos he often used the device, but he rarely deployed it as effectively in his charts as he does here. "Double Arc Jake" is one of the great cuts of the '80s. Another treasure for those vinyl pigs willing to go truffling.

[April 2004]

POSTSCRIPT 2016: *Honestly, people, what are we waiting for? It's been more than thirty years, and this needs to be dusted off and made available pronto.*

Mike Osborne Trio, *Border Crossing*
(Ogun, 1974)

It's about time for a retrospective of the work of British alto saxophonist Mike Osborne. A few things are available on CD, including his 1970 debut as a leader (originally issued on Turtle—try finding a vinyl copy of that!) titled *Outback*,

MIKE OSBORNE TRIO

BORDERCROSSING

Ogun

which was reissued by FMR. But the bulk of this great musician's catalog, most of it recorded for the Ogun label, remains out of print. If you get lucky, you might score an LP version of his 1977 quintet session *Marcel's Muse*, or one of his two dates with pianist Stan Tracey. You can hear him to advantage on various Chris McGregor's Brotherhood of Breath records (including recent trips to the tape vaults via Cuneiform Records), as well as the outstanding concert recording with bassist Harry Miller's sextet Isipingo, *Family Affair* (Ogun, 1977), and he's one-third of S.O.S., the saxophone project with Alan Skidmore and John Surman, on their eponymous Ogun record from 1975. Alas, that too is unavailable.

My preferred setting for Osborne, though, is with his classic trio, which featured two South African members of the British new jazz scene: Miller on bass and Louis Moholo on drums. It's the same rhythm section that Peter Brötzmann would deploy later in the decade, to quite different ends, and it's a pairing that reminds one of the bassist and drummer's common roots in jazz groups under apartheid. The Mike Osborne Trio worked somewhat regularly from 1969 throughout the mid-'70s, during which time they recorded the scorching *All Night Long* (Ogun, 1975) and my favorite, *Border Crossing*, a live date from 1974. It's not a perfect record, with a couple of untoward edits (for length, no doubt, as they've no problem coming up with material), but it's a wonderful document of an essential ensemble.

Osborne doesn't have the sour intonation of Dudu Pukwana, but he and Pukwana share some similarities in spirit, most notably an ability to balance energy and buoyancy. With a continuous tableau of pieces, basically a festival set, the music ebbs and flows naturally, moving from tune to tune with everyone playing all the time. No extended bass solos or drum breaks or saxophone sections here—this is integrated ensemble music, shifting gears from freebop to free jazz and African-inspired vamping. The beauty is in the trio feel, the sense of seamlessness between them, and the way they turn that to their own advantage, elaborating a piece until it's intuitively evident that it's time to move to the next one, a methodology that recalls Don Cherry's '60s episodic suites.

Border Crossing starts with an easy 4/4 on Osborne's "Ken's Tune," seguing into the feverish "Stops and Starts," which together set the table for a forty-minute feast. The bassist's Ornettish "Awakening Spirit" is, fitting its title, abruptly faded after a few minutes, leading to the meditative introduction to Osborne's "Ist," which in turn explodes into a dramatic, terse little rising theme, springboard for a short, ferocious bass solo over skittish drums.

Side two is an equally absorbing unfurling of nonstop trio energies, the alto soaring and growling over Miller's driving bass and Moholo's deceptively propulsive, but never belligerent, drums. During the transition between "Animation" and "Riff," the saxophonist so subtly changes tempo and feel that a listener might suddenly wonder how he or she got here from there. Only a band with an innate sense of its own potential can make those confident moves, and the Mike Osborne Trio was unquestionably one of those groups.

[May 2004]

POSTSCRIPT 2016: *Later in 2004, Ogun reissued* Border Crossing *as a twofer with* Marcel's Muse. *Meanwhile, Louis Moholo (now Louis Moholo-Moholo) is the final South African jazz musician still in action. Last man standing.*

The Three Souls, *Dangerous Dan Express*
(Argo, 1964)

We return once again to the vaults of Chicago's Argo label. Why? Because they're so deep, so fun, and so action-packed. And so unmined. Here's a terrific soul-jazz LP from the mid-'60s, something that's surely got a contemporary audience waiting out there for it, but something that remains needlessly obscure to all but a few freaks.

Cincinnati-born alto saxophonist Sonny Cox started a trio together with Ken Prince, a Hammond B-3 player he met in school during the '50s at Kentucky State, and Chicago drummer Robert Shy. They'd probably heard of the Three Sounds, Blue Note's resident soul-jazzers, when they called themselves the Three Souls. In any case, their swinging debut was recorded in January and

February 1964 and paid tribute in its title to the Dan Ryan Expressway—the highway to the South Side of Chicago, widely reputed as the most perilous thruway in town, the main drag for underage dragsters, drunk drivers, and other speed demons. On the cover, our fearless Three hug the side of the highway, their gorgeous red roadster behind them, Shy crouching like he'll leap into oncoming traffic, Prince clutching some scores, and Cox tooting into the backwhoosh of a passing automobile.

On *Dangerous Dan Express*, the Three Souls are augmented by a fourth and sometimes fifth Soul—one of two guitarists and an occasional bongo player. I don't know anything about guitarist Gerald Sims, except that he's got an appealing sound (unusually trebly for the day) and plays some especially welcome licks on "Greasy Sonny," a chugging blues vehicle, based loosely on "Fever," by and for Cox. Sims appears on half the record, where the other half is covered by an important, rather overlooked guitarist in Chicago jazz history, George Eskridge.

Eskridge at one time had a working quartet that many would die to hear, with an unnamed bassist, drummer Robert Barry, and tenor saxophonist John Gilmore. The band stayed together for more than a year, apparently, in the mid-'50s, around the time Gilmore was first working with Sun Ra. Eskridge is more harmonically adventurous than Sims, as evidenced when he and bongo player George Harris fill out a bossa nova version of "Our Day Will Come," which also gives Cox a chance to show off his soul credentials.

Shy is still one of Chicago's great trapsmen, and on this early recording he acquits himself wonderfully, whether laying down a kick-back groove under yet another blues number—like the collectively credited "Fannie Mae," the cooking title track or Cox's "Past Due"—or lending a sensitive touch to a chipper version of "Ol' Man River."

The LP's odd man out comes at the start of side two, with a quick version of "Milestones" (for some reason, probably monetary, credited as "Mile Stones"), Prince pecking pert chords behind a roller-coastering Cox. This leads directly to a riotous version of the Tommy Tucker hit "Hi Heel[ed] Sneakers." Venerable Chicago jazz presenter Joe Segal provides liner notes whose faint praise borders on the apologetic ("travelling the middle road of listenable, danceable improvised Jazz"). Not necessary, though: there's nothing to apologize for on this supersoulful, listenable, and danceable Chi-Town outing.

[June 2004]

POSTSCRIPT 2016: *Robert Shy remains a bit under the radar, kicking ass regularly on the Chicago mainstream jazz scene.*

Steve Lacy, *Raps*
(Adelphi, 1977)

With the passing of Steve Lacy (1934–2004), the jazz world has lost one of its most accomplished record makers. As a youngster, Lacy was something of a vinyl freak himself. He once told me about the thrill of having hustled over to buy acetate bebop airchecks from Boris Rose, hot off Rose's disc cutter in Manhattan.

Lacy started making records under his own name in 1957. His catalog is the stuff of legend, so plump that there are entries Lacy himself forgot about. Though his output slowed to a more manageable level over the last decade, Lacy produced an astonishing quantity of LPS in the '70s and '80s—by my count, he'd released nearly fifty LPS as a leader or principal in the '70s alone—the vast majority of them for small European or Japanese labels.

A partial checklist of great Lacy vinyl not currently available on CD includes *Wordless* (the first version of his "The Way" suite, from 1971, for Futura); *The Gap* (his 1972 quintet date for America Records, first collaboration with Steve Potts); *Shots* (1977 meeting with traditional Japanese percussionist Masa Kwate, on the French Musica imprint); *Points* (a quartet recording from 1978 on Chant du Monde); and several LPS on the criminally unreissued Horo series, from Rome, most urgently the duet with bassist Kent Carter, *Catch* (1977). Lacy's solo albums are some of his most important; a number are still vinyl-only, including two exceedingly rare Japanese LPS, *Torments* (Morgue, 1975) and *The Kiss* (Lunatic, 1986). Why hatOLOGY hasn't reissued the early Lacy LPS in the old Hat Hut line, *Clinkers* (solo, 1977) and *Stamps* (quintet, 1977–78), is beyond me.

The LP I'd like to center on here, however, is an American release from the '70s (one of only three or four such outings), recorded for Adelphi Records, a label that has several great LPS ready for reissue, including primo Arthur Blythe and David Murray. *Raps* is one of the more easily obtained Lacy LPS, popping up in used bins, often cheaply, but don't let the price tag fool you: this is sensational music.

Recorded in the studio in January 1977, after a run of gigs at Rashied Ali's loft venue, Ali's Alley, *Raps* was produced by Michael Cuscuna, and it consists of material from Lacy's late-'70s working songbook, including familiar favorites "The Throes," "Blinks," and "Stamps." Potts, Lacy's right-hand-man during these years, plays soprano and alto saxophones, with Ron Miller (never heard of him before or since, but he acquits himself well) on bass, and Lacy Quintet drummer Oliver Johnson.

Johnson's swaggering, sometimes brutish drumming helps push this quartet over the top, injecting pneumatic energy into the rising and falling scalar slopes of "Stamps" and the stabbing four-note repetitions of "The Throes." By the early '70s, Lacy had returned to composition after a few years experimenting with free improvisation, but his pieces were still highly reduced, terse and potent, meant to serve as jump-off points for improvising rather than as end points in themselves. Anyone who knows the perky "Blinks" from later recordings might find this version a tad hallucinatory, as they take it at roughly half the tempo Lacy did in subsequent years, but it works well at this lope, and Potts takes a positively broken alto solo over Johnson's restless drums, Lacy snaking in to lend altissimo support.

The title track is an irresistible bluesy grind on which Lacy and Potts jointly play a sweetly harmonized, singing little line that's pure Lacy—a sound whorl of devilish joy. On the tremendous "No Baby," the LP's peak moment, Johnson sets the tempo by stating the title repeatedly, and we're left to wonder: Is it an admonishment or a statement of being "babyless"? Lacy takes the three syllables of his title and runs with them, permuting and further distending the words' natural rhythms.

[August 2004]

POSTSCRIPT 2016: *Most of the Lacy records I mention in the column remain unexcavated, but in 2014 Hat Hut reissued* Shots, *beautifully remastered from clean vinyl, to which I contributed liner notes. My label, Corbett vs. Dempsey, bought the complete Lacy master tapes from Hat Hut that year, and we have started releasing them one at a time with* Tips, *featuring Lacy and Steve Potts on saxophones, with Aebi singing painter Georges Braque's aphorisms.*

Halki Collective, *Halki Collective*

(Larisa Improvisers' Guild, 1984)

One artifact of the abrupt switch from
LP to CD in the mid-'80s is the fact that
you can still find caches of vinyl records produced at that time. Independent
productions—ones that would normally
have taken some time to sell—got cut
adrift during the sea change, and if you
hunt a little you can find piles of unplayed vinyl, circa that period, that have
simply been waiting, neither being discarded nor finding an adequate avenue
into the marketplace. The upshot is that
for vinyl freaks there are basically "new"
out-of-print records to find.

In Greece recently, I stumbled on just such a reserve in the backstock of a
small distributor. Among the LPs available from them were two super-rarities
by pianist Sakis Papadimitriou, one self-produced solo—his first record, a
veritable demonstration of extended piano techniques for the improviser,
also exhaustively documented in Papadimitriou's book on the subject, *The
"Other" Piano*—and one duo on Praxis with German percussionist Gunter
"Baby" Sommer. Having spent many hours trolling for European improvised
music, it sets the heart aflutter to uncover records one's never even heard of
before, and to find them new was even more of a kick.

But there was another record in this stash that caught my attention not
only by being an LP I'd never seen, but featuring a group of Greek improvisers
unfamiliar to me. The Halki Collective is a local improvising ensemble from
the city of Larisa. Their first and only record, recorded in 1984, was issued on
the Larisa Improvisers' Guild imprint; it featured live performances mounted
with the support of the Cinematic Cultural and Arts Union and Ministry of
Youth, recorded in Piraeus, the major port city near Athens. Players include
drummer Sakis Grimboulis, bassist George Kostoulis, tenor saxophonist
Casilis Sitras, and Hristos Papageorgiou on trombone, electric guitar, and
violin.

The Halki Collective's music is totally improvised, with roots in both
American free jazz and European free play. When Kostoulis moves up into

the higher registers, he suggests that he's listened attentively to Peter Kowald, the late German bassist who, early in his life, translated Greek poetry, and who remained a lifelong Grecophile, probably playing more often in Greece than any other northern European improviser. Side A features tenor (Sitras is absent completely on the second side) and trombone in a "front line" that is well integrated, if sometimes tentative. There's a self-taught quality to the band, a familiar exploratory rawness that many players experience when stepping into the ring without composed material. During some passages, they rely too much on long notes and pedal tones to create a sense of cohesiveness. But the group works nicely together, Papageorgiou manipulating a good variety of sounds on trombone, including some husky blatting.

Without the saxophone and with Papageorgiou switching to strings, side B is skronkier and more explosive. There's little difference between the sound of violin and guitar as played here; they're both generally used for scritchy impact, except when Papageorgiou makes a couple of unwarranted stabs at guitar heroics and a silly diversion into chugging 4/4 punk, alongside Kostoulis's menacing electric bass. Drummer Grimboulis is adept at keeping things from grinding to a standstill, as his propulsive kitwork bubbles underneath and directly interacts with his comrades. Theirs isn't an especially delicate or sophisticated music, but Halki Collective has its charms.

[September 2004]

POSTSCRIPT 2016: *The Halki Collective LP was never issued on CD, but they have jumped to free downloading and made it available that way. A simple search will yield the music.*

The Amram-Barrow Quartet, *The Eastern Scene*
(Decca, 1957)

Were it not for the fact that it's got more scratches on it than the average breadboard, my copy of this extremely rare 1957 LP would be worth some real money. I've seen it listed for between $60 and $250 in decent shape. Crackles and all, it's still a pleasure to own—David Amram and George Barrow concocted a quite unusual and worthwhile sound with their modest little working band.

Recorded as the sixth installment of Decca's Jazz Studio series, which included outings by John Graas, Jack Millman, and Ralph Burns (featuring musicians such as Gerry Mulligan, Curtis Counce, Frank Foster, Jimmy Giuffre, Hank Jones, and Kenny Clarke), and which might be well served by a complete reissue from someplace like Mosaic (hint, hint). Amram is featured on French horn, which, like Graas, was Amram's main ax, but also on the tuben (a smaller version of the tuba), which he plays to great effect on his own terse, hard-boppish tune "Lobo Nocho."

When he puts down the horn, Amram sits and accompanies on piano, which he plays with an ear for dissonance that reminds one that Cecil Taylor's first recorded solo—much more "inside" than might be expected, in turn betraying Taylor's debt to Dave Brubeck—was on a film soundtrack Amram scored a few years earlier, a recording that was never commercially released. (A side note: the anonymous liner notician here reasonably suggests a comparison with Monk, who he refers to as "Thelonius." Why is it that so many competent writers and well-meaning musicians have misspelled Monk's name? What's with that missing "o"? It must be the most common copyediting mistake in jazz. Seriusly.)

The title *The Eastern Scene* was surely meant to set this record apart from the West Coast orientation of the other "Jazz Studio" releases, though it's got plenty of chamber-jazz classical elements about it. Amram's arrangements of Irving Berlin's "The Best Thing for You" and Cole Porter's "I Love You" are hands-on and harmonically nuanced, emphasizing counterpoint and structure, while an interpretation of the standard "Darn That Dream" is particularly proto–Third Stream.

The most unusual piece here is a sensitive and forward-looking arrangement of the classic American song "Shenandoah," which is treated in a way that might be of interest to contemporary genre-hoppers. Indeed, today's East Coasters (and Dutchfolk, too) might well find this whole record an inspiration or at least a nice place to visit.

What makes the band's case for its "Eastern" quality, perhaps, is the swinging rhythm section of bassist Arthur Phipps and drummer Al Harewood, and moreover the gorgeous tenor saxophone playing of Barrow. This record makes me wonder why Barrow isn't a more common name. He's without pretense, playing nothing extraneous, with a serious-minded sound that rings clearly in the bottom of the horn. Playing the charts, he blends beautifully with Amram's brass, and when he kicks into a solo, his authority is immediately evident. It's time to comb the collection for more Barrow, for us to sit up and take greater notice.

[October 2004]

Charlie Parker acetates
(no label, early 1950s)

Let's call this "Notes from the Acetate Underground." In the '40s and '50s, before the magnetic tape revolution and cassette technology inspired widespread self-production and the subcultures of mixtape and bootlegging, there was a cruder, and in some ways more beautiful, technological precursor: the acetate.

Say you were a Charlie Parker fanatic, or a student fascinated by Duke Ellington's arrangements, and you heard something wonderful on the radio—those were the days when live jazz was often heard on the airwaves. If you wanted a chance to listen to it again, what could you do? If you lived in Utah and didn't have a disc cutter of your own, you were out of luck. But if you lived in New York, you might have had the opportunity to listen to this music once again.

A few years ago, Steve Lacy and I were at my house talking about his early experiences in New York. I asked him what records he was buying at the time, and he said that aside from the commercially produced ones, he used to go to a guy from whom, for a few bucks, he could acquire handmade acetates of airchecks. I excused myself, made my way into my records, and retrieved four of the collection's crown jewels. Steve looked at them, shook his head, and whispered, "Boris Rose."

Boris Rose supplied hand-cut acetates of radio airchecks to jazz fans for decades. When LPs came along, Rose began making what would later be known as bootlegs, replete with personally designed Xeroxed covers; his recordings of Parker, in particular, have circulated widely. We should thank goodness that someone was documenting these broadcasts, or they might have been lost forever.

My Rose acetates are among a small group of records in my collection that I won't play. I've got the music elsewhere, and they're on a medium that doesn't last particularly long—eight or ten plays, and it's history. Having bought them used, it's anybody's guess how many times they've already been

played. But they're special for other reasons. Highly tactile, they have the leaden weight of an acetate—a serious, substantive feel that signals a precious cultural object. They also have the unmistakable smell of whatever compound that's exploring its own half-life as an acetate decays.

What is so wonderful about these unplayable, heavy, stinky old albums, however, is their covers. They sport handmade collages, with photos of the musicians cut and taped to the covers of other LPs (one an Art Tatum / Errol Garner collection, another *The Art of Jazz* by Gus Johnson and John Williams), the text of which has been blacked out with marker. On the front of one, which includes music by Charlie Parker recorded at the Bandbox (and a twenty-minute interview with Bird that I'd not heard before—OK,

I played that one), the word "Keyboard" has been altered so that the last part of the word is covered by the name "Charlie Parker"—hence, it's "Key Charlie Parker." Elsewhere, text is either cobbled together like a ransom note or handwritten. One of them even includes quite extensive liner notes, in cursive! On the inner label, the basic information is typewritten, and titles to the Royal Roost recordings (and other performances from unidentified venues) are provided in little mimeographed scraps taped to the covers.

These "Collectors' Series" records are marvels of early self-production, glorious little artworks by an autodidactic designer, someone who gets props for keeping the freak alive, and for helping spread the bebop gospel.

[November 2004]

Tommy "Madman" Jones, *A Different Sound*
(M & M, circa 1961)

Just Friends
(Apex, 1959)

In the 1980s, tenor saxophonist Tommy Jones moved to Amsterdam, where he opened a soul food restaurant and would sometimes play saxophone while cooking. A legendary and beloved character, Jones started out his musical life in Chicago, where he was modestly successful as a jazz musician, but perhaps more so running a record label.

This was a time when artist-run organizations were barely known. There was Debut, the label Charles Mingus and Max Roach instigated in New York in the early '50s, and classical composer Harry Partch was running his Gate 5 label from his temporary mid-'50s Chicago abode. Sun Ra and his business manager, Alton Abraham, started Saturn Records in about 1956, and a few years later Saturn had some collegial correspondence with another musician-run label in the Windy City: M & M, so-called for its inaugurator's nickname, Madman.

M & M (and Mad, Jones's other label) issued some hot doo-wop-ish singles; I've managed to sniff out a few of these rare sides, and they're great raw black pop. But "Madman" Jones was a hard-core Chicago saxophonist, and he also issued singles by other jazz folks, like E. Parker McDougal and Red Holloway, as well as singer Oscar Brown Jr. A big, lanky guy, he got his

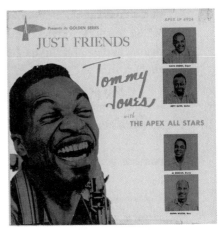

nickname for the wild gesticulations he made while blowing. His music is not particularly free or wild, and in truth it proves Jones to be as sentimental and woozy as a balladeer can be without losing his punch.

Don't get me wrong, he's punchy. But boy does this guy want to get cozy, too. He makes Ben Webster seem a little standoffish. With giant, swooping slurs, glisses that literally laugh or cry, tongue flutters that tickle the ear, gentle, quick little trills like butterfly kisses, and a huge, radiant sound, he's a man after someone's heart. Nearly everything on these two records—one waxed for his own imprint, one for the Chicago indie Apex (in which he also had a financial interest)—is romantic. Jazz with one thing in mind: the caress of love.

With their perfect lounge music, Jones and his ensembles could slip into one of the remaining South Side jazz dens nowadays and please everyone. Take Gene Ammons and distill him down to all the romantic tricks—the softly articulated trips to the bottom of the horn, the piercing Hawkish tone, the Johnny Hodges arching notes—and you've got the right music to cry into your martini glass or to nuzzle your baby behind the ear.

On *Just Friends*, Jones deployed a fine quintet, the Apex All-Stars, with Floyd Morris on organ and piano, Al Duncan on drums, Quinn Wilson on bass, and William "Lefty" Bates on guitar. The material is a bit more up-tempo, but still made for lovin'.

On *A Different Sound*—an LP that the extensive Mad / M & M discography (hub cap.clemson.edu/-campber/mad.html) doesn't list and probably doesn't know about (it's LM-27)—Jones compiles tracks by two groups, one featuring pianist Jack Wilson, Donald Garrett on bass, Roland Falkner on guitar, and Harold Jones on drums, the other featuring undersung pianist Willie Jones, Betty Dupree on bass, Marshall Thompson or Gil Gay on drums, and Leo Blevins on guitar. Along with various sumptuous romantic morsels such as "Snowfall," "I Don't Stand a Ghost of a Chance" and "Baubles, Bangles and Beads," the LP contains five originals, all nicely crafted, if unexceptional, jazz tunes. They're proper vehicles for the man driven mad by sounds of *amore*.

[December 2004]

POSTSCRIPT 2016: *I have been unsuccessfully trying to locate any Madman kinfolk, with the hopes of reissuing either or both of these gems. If you're out there, look me up.*

The New York Art Quartet, *Mohawk*
(Fontana, 1964)

Many of the canonic jazz records—the absolutely necessary ones, urgent for any comprehensive jazz history or aspiring collection—have been issued on CD. That's even true of the self-produced or small-label productions; consider that the signal New York underground company ESP has had most of its catalog in print—albeit sometimes in badly remastered form—almost continuously since the '60s.

The Vinyl Freak column usually focuses on albums that slip through the cracks, rather than the major watershed events. The canon needs to be wider than it is, including all sorts of oddities. Those unusual items tell as significant a part of the story as the "classics." The waste pail of history is, for an audio archaeologist, often more fruitful than the pantry.

But there remain a few items that should, by any account, be staples prominently placed in that pantry that haven't been properly restocked. In the early '60s, one of the forefront labels documenting the new jazz was a Dutch company called Fontana. A few of its important productions were reissued on LP by Freedom, enja, and Arista in the '70s—Dewey Redman's

Look for the Black Star, for instance—but some of its early entries in the New York underground remain inaccessible. In many ways, Fontana was the sister label to Impulse! and ESP. It helped capitalize on mounting interest in free jazz in Europe, having been better distributed and more broadly collected there.

Tenor saxophonist Archie Shepp and alto saxophonist John Tchicai produced a tremendous quartet outing, *Rufus*, which, only ever having been reissued on French LP and in a tiny batch in Japan (where some of the rarest Fontanas have somehow made their way onto CD), joins Marion Brown's *Juba-Lee*, the first record to feature pianist Dave Burrell and a tenor-only recording of Bennie Maupin, in the super-obscure Fontana category. Of Fontana LPs that have languished in obscurity, however, one is an absolute classic and should be reissued immediately. If they did they'd have to pay more historical homage to the group that made it.

The New York Art Quartet's *Mohawk* was recorded in July 1965. It's got pristine sound for a free jazz LP, having been recorded in Rudy Van Gelder's studio, which is good because the details are meaningful. The lineup includes Tchicai on alto, Roswell Rudd on trombone, and Reggie Workman on bass. But it's the remarkable drumming of Milford Graves that makes this record more than another nice entry in the "New Thing" discography. Indeed, this LP is a major event, perhaps the best evidence of what a totally new rhythmic concept Graves had invented, and the top recording of unpulsed drumming, bar none.

Graves was just at the point of discarding his snare in '65, and he's still playing it on about half of *Mohawk*. Anyone who questions Graves's prowess on snare will have to reckon with this record, where his playing is as shocking and revelatory as Tony Williams on Eric Dolphy's *Out to Lunch*, and perhaps more so. Listen to him start and stop on the Rudd-less "Everything Happens to Me," as Tchicai brilliantly and gently abstracts the beautiful melody. Or listen to the sensational "Banging on the White House Door," where the rhythm is at once precise and clotted.

Graves proves that it's possible to imply forward motion and at the same time resist the simple groove. His metrical overlays and wavelike fluidity are as astonishing now as they must have been then, in part because so few players have had the discipline to pick up on and develop them. Here's an example of free jazz that's ceaselessly creative and puts something new on the table. Happy hunting.

[February 2005]

POSTSCRIPT 2016: *A label called Cool Music reissued* Mohawk *in 2014, apparently as a bootleg, along with several other excellent Fontana titles. John Tchicai passed away in 2012.*

Paul Gonsalves / Tubby Hayes, *Just Friends*
(Columbia [UK], 1965)

Tubby Hayes and the Paul Gonsalves All Stars, *Change of Setting*
(World Record Club, 1967)

The sleeve notes to *Just Friends* tell one version of the backstory nicely. In 1964, the Duke Ellington Orchestra was at the Royal Festival Hall in London. Tenor saxophone hero Paul Gonsalves grew too sick to perform just before showtime. Rooting around in the audience for a replacement, Ellington singled out Tubby Hayes, who was happy to participate, and who wowed the band and the crowd at the venerable venue.

In fact, it was revealed later (not in these liners, to be sure) that Hayes got the call earlier in the day and was planted in the audience, his emergency performance something of a publicity stunt (probably to keep the fans from being disappointed at seeing a "local" rather than the big out-of-towner). That he played splendidly, however, comes as no surprise at all. A fluid, dynamic tenor saxophonist, Hayes had been adeptly swinging alongside American comrades since the early '60s, when he'd made a classic recording with Clark Terry.

A rehabilitated Gonsalves joined Hayes a few days after the switch and sat in with his band. An intermittent string of sessions ensued, resulting in these two wonderful rare British LPs, neither of which has been reissued on CD. They each allow for a comparison of the two men's complementary sound. Hayes had long claimed Gonsalves as a favorite, but they're quite distinct—Hayes with a slightly harder tone and evidence of John Coltrane's influence in his phrasing.

Timed to coincide with the next Ellington appearance in London, the earlier of these two dates was organized by baritone saxophonist Jackie Sharpe, who assembled a superb all-British band to back the two tenors, with Jimmy Deuchar and Les Condon on trumpets (both of whom were, with Sharpe, members of an early Hayes group), Keith Christie on trombone,

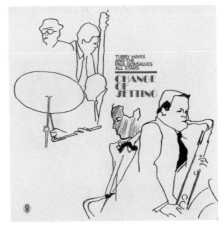

Lonnie Bush on bass, Ronnie Stevenson on drums, and the amazing Stan Tracey on piano.

Gonsalves sticks to his tenor, while Hayes doubles on alto and vibraphone, the latter featured on Hayes's "Souraya." Two pieces (the Spanish-tinged "Pedro's Walk," which spotlights the ingenious Tracey, and "Mini Minor") were written especially for the session by absent trumpeter Ian Hamer, while Tracey contributed "Baby Blue" and trumpeter Deuchar penned "Amber Mood" and arranged the title track (both vehicles for the powerhouse Gonsalves).

Like its predecessor, *Change of Setting* is a carefully arranged set of pieces—not a whiff of blowing session in the air—featuring the compositional talents of Londoners such as trumpeter Condon, drummer Tony Crombie, and pianist Harry South, none of whom play on the LP. The lineup is similar, though instead of the brass section, the two tenors and Sharpe are augmented by Ronnie Scott on tenor and Tony Coe on alto. Fellow Ellingtonian Ray Nance joins in on violin and trumpet, and Tracey is replaced by the more commonplace Terry Shannon on piano. The stellar Hayes piece "Don't Fall Off the Bridge" is an up-tempo showcase for the tenor players, and having Scott in the mix only ups the ante.

[March 2005]

Anthony Braxton, *New York, Fall 1974*
(Arista, 1974)

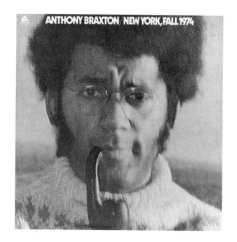

In the 1970s, the Arista imprint released a run of great LPs, some of them groundbreaking, that the label made so widely available that you could scarcely visit a record store without seeing them. More than two decades out of print, they're still relatively easy to obtain, which is an excellent thing, since many of the best of them haven't made it to CD.

Anthony Braxton's enormous catalog from the '70s includes a pile of stunning Aristas, all of them produced by Michael Cuscuna under the executive production of Steve Backer. Good thing these guys were on the ball, or great pieces like cut three, side one of *Creative Orchestra Music 1976*—Braxton's outstanding, outlandish marching band piece, which sounds like Sousa gone wonderfully awry—might never have been waxed. Records with fellow AACM alumni, like a duet with Muhal Richard Abrams and an LP with two trios (Braxton plus Henry Threadgill and Douglas Ewart on one side, Roscoe Mitchell and Joseph Jarman on the other) are significant entries in the Chicago new jazz legacy.

Cuscuna had the good sense to record some of Braxton's most challenging music, like a piece for two pianos performed by Ursula Oppens and Frederic Rzewski, and Arista was open enough to sink some money it was sure to lose into documenting one of Braxton's multiple orchestra pieces, resulting in a three-LP set that's as important for its liner booklet as for the slightly shaky reading by a student orchestra at Oberlin. In the notes, the composer foresees producing a piece to be scored for different star systems (by 1995) and different galaxies (by 2000). For Braxton, the problem in mounting such projects is always material, never creative—give him the means, and I have no doubt that he'd have intergalactic symphonic music happening tout de suite.

Braxton's music of more modest means is also highly ambitious. Check out, for instance, one of his finest records, among the signal vinyl releases of the '70s: *New York, Fall 1974*. The main part of the LP is given over to Braxton's exceptional working group with trumpeter Kenny Wheeler, bassist Dave

Holland, and drummer Jerome Cooper. With this ensemble, Braxton explored some of his most exciting jazz compositions, introducing pieces with unison sax/trumpet melodic lines that extend far beyond conventional song form—a further elongation of Lennie Tristano's drastic-elastic phraseology.

One molten cut with this group finds Braxton on contrabass clarinet; he loves the registral extreme, playing his super-low instrument against Wheeler's quicksilver muted trumpet and guest Leroy Jenkins's violin. Two tracks with Braxton on alto should be mandatory listening for Brax detractors. The leadoff cut is an up-tempo burner with an absolutely gorgeous saxophone solo, Holland locking in perfectly with Cooper under Braxton's excoriating climax.

Elsewhere, a piece for clarinet and the synthesizer of Richard Teitelbaum visits different textural vistas, as does a historic saxophone quartet, with Braxton and Julius Hemphill on altos, Oliver Lake on tenor, and Hamiet Bluiett on baritone. Sound like a familiar lineup? It's the World Saxophone Quartet, pre–David Murray, assembled to perform a forward-looking composition structured around gently pulsing clusters and chords and dialogue-based improvisations.

[April 2005]

POSTSCRIPT 2016: *In 2008, Mosaic Records issued an eight-disc box of Braxton's total output for Arista. Any sensible person should have these both as LPs and in this marvelous compilation.*

Herbie Fields Sextet, *A Night at Kitty's*
(RKO Unique, 1957)

I'll be the first to admit it: sometimes, I buy a record just for its cover. And I might never listen to it, not wanting to disturb my vision of it with what promises to be dull or unpleasant sounds. This was the case with the Herbie Fields Sextet's enticing *A Night at Kitty's*, which was bought for a buck at some garage sale and made a proud part of the collection for years, until a few weeks ago when I pulled it out on a whim and put it on the turntable.

It's a great record cover, slightly kitschy, with a carefully posed snapshot of the interior of that beautiful bar, Kitty's Show Lounge in Columbus, Ohio, where the recording was made. There's the woman at the bar, cocktail ready, and in the background a tape deck, engineer, and helpful assistant, poised to document the proceedings. It's the perfect setting for a film noir or a lost weekend.

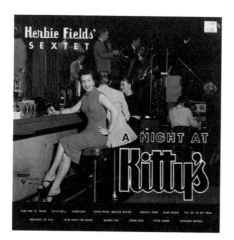

Little did I know what bodacious music was lurking in those grooves. I can't say that it's great music, but it's uproariously energetic and playful, which is much more than I expected. And Fields is a hilarious saxophonist. In fact, *A Night at Kitty's* serves as a showcase for a showboating show-off. The taste is not always tops, but the point here is to generate enthusiasm, and Fields manages to crank it up pretty far.

Listen to the start of "How High the Moon," a notorious throw-down for speed freaks. Fields sounds like he's been shot out of a cannon, which makes it that much more of a shock when the band drops down to quarter speed for the second half of the tune. On the alto version of "You Go to My Head," Fields rushes to say everything at once; he's the kid who's a bit too dexterous for his own good, flailing around with his prodigiousness.

Everything here is overstated and excessive, which is part of what makes it so fun. Fields himself is technically off the charts, a regular Rudy Wiedoeft. On two baritone features, "Satin Doll" and "Song from 'Moulin Rouge,'" he's totally in control of his horn (James Carter, check this out), and for him expressiveness isn't a stretch, but maybe on the contrary it's something to try to rein in. And he doesn't, at least not much.

Fields is too busy flutter-tonguing, slap-tonguing, and pulling other feats of fancy articulation. He hits piercing high notes, blats low notes, and on "Bernie's Tune" even gets into some completely wild, edge-of-the-seat mania with more teeth than plenty of free jazz saxophonists. An absurdly hyperbolic, Latinized clarinet piece, "Mambo Inn," ends with a requisite: "Gracias!" Fields takes the horn out of his mouth long enough for a weird scat break on "Undecided."

The rest of the band is fully on board for the shenanigans, though Joe Black's piano gets short shrift as it's unmiked—every time he solos, the entire recording level is raised, so the cymbals and ambient noise get much louder. Between phrases on "Satin Doll," the bar's phone rings, almost on cue. But these elements just add to the feeling, which is in a way as accurate a portrayal of a great night at a jazz lounge as I can think of. A night at Kitty's sure sounds fine.

[June 2005]

I had every intention of seeing Air, but it wasn't in the cards. The album title *80° Below '82* always reminds me why. It had to do with an Air gig in Cedar Rapids, Iowa, during the frigid winter of 1982, something about a patch of ice and totaling my parents' car. But never mind that. There's the record to wonder about.

What a fantastic expanse of vinyl it is—one of Air's best, though their catalog from that period is pretty, pardon me, airtight. Can't fault the Nessa, the India Nav-igations, or the fabulous Aristas, includ-

ing their versions of Scott Joplin (on *Air Lore*, 1979), and my favorite single track waxed by Air, "The Jick, or Mandrill's Cosmic Ass" (on *Open Air Suit*, 1978).

Nevertheless, *80° Below '82* is the one I always return to, and I'd argue as a whole it can't be topped. Henry Threadgill's compositional vision, coupled with the unparalleled group dynamic, made Air one of the most exciting bands of its time. On this LP the reasons are abundantly evident and succinctly presented.

Proceed straight to their astonishing take on Jelly Roll Morton's "Chicago Breakdown" to hear exactly why they sit so high on the shelf. The architecture of the composition is clear—Morton's appealing melodic line tipping its hat and tapping its cane with grace and good humor. But Air reinvents the piece, toying with the idea of the breakdown. Bassist Fred Hopkins and drummer Steve McCall mark breaks with joint stop-time hits, and Threadgill's saxophone plows ahead as if to insist that the show must go on. Persevering through several convincing false endings and shifts in time feel, Air glides into the finishing moments of the piece, only to hit the ground with the elegance of a frigate-bird. It's a beautiful, upended ending.

Part of what's so winning about *80° Below '82* is the outstanding perfor-mance by the late, lamented Hopkins. Hopkins was, on the face of it, every-thing I detest in a bassist: electric, overamped sound; slippery and sometimes sloppy articulation. But through some alchemical process he made all those faults work to his advantage, and his playing is completely inspired. Indeed, it helps make Threadgill's compositions and arrangements work so delightfully, lending them an open, spontaneous feel and sense of transparency.

When one of the Air band members plays unaccompanied, it often doesn't feel like a "solo," but more like it's a moment in a larger arrangement—an arrangement that's sketched out and then filled with potential, rather than mandatory, events. The core structure is implicit; its manifestation can take many forms. Even on a more straightforwardly constructed cut like "The Traveller," the bass ostinato doesn't completely dominate or ground the rest of the activities. It conspires to present Threadgill's dramatic voice and McCall's tender swing.

In that sense, Air was among the most democratic of ensembles. Instrumental roles were neither trashed nor revered—a bass can play like a bass or adopt any other instrumental role it wants. In some spots, McCall picks up melodic duties, and elsewhere Threadgill and Hopkins might swap that task. Everyone's not there to do his own thing, but to contribute to the collective cause. And in the case of *80° Below '82*, it certainly was a joyous, gritty, sophisticated cause.

[July 2005]

POSTSCRIPT 2016: *Hard to swallow that this major LP is still unavailable as either CD or digital file. Is anyone paying attention? In the words of John Wayne, it's getting to be rigoddamndiculous. This opens a gap in available post-AACM recordings. In any case, Threadgill's whole Arista catalog was reissued, like Braxton's, by the kind folks at Mosaic, along with the essential RCA and Columbia releases that followed.*

Guy Warren with Red Saunders Orchestra, *Africa Speaks—America Answers*
(DECCA, 1955)

Among the engrossing stories of the '50s, that of Kofi Ghanaba, aka Guy Warren, is one of the most woefully forgotten. A Ghana-born percussionist who posed for a famous late photo swapping clothes with Charlie Parker, Warren was a fixture on the New York jazz scene of the mid-'50s, jamming with Thelonious Monk and John Coltrane, and even gigging at Birdland with Sarah Vaughan and Lester Young. Before his stint in the Big Apple, Warren had spent time investigating Chicago's jazz environs, and prior he'd spent some time in London, playing bebop bongos with Kenny Graham's Afro-Cubists. But it was the Chicago period in which Warren made the contacts for his groundbreaking first solo record, *Africa Speaks—America Answers*, arguably the original world-jazz outing.

Recorded with drummer Red Saunders and his orchestra—sadly not detailed on the sleeve—under the direction of pianist Gene Esposito, the LP was popular in its day, reputedly selling more than one million copies. That's strange given that it's so infrequently seen in second-hand shops, but it is quite rare now. What is particularly intriguing about *Africa Speaks—America Answers* is the liaison with Saunders. The workingman drummer had a band for which Sun Ra had arranged at Chicago's Club DeLisa. Saunders was also fundamental in integrating the musicians' unions in Chicago, probably his claim to fame.

If you consider Warren's popularization of African percussion—he was the musician more than any who introduced the talking drum to American audiences—it's not hard to triangulate a Ra connection, given the Arkestra's experimentation with exotic African sounds. There's no direct evidence for this, though; neither is there much to be made of the collaboration with Esposito, who has the misfortune of being best remembered (at least in my circles) as the pianist who was fired from his own quartet to create the Joe Daley Trio.

As early Afro-jazz exotica goes, *Africa Speaks—America Answers* is surprisingly varied and engaging. The title track marks the transition suggestion in the record's theme, moving from echoed-out voices and African percussion to traps and piano, played sparely with talking drum and balaphon soloing delicately over them. "Duet," a dialogue between Warren's talking drum and Saunders's full kit, is the most convincing and simplest of the syncretic cultural mind-melds. Less so are pseudoclassical pieces like "Ode to a Stream," a slightly Ravel-ish chromatic study with poetry recited by Warren, and "My Minuet," a geeky pre–Jean-Pierre Rampal contrapuntal jaunt. Fulfilling the straight exotica quotient is "Invocation of the Horned Viper," with spooky snake-tongue sounds courtesy of Warren.

Four highlife tracks recall the fact that Warren cofounded the seminal band the Tempos in Ghana during the early '50s. On "Highlife Song," the unnamed Saunders saxophonist runs bebop licks with the off-pitch African sound, while "High Life" jump-cuts between light African pop and swinging jazz. "J.A.I.S.I. (Jazz as I See It)" has a B-movie soundtrack bump 'n' grind, with a great baritone solo and African percussion, the bass and African percussion breaking for a little walking and talking. But the track that comes closest to a real merger of American and African musics is "Eyes of a Faun." With its loose, neat horn arrangement, it's got a distinct Art Ensemble of Chicago vibe, way out ahead of the AACM.

[August 2005]

POSTSCRIPT 2016: *Full name, Kpakpo Kofi Warren Gamaliel Harding Akwei, died in 2008.* Africa Speaks—America Answers *was remastered by Trunk Records and made available as a download on iTunes.*

Barry Altschul, *Another Time, Another Place*
(Muse, 1978)

A few years ago, I saw a very nice group at Fred Anderson's Velvet Lounge in Chicago. Paul Smoker was on trumpet, John Tchicai on saxophones, and young Adam Lane was on bass. This impressive lineup would have had me out that evening, but the biggest draw for me was an opportunity to hear drummer Barry Altschul, who for many years was MIA in my books, and he surely didn't disappoint one iota.

Altschul was an important youngster himself in the New York scene of the late '60s, but his records of about a decade later place him securely as one of the most important figures of what Anthony Braxton—a long-term compadre of his—called restructuralism.

Big drag, then, to discover how few of his wonderful records are available on CD. Among those still available, don't miss his Black Saint trio with bassist John Lindberg and trombonist George Lewis, *In and Out*, especially for the essential tune "Be Out S'Cool." I adore his Moers outing, now impossible to find, and there are some obscurities worth looking for, too.

Of the lost sessions, this one, made for the Muse label and never excavated for digital purposes, is one of the best. It's a mixed record, featuring different ensembles and one short, nicely structured drum solo. The bands include a string-group-plus-drums playing a Dave Holland tune, Holland on bass along with Brian Smith and the great undersung cello of Abdul Wadud, and even more obscure Peter Warren.

Much of the record's success revolves around Altschul's inventive writing, which has the complexity of classic Braxton but also a driving clarity and forthrightness. Ray Anderson is the perfect foil for these pieces, and the trombonist plays with all the grit and wah for which he's known best on *Another Time, Another Place*. This is perhaps one of his best outings, little known as it is.

The track that I want to spotlight, however, is a lengthy Thelonious Monk medley that's so splendid—and so free of the nasty clichés that now plague covers of Monk—that it's really worth singling out. Alto saxophonist Arthur Blythe joins the fray, along with odd-man-out guitarist Bill D'Arango, a more conservative elder jazzer who plays low-profile but fits in nevertheless, but the medley has a way of taking "Evidence" and "Crepuscule with Nellie" and making them sound fresh and alive. It's just like Monk would have wanted.

The band moves seamlessly between the tunes, bridging them with open improvising and loose arrangements. Blythe was a fiery fiend back then, and the drummer spurs them on with his limber-jointed combination of swing and obtuseness. I'm happy to report that Altschul's playing on the night I saw him was still just as tasty as this, but for a durable spot of vinyl with his singular artistic imprint, hunt down this not-too-rare LP.

[September 2005]

The Korean Black Eyes, "Higher"
(Vitoria seven-inch, circa 1970s)

People collect records for all sorts of reasons. For value, of course, though that's a relatively silly motivation, since there are virtually none that have the monetary worth of a Honus Wagner baseball card or upside-down airplane stamp. Folks hunt vinyl to fill in parts of the music history puzzle, searching out rarely heard moments. Or they revel in the diversity of material culture, looking for a special pressing, maybe a better-sounding "deep groove" Blue Note or a scarce monaural copy of their favorite Riverside album.

These are all classic rationales for vinyl freakishness, but there's another one that's less often cited: the celebration of human weirdness in all its

unimaginable splendor. Onto those little black spinning discs have been projected some of the most outlandish concoctions of human imagination. This month, we consider the activity of collecting the bizarre productions that make you say, "What were they thinking?!"

A few years ago, I was digging in the most unpromising environs of a record shop in Lisbon, Portugal. The basement was filled with stacks of '80s synth-pop LPS, and in bins below the LPS were thousands of picture-sleeve fado singles, mostly from the '60s. They held some curious appeal; and right there, unprepared, I discovered what might be the strangest record of my collecting career.

In general appearance and feel, it was at home among the other singles. But this one made me halt in my tracks. Where the fado records sported romantic Portuguese men and women smiling tenderly or grimacing into a microphone, this one depicted a group of heavily made-up Asian women on a lawn in front of some monument, with a saxophone and two guitars strewn in front of them. The Korean Black Eyes is a band name much too suggestive for me to pass up, so I tossed the enigmatic item in my short stack and promptly forgot about it until I got back to the States.

Whereupon, I was shocked and thrilled to actually spin it. I know little about the group, but here's what I can tell you. The Korean Black Eyes appear to be a Korean girl group from Portugal from the early 1970s. Based on the four songs of this single, they specialize in adaptations of American pop songs. Also, I'd wager that not one of them knows more than a few words of English. Perhaps there is the twisted genius of a Portuguese producer lurking behind the record, or maybe it was just a flock of immigrant gals eager to share their passion for Elvis Presley, Johnnie Taylor, and Sly Stone. Whatever prompted it, the result is a hilariously original train wreck of cross-cultural misunderstanding.

The bedrock of this ultrastrange aesthetic is phonetic transliteration, the means by which the Korean Black Eyes make use of song lyrics. On the record's centerpiece, a version of Sly & the Family Stone's "Higher," it's only at the exclamations of "Hey"—which they shout like they're kick-starting a political rally—that they appear to have any feeling for what the words are about. Elsewhere, above percolating organ, distorted guitar, and sour saxophone, with gleeful verve and determination, they mangle the text, at one point pronouncing a line with a distinctively Portuguese sound that doesn't appear in the English language.

Take note, however: they don't translate anything. It all has the vague, distant shape of the original lyrics. By the time they get to the "Boom-shaka-laka" break, the Black Eyes are completely lost, but wonderfully so. They massacre Presley's "Burning Love" and even more so Taylor's "Who's Making Love?" Korean women in Lisbon singing about mutual infidelity through the eyes of an African American man—what a wonderful world we live in!

[November 2005]

Rufus Jones, *Five on Eight*
(Cameo, 1963)

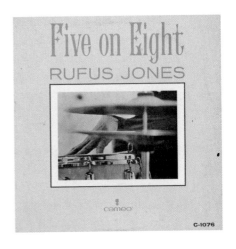

Though he was the drummer in a string of successful jazz bands, including outfits led by Lionel Hampton, Maynard Ferguson, Count Basie, and Duke Ellington, Rufus "Speedy" Jones never achieved the level of recognition that folks like Sonny Greer or Papa Jo Jones did. But he was a wonderful player, motoring such milestones as Ellington's beloved *Far East Suite*. His nickname was no joke—Speedy was quick-wristed and lightning fast, and when he let it rip on a snare, he could make a drum corps drop their sticks in awe.

In 1963, at the beginning of his stint with Basie, Jones took a minute to make an LP as a leader. Recording for the little Cameo label, he wisely chose Jaki Byard as his pianist, with Teddi Smith and Major Holley alternating on bass, and guitarist Gene Bertoncini (on side B) rounding out the exceptional rhythm section. Indeed, the first side of the album centers on Byard, an added bonus on this rarity. The pianist's composition "Just Around That Time," the first track on the LP, is little more than a progressive hard-bop sketch draped over a continuous and quite astounding drum solo—Speedy going for broke, giving his skins a serious workout. Clearly the centerpiece of the LP, it's reminiscent of the drum features that Max Roach liked to orchestrate with his small groups.

"Rollin'" is a Byard blues, and it allows Joe Farrell, the saxophonist on this side of the platter, to take a laid-back solo. Trumpeter Tommy Turrentine (another Roach small-group connection) complements it with a cup-mute solo that's more swing than we're used to from him. The ballad feature for Byard, "A Secret," contains some lovely piano in the double-time section, thick with imaginative harmonies. "Aluminum Baby" sports an arrangement that builds a fascinating bridge between swing and hard-bop.

The second side of *Five on Eight* is a mini concept suite of soundtrack themes, featuring the imposing Seldon Powell on tenor saxophone. After Jones's explosive introduction on side A, the drummer took a more familiar backseat on the session, but he shines again on "My Special Dream" with a light, pillowy touch and propulsive drive. "Bird Brain" (from *Singin' in the Rain*) features a beautiful, buoyant treble meter and a guitar solo that cleverly integrates "Nobody Knows the Trouble I've Seen." Henry Mancini's "Ebb Tide" includes tasty inserts from Byard, whose insights across the board make this record especially worthwhile, more than just a bone thrown to the skinsman.

[February 2006]

POSTSCRIPT 2016: *Another LP that's been made available, finally in 2013, for download on iTunes.*

Johnny Shacklett Trio, *At the Hoffman House*
(Universal Artists, 1969)

Given the genre's popularity, it's surprising that there are any groovy guitar records left in the wild. Grant Green and Wes Montgomery are pretty well covered, as are slightly lower-profile folks like Boogaloo Joe Jones and Melvin Sparks, the latter of whom was treated to an excellent twofer recently. If you dig around you can still find some terrific soul-jazz guitar LPs. A Japanese Montgomery fan club Web site (www.ne.jp/asahi/wes.fan/club/right/modoki /wes_ha1.htm) mentions a few, including a scarce one from Madison, Wisconsin, by guitarist Johnny Shacklett and his trio, recorded in the summer of 1969.

It's a well-recorded LP, mixed in an odd way with the guitar entirely panned right, the band to the left, isolating the parts the way early Beatles records did with the vocals and the instruments. The guitar is also mixed quite forward, which is augmented by Shacklett's ear-popping sound, thumbed, with lots of Montgomeryish octave unisons.

On "Hoffman House Blues," he peps these up with an active bass line, ornamenting the higher octave with the lower notes rather than the other way around. It's a fancy trick and kept funky by Shacklett's prestidigitative skills. Mid-solo, he transforms the octave work into full chords, playing a chordal solo that might have given Niles Rodgers something to think about. This becomes a formula across the record, moving from Montgomery octaves into full-blown chords. But every soul-jazz record needs its formulas, and when they're original and groovy, there's no problem. Even on more mellow numbers—generally less interesting here—there's heavy chording. On "Polkadots and Moonbeams," he even gets into some pre–Stanley Jordan two-hand hammering, a weird and dissonant effect given his lack of control.

The punchier the better. Shacklett's version of the Dizzy Gillespie classic "Birk's Works" is blues, featuring plosive plucking and evidencing no fear of trebly twang. In fact, Shacklett lets the instrument's rough edges show through in an attractive way. Organist Melvin Rhyne and brother Ronnie Rhyne on drums are mostly in the background. This is for sure the Shacklett show, and he showboats mercilessly. Mel Rhyne—who is still making strong funky jazz records today—takes a solo on the Gillespie number, displaying an acid sound and tempestuous, but organized, expressivity.

"Haskell's Tune" is an original by Shacklett, a killer on which the guitarist doesn't avoid the dark bottom of the guitar, but plays all over the neck. Single-note runs range into fat chords. The record ends with a surprise, one that might not have been the Cracker Jack present we'd have wanted but one that turns out to be a treat nonetheless. Shacklett turns in a solo version of the Luiz Bonfa / Carl Sigman ditty "A Day in the Life of a Fool" (miscredited to Lennon and McCartney), and it's surprisingly successful. Indeed, if you put it on a CD by an up-and-coming young jazz guitarist, it would seem quite contemporary. I'm not sure if that says something about Shacklett or about this generation of guitarists, but it makes for a wonderful coda to a percolating piece of vinyl.

Now, as for the cover . . . what the heck is that multinecked thing?

[March 2006]

The Mad-Hatters, *The Mad-Hatters at Midnight*
(20th Century Fox, 1964)

One of the amusing things about the Internet is the way that mixed-up information is sometimes passed off as cold, hard fact. If you Google *The Mad-Hatters at Midnight*, you'll get a few sites that list that album, together with its correct release date, and go on to describe them as cocksure as could be as a quintet from Washington, DC, that is "very heavily influenced by the Beau Brummels, the Byrds, P. F. Sloan and Bob Dylan." Combine that with a reference to their lead singer, and you'll know right away that this is a faulty hybrid factoid—there were, in fact, two groups with the name the Mad-Hatters, and they've magically been fused into one.

That said, I still can't claim to know too much about the Mad-Hatters who released *At Midnight*. I know they're not a folk-rock quintet. They have no singer. They're a soul-jazz quartet with a vibes and B-3 front line, guitar, and drums. Dapper, in matching pale blue suits, they appear to be swinging like heck in concert on the cover. The rest of the band is deeply into their thing, while the B-3 player has spied the camera and is beaming for it, his arms crossed up like a signifying gang member. Very unhelpful liner notes tell us little more than the fact that this is music "in the modern manner, music with a beat designed for the Swinging Sixties, and music that has kept toes tapping in major night clubs through-out the United States." Thanks, guys.

From the songwriting credits, we can infer that one Vonn Williams is a member of the band, perhaps its organist. I'd further venture that Johnny Banks, Larry Coakley, and Jimmy Daniels are the other three—they each get a little taste of the compositional pie, albeit for contributing music that might have been drummed up on the spot. All tracks are jukebox single length, clocking in under four minutes. "Monkey Children" features a glorious cascading guitar solo, and "Mat-Hatters Stomp" is a generic blues of the sort that often starts soul-jazz gigs. "That Sanctified Thing" features a wonderfully nasty electronic organ setting, and a perky "Poinciana" bursts from a particularly goofy rendition of its silly theme into a hot vibes solo, the organ speed-walking its bass line beneath.

An idiotic piece of Orientalism, "World of Suzie Wong," doesn't hang the show up for long, and the Hatters are back on track with "Soul Sister" and Marvin Jenkins's "Big City." The vibes/organ combination is sometimes clumsy—this is no Johnny Lyttle group, where that instrumentation is always smooth sailing (check out *Swingin' at the Gate*, Pacific Jazz, 1967)—but they'd clearly been working together regularly by the time they waxed this winner. When the vibes sit out on "Ebb Tide," the organist takes the chance to kick up some swells that are positively swollen. For all I know, that might well be the secret P. F. Sloan influence they're talking about so confidently on the web.

[April 2006]

Klaus Doldinger, *Doldinger Goes On*
(Philips, 1967)

Maybe somebody out there can help me find something. It's not an old LP, though. It's a film clip. In the mid-'60s on German national television, Klaus Doldinger and Peter Brötzmann engaged in a conversation that turned ugly, reputedly almost coming to blows.

Seems that Doldinger, upholder at the time of mainstream jazz values in Deutschland, speculated that Brötzmann, the enfant terrible of the German new jazz scene, couldn't play a C-major scale. This, naturally, didn't go over well. Now the encounter is legend, and I'm anxious to view it for myself. Bonus: there should be performance footage from both of them, and I'm betting that the aggravation made for an especially potent Brötzmann Trio segment.

Whatever one thinks of his later projects—the best-known of them are his band Passport and the soundtracks to films like *Das Boot*—Doldinger's early music has aged rather well. *Doldinger Goes On*, a rare 1967 outing, is described thusly in Siegfried Schmidt-Joos's liner notes: "Auf seiner neusten Schallplatte präsentiert der Meisterjazzer soul-food, groovy down home cookin', Blues für schwarze and weisse Seelen, yeah!" One must wonder how many "schwarze Seelen" (black souls) actually ever laid ears on this *schallplatten*, though if they did, there's plenty of soul-food, groovy down-home cookin' to gnaw on.

On the most soul-jazz tracks, like "Shakin' the Blues" and "Run, Baby, Run," Ingfried Hoffmann's organ infuses everything with gospel, maybe a tad too insistently, like tourists in a black church clapping too hard and shouting too loud. But Doldinger's irrepressible tenor cuts through any overreverent cultural precaution, and the strong support of Dutch drummer Cees See and bassist Peter Trunk—both mainstays of the European mainstream—doesn't hurt either.

Doldinger's sound is big and meaty, steeped in R&B and Coleman Hawkins. In places, you can sense a Johnny Griffin–like love of speed and dexterity, and "Watch It"—like all the compositions, a Doldinger original—has enough interesting harmonic surprises to help keep the clichés at bay.

Another treat on *Doldinger Goes On* is guitarist Volker Kriegel, later familiar in the United Jazz and Rock Ensemble. Here he shows his funkier roots, dipping into a little chicken scratch and some popping single-string solos. On "Five for You" Kriegel lays down a nifty 5/4 Latin groove on guitar, with percussionist Fats Sadi bongoing along. This leads Schmidt-Joos to say, "Diese musiker sind meister der afrikanischen ekstasetechnik" (These musicians are masters of African techniques of ecstasy).

That's taking it more than a bit too far, but it's interesting to think of this rib-tickling, sometimes world-music-y funk being the runway for the later fusion excursions. Soul-jazz was the precursor to other electric adventures. Along with the soul stirring, side one includes two acoustic tracks featuring Doldinger's soprano sax, both in treble meter.

John Coltrane's inspiration is, naturally, front and center. On "Quartenwalzer," Hoffmann's piano is studiously blue, while on the track "Tears" (the most stripped-down setting on the LP, a quartet with Hoffmann, Trunk, and See), Doldinger is too imitative of Coltrane's radiant tone. The influence was hard to avoid at the time, though, given the newness of soprano as a lead instrument. Folks all across Europe were digesting Coltrane's ideas and testing out his sound, sometimes a bit too close for comfort.

[May 2006]

POSTSCRIPT 2016: Doldinger Goes On *was reissued on vinyl in 2010.*

In the mad rush to reissue out-of-print LPs, solo drum recordings haven't exactly sped to the front of the line. Unaccompanied drumming is, at album length, something of a hard sell, perhaps rivaled only by bass duets or "special" encounters for three pianists. In fact, some great lone drummer dates remain in the queue.

I was astonished to discover that the first such record, by Baby Dodds, was unavailable as I endeavored to reissue it a few years ago. Now someone's got to license the Papa Jo Jones double LP on which he describes and demos various historical techniques. Pianist Steve Beresford once played it for me, and I've never been able to get Jones's vocal mannerisms out of my head.

Max Roach recorded solo a couple times, including tracks on the fabulous *Chatahoochie Red*, released by Columbia in 1982, and also out of print. A few years earlier, he'd made this less well-known LP, which was issued on the Japanese Baystate label and recorded in 1977 at a studio in Massachusetts. It was an expansive time for the pioneering bebopper. He was busy performing and recording with his own excellent quartet, as well as such unexpected partners as Cecil Taylor, Archie Shepp, and Anthony Braxton.

In this period, Roach was perhaps the best argument for the continuity, rather than rupture, of the jazz tradition as represented in movements from the "New Thing" to restructuralism. He managed to keep his integrity, playing music that was unequivocally Max Roach, while establishing fruitful collaborative strategies in tandem with a panoply of different players from various backgrounds. In the early '80s, I saw him play duets with trumpeter Cecil Bridgewater. It was an inspiring concert, the highlight of which was Roach's solo on hi-hat.

That patented approach to sock-cymbal is well documented on *Solos*. The title "Mr. Hi-Hat" makes explicit what's to come, and Roach provides a four-and-a-half-minute workout on the instrument that's a primer on the virtues of technical mastery. It's showy, with Roach swiping the sticks up and down to strike both the upper and lower cymbal, but it has real substance, an architecture and drama.

The hi-hat is central to "Jas-Me," one of Roach's swinging, rolling pieces, which features a great snapping shut of the jaws of the hi-hat as a signature. Interplay between the bass drum and hi-hat structures the 5/4 groove on "Five for Paul."

"J. C. Mose-Is" is ferocious, with a motoric pattern that changes tempo but keeps a clenched-fist sense of tension. Likewise, "South Africa '76" interposes a chugging train rhythm with sharp whacks on open tom, creating a sense of call-and-response out of the pattern.

Many of Roach's solos revolve around ingeniously varied patterns, and his celebrated "melodic drumming" has as much to do with a manner of phrasing as it does tonality. Roach implies a line on "Big Sid," introducing a pattern that serves as a theme just as a melody might. There's tonal content, but not much more than on an Art Blakey solo, for instance. It's the way he phrases, the linearity of his ideas that imbues his drumming with something singing as well as swinging.

[June 2006]

Dick Johnson, *Most Likely . . .*
(Riverside, 1957)

How about most unlikely? To be reissued, at least. And perhaps most unlikely to have been issued in the first place, not based on the music or the musicianship, but on the simple combination of factors—the specific grouping, the pairing of alto saxophonist Dick Johnson with Riverside, the whole knish.

Johnson's second leader date was recorded in October 1957. The Bostonian elegantly combines different styles, synthesizing some of the edgier post-bop sounds with the gently dazzling dexterity of Lee Konitz. It's a hip result, and one that deserves to be heard. But with its terrifically horrible cover and weird lineup, it's doubtful that Fantasy will be putting *Most Likely . . .* high on its list of reissue priorities.

The band, which appears to have been assembled by producer Orrin Keepnews, starts out with an obvious pairing of Johnson with his old chum Dave McKenna on piano. The twosome first played together when they were in high school, probably somewhere in Massachusetts. It is an excellent match, with McKenna sounding crisp and totally at home in the company of Johnson's subtle but driving saxophone. With their precision and grace, it's evident that they both put in time in big bands, but they're comfortable playing modern midcentury small-group jazz.

If they've got a Boston cool vibe, the session surprise—and delight—comes in the form of the rhythm section, a New York special of bassist Wilbur Ware (by way of Chicago) and drummer Philly Joe Jones. Nifty to hear the New Englanders adjust to the Riverside way, but it's equally interesting to hear Ware and Jones shift into a slightly lighter-weight swing mode. Listen to Jones's rimshots on the corniest piece, "Folderol." It must have seemed odd to a hard-bop master to play like this, but he imbues it with life, and the result is charming.

Compass points are set at the opening with "Lee-Antics," Johnson's snaky alto conveying his interest in Konitz and the Lennie Tristano approach. On "The Loop," one of five original compositions, Johnson shows what he's capable of at high speed, and he's quite impressive, evoking the requisite Charlie Parker component, but also showing an angularity that briefly hints at Eric Dolphy as well as Konitz. The softer side is emphasized on the record's ballads, like "The End of a Love Affair," on which Parker-esque bursts intrude on sweet, overtly Konitzy cooing. The Boston contingent celebrates its partnership on "Me 'N' Dave," a tough, fast, tandem melody line in the Tristano mode showing their shared roots. It lacks the contrapuntal complexity of the original, but it's got zip and drive, and that's enough to make it work.

Johnson is best known now as a clarinetist, and as leader of the Artie Shaw Orchestra, and McKenna's excellent work continues, albeit in a somewhat different vein from this date. Alas, Ware and Jones are no longer with us, except in the form of their recordings, many of which are readily available. For the intrepid collector unafraid of strange combinations, *Most Likely . . .* will add an intriguing twist to that discography.

[July 2006]

POSTSCRIPT 2016: *Dick Johnson passed away in 2010. The LP has never been reissued.*

Phil Seamen, *The Phil Seamen Story*

(Decibel, mid-1970s)

Record collecting inevitably gets mixed up with personal history. An evening spent in someone else's collection—discovering, sharing, arguing, reveling, maybe having a drink and generally enjoying the social aspect of recorded music—is vinyl freaking at its finest. Like all memorable social experiences, these evenings are fleeting, ephemeral, and one day you awake to discover that not only has the collection's owner moved, but their precious holdings have been dispersed, sold off and scattered to other hungry freaks. Their collection continues to exist only as a memory, a moment of communal listening that inspired thoughts and fantasies and maybe spurred you to search out a particularly awe-inspiring record.

I already knew about *The Phil Seamen Story* before bassist Torsten Müller played it for me in Hamburg one such night. The LP is legendary, but its legend is compounded by the notoriety of its subject. I've long considered compiling stories about two jazz musicians: South African alto saxophonist Dudu Pukwana and British drummer Seamen. Both of them, in their own different but related ways, redefined what it meant to be a colorful character. Over the years, Seamen stories have flowed in a seemingly endless stream, always full of hilarious high jinks, great musicianship, and an ocean of alcohol. The best of the ones I've heard have come from Evan Parker, Paul Rutherford, and Paul Lytton, some of them closely studied, some probably embellished or transformed from other versions. My favorite, which has been recounted in exacting detail by several sources, involves Seamen nodding off while at the kit—something he was known to do. Thing is, he was playing a cruise gig, and moreover he was on deck. Falling asleep meant falling overboard.

On the first side of *The Phil Seamen Story*, we're treated to a Baby Dodds–style narration and demonstration, with Seamen playing and explaining, but most gloriously telling his own tales. "I was asked to do *The Phil Seamen*

Story," he starts, "which pleased me greatly, being an egomaniac, and here I am!" In his own ultradroll, five-pints-worth woozy voice, he shares horror stories and mishaps, explaining that until he played with Jack Parnell he'd never played a paradiddle. "I thought a paradiddle was some sort of sexual orgasm," he explains. The second side fills out the story with a chronological sampling of his work from the 1940s to the '70s, featuring different bands, including Kenny Baldock, Brian Lemon, Tony Coe, Jimmy Witherspoon, Harry South, Phil Bates, and Dick Morrisey. It's a simple and concise indication of what a masterful musician Seamen was, a perfect complement to the rambling egomania of the other side.

Many of Seamen's fine recordings with Tubby Hayes, Ronnie Scott, and Roland Kirk are available on CD; there's even a DVD of Kirk in London with Seamen clearly asleep at the wheel but still driving the band like crazy. This record may take a while to get reissued, but it's a rarefied treat to be enjoyed with a friend or two, listening to Seamen's akimbo wit and barroom wisdom.

[September 2006]

Paul Smoker Trio, *QB*
(Alvas, 1984)

Coming of age in Iowa felt about as removed from the epicenter of jazz as if I'd been in Novosibirsk, Siberia. In fact, before I left for college, I never saw a live jazz concert. But our university town had a record store with a huge jazz section, so I was safe: my pockets were empty and my ears were buzzing even neck deep in the heartland. Little did I know, just a short drive away in Cedar Rapids, a serious little hub of in-the-flesh jazz activity was brewing, all of it centered around the extraordinary trumpeter Paul Smoker, who was teaching at Coe College.

Smoker's main vehicle was his trio with drummer Phil Haynes. Later it would include bassist Drew Gress, but in one phase it featured the too-little-known bassist Ron Rohovit. Trumpet-led trios are rare—think of the novelty of Dave Douglas's Tiny Bell Trio, which will someday be looked back on as a rather prescient threesome. Maybe this is because it's hard to keep from having your lip give out. Or, perhaps it's because trumpet can be a wearying instrument to listen to without another timbre for contrast. In the right hands, and with the right lips, it's no sweat, and listening back to the fantastic records Smoker made with his trios, including his better-known Sound Aspects releases, confirms that he has a commanding presence.

Another feature of Smoker's Iowa activities had to do with bringing luminaries in to play, sometimes on their own and sometimes as guests with his group. In 1984, Smoker brought Anthony Braxton, with whom he would go on to collaborate many times over the years, to Iowa. They hit the studio in my town, Iowa City, and waxed an LP. *QB* could stand for "quarterback," maybe suggesting the role Braxton played, or it could simply mean "Quartet Braxton," using a distinctly Braxtonian, math-like abbreviation. With Rohovit and Haynes as the rhythm section and a front line of Braxton and Smoker, this is a record that deserves to be remembered by a group that should be revived. An intense, roiling set of originals by Smoker and Haynes, the seven tracks have the sort of explosive germinal material and driven blowing that mark them as coming out of other 1970s Midwest movements, the AACM and BAG camps most clearly. Right out of the gate, on Smoker's "Slip-Knot," the quick little theme catapults the trio, sans Braxton, into a brisk, physical, lurching series of solos, pushed out onto the canvas like paint right out of the tube.

Rohovit is powerful, pushy even, but in a good way, recalling bassist Fred Hopkins in both tone and temperament. Braxton joins the gang for three tracks, including Haynes's brooding, building "Saeta," on which his alto (his only horn here, a bit of a rarity in those days) slowly crescendos and rises in pitch to a febrile peak, Rohovit's one-note ostinato mounting tension the entire time.

The trumpeter's "Baps" is a swinging tune with a tricky little Art Ensemblish break. On the title track you can hear plainly what a wonderful, creative soul Smoker is, his trumpet a marvel of brassy forthrightness. Dig the smeared sounds he makes with Braxton, whose fans had better get hunting to find a copy of this self-produced classic.

[October 2006]

POSTSCRIPT 2016: *Smoker died in May of this year.*

Khan Jamal, *Drumdance to the Motherland*
(Dogtown, 1972)

Franz Koglmann, *For Franz / Opium*
(Pipe, 1976)

In all my perambulations during three decades of record hunting, I have never seen a copy of Khan Jamal's *Drumdance to the Motherland*. It's so rare that I'd never even heard of it, despite liking Jamal and generally looking for unusual 1970s free jazz. And, despite the fact that it has now been lovingly reissued, I still have no idea what the record looks like.

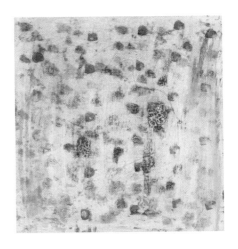

So, let's get extra-geeky and talk about record covers. When Eremite re-packaged *Drumdance*, they put a nice new image on it. The original issue, on the microscopic Dogtown label from Philadelphia, came with individually designed covers, a probable nod to Jamal's then-fellow-Philadelphians in Sun Ra's Arkestra, who regularly decorated records by hand, often just before a big gig. There's more than just the cover about *Drumdance* that's Ra-esque. Wave upon wave of tape delay recalls the Ra LPs, nearly a decade earlier, on which drummer Tommy "Bugs" Hunter first accidentally put the microphone into the wrong jack and discovered the supernatural, spaced-out powers of overdriven echo. Jamal's is a fantastic record, with funky grooves and mania-cal blowing periodically reflected in the funhouse mirror of slapback.

Jamal's vibraphone and marimba are, in some sections, featured in an un-fettered and undistorted way. It's a real treat, as is Monnette Sudler's aggres-sive guitar. An absolutely unique LP, *Drumdance* is testament to the liberating powers of the underground, the shared do-it-yourself mentality that links fringe jazz and punk. Hats off to Eremite for dredging it up, even with its new visage.

I may never find a copy of the three hundred original issues of *Drum-dance*, but I've got a first edition of Austrian trumpeter Franz Koglmann's *For Franz / Opium*, which was reissued a little while ago on the Between the Lines label. Documenting studio projects undertaken with fellow trumpeter

Bill Dixon (*For Franz*) and Steve Lacy (*Opium*), it too is an enjoyable oddity. Bonus points, aside from the marquee stars, include bassist Alan Silva, who joins the Dixon festivities, and drummer Aldo Romano, who is present on the Lacy material. In both cases this makes sense, as Silva worked with Dixon at that time, in the mid-1970s, and Romano had played extensively with Lacy in the '60s.

The initial run of these records came with sensitive, pastel-toned cover paintings, all original, by Koglmann himself. The reissue didn't take its cover from one of these, but imposed something consistent with the Between the Lines cover concept. Too bad, since the original art was, in its own way, a beautiful exhibition of multidisciplinarity on Koglmann's part.

The fact that the cover art hasn't been reissued just means the original was never fully reissued. The music, if it was meant to be augmented by the cover, is just a little bit lessened by the lack of dialogue with the visuals. For die-hard freaks, we have to have the whole package.

[November 2006]

Brand New Secondhand: Record Collector Subcultures

In a way, it doesn't really matter what it is. Any material object that can be collected, it seems, will gather together a subculture to celebrate, venerate, and debate it. If the subculture is big enough, there will be stores. Even shopless objects, if beloved fervently enough, provide occasion for conventions and fairs, little pagan rituals of commercial worship at which panels are sometimes convened and booths are erected and people sit waiting for the right devotee to walk in, strike up a conversation, and buy something. These are places where freaks go to be with other freaks.

The truth of this statement was brought home to me once at a convention in rural Illinois dedicated to shellac records. My friend Hal Rammel, himself a collector and scholar of odd and unusual musical objects, many old-timey in nature, and one of the few deejays specializing in the antiquated 78-rpm discs, discovered that the convention was convening, and we set out for a wee town in the northernmost part of the state. At the time, I had no 78s to speak of; like most of my generation, I was used to buying records in two possible speeds, 45 and 33⅓. They were no longer building machines to play 78s, and it seemed far-fetched to me that there would be a fan base for the derelict medium. Boy, was I wrong.

Walking the aisles in the convention's big tent, I was filled with a sense of both disorientation and delirium. The former came from being in a context of collectors so similar to me but in another way so very different, like landing on a planet where everything is exactly the same, but the inhabitants wear their socks on the outside of their shoes. The delirious feeling came as a contact high from the intense aggregation of nerds, a species so myopically loyal to its object of adoration that nothing else, not even something quite close, suffices in satisfying the urge. Connoisseurs of seventy-year-old musty recordings of Hawaiian string music or early down-home blues, Bix Beiderbecke completists, aficionados of the Victrola, the phonograph, the gramophone, the phonogramophone.

I walked into a booth and promptly had a twenty-minute conversation with the dealer about types of needles for 78s. I'm sure, to him, it was like telling a child how to eat with a fork, but for me it was hilariously, wonderfully new. Hal and I ducked in and out of the various vendors, rifling through the awkwardly heavy, glass-like discs, looking for a way in. I bought a couple of Greek rembetika 78s, he found some Mound City Blue Blowers on Brunswick, and we were off to the races. I can't say that I've joined the 78-rpm Collectors' Community (a website and social network for this particularly splinter group of freak) or become a collector on the scale of the greats, like R. Crumb, Dick Spottswood, or Joe Bussard, folks who pose in front of acres of shellac in their basements—always in the basement, where there's no floor to collapse under the weight of these monstrously heavy things—but now I pay attention whenever there's shellac around, and I can have a relatively intelligent conversation with a 78 fanatic.

I think the thing that's always fascinated me about records is the play between understanding them as objects of solitary attention and as the focal point of social interaction. And the social part of the equation can come at any moment, from when you're shopping to when you already know a record backward and forward and just enjoy sharing it with others. I'm the type who loves to understand as much as I can about a record, from details about the lineup to how many were pressed and in how many editions and how the editions differed from one another. Records are an excuse for research, for comparison and contrast, the two most exciting things in life. But they're also simply a source of pleasure, to be listened to and enjoyed. I can do that via earbuds on the bus, or I can do it with a bunch of folks sitting around a bottle of scotch and some ribs.

When I was fifteen, I got a job at Co-op Records in Iowa City. I'd been hanging around the store for a couple of years already, and now and then the manager, Michael, would ask me to watch things while he went out for a smoke or ran to the bank. After a while, he said it would make more sense for me to just work there, so I did. We also sold a selection of pot-smoking paraphernalia, elaborately tubed objects made of glass, housed in a vitrine under the front desk. The store's logo, as a matter of fact, featured the chain's name covered in a garland of grape vines with pot leaves surreptitiously standing in for the grape leaves. Somehow, despite my wearing the store's T-shirt all the time, my folks never noticed the dope reference. They did, however, notice when my grades declined after I'd been employed at Co-op for a year—no wonder, I spent all my time and all the money I made at the store, waiting for the latest shipment from Jem Imports to come in and update my understanding of what musicians were up to in London and Kingston.

Working at Co-op Records was an education and a constant social experience. We didn't just sell records, we played them all day long, commenting on them, replaying favorite passages, one-upping each other. I liked spinning stranger and more strident selections, and Michael finally asked me to tone it down so as not to scare away the customers. At the front of the store were bins of cutouts—records that had been discontinued and were therefore substantially discounted—which is where I bought my first Sun Ra Impulse! LPs. Michael introduced me to formative records, including Little Feat's *Waiting for Columbus*, Prince's *Dirty Mind*, Parliament's *Mothership Connection*, Sparks's *Kimono My House*, various and sundry by Todd Rundgren and the Tubes. Before I'd joined the small staff, Michael had given me the debut Elvis Costello LP, hot off the shelves, my first promotional copy. Like heroin—the first hit is free, the next one costs you your soul.

In addition to the undercurrent of light drug use, there was also an air of sex to the shop, or at least as an adolescent kid I felt the gnawing presence of Michael's girlfriend and ex-girlfriend, both of whom worked there; the latter was a sweet, slightly airheaded blonde with tight curls and dolly cheeks who liked to break Michael's rule against getting me stoned, and the former was a razor-sharp, makeupless, straight-haired brunette who once verbally called me out for looking down her shirt while she inventoried records. Rightly so. When I got a C in chemistry, my folks pulled the plug, as they should have; if they hadn't, I might still be working there. Co-op was one of the most enjoyable places I was ever employed, and I guess in retrospect I've always tried to replicate the sense of discovery and delight in subsequent workplaces.

Co-op had a rival store called BJ's Records. I felt no particular allegiance, being a freak, so I often bought from BJ's, quizzing the guys behind the counter, who I would know on and off in record stores across the Midwest for the next forty years. When one of them accused me of liking everything because I would listen to the Vibrators and Van Halen with equal relish, it caused me no end of anguish and outrage. I clarified my omnivorous attitude when a dour punk I liked came up to me at Co-op and said basically the same thing, asking me how I could be interested in Steve Howe's virtuosity—I had Yes's *Close to the Edge* on the house system—and the deskilled attitude of the Fall at the same time. I listen to them for different things, I figured, and nobody makes me choose sides. I stick to that program, even if now I am much more selective in what I like than I was as a wide-eared lad. Because they're all on record, there's a distance, and it's easier to be thoroughly relativistic, unlike rooting for a sports team or being affiliated with a club. But having catholic taste doesn't mean liking everything. One can be a vinyl connoisseur with ranging interests.

I had a listening buddy, older than me, much more seasoned. He turned me on to lots of new music, urged me to cross over from the Pop & Rock section to the vast sea of Jazz, about which I knew nothing. I was always slightly jealous of him because every time I went to his place he had a pile of new records, all the expensive imports that I had to save up for, even with my cherished employee discount. One day I turned up at his house, and he was pretty bummed out. It turned out he'd been stealing them, armloads at a time, and got caught red-handed on the way down BJ's stairs. As a goody two shoes who'd never stolen a pack of gum, I was scandalized. But being a freak is not too far from being a druggie or a sex addict; the calculus of want and the algebra of need have situational senses of ethics. I took his travails as a personal warning.

There were years when record stores were more home than home. Like all good hobbies, record collecting provides a refuge from responsibilities you don't want to face and can help sublimate unwanted emotions into a set of urgent preoccupations. For a while, with one girlfriend, shopping for records represented something about personal space and identity. We crossed Europe taking turns between vinyl and shoes, indulging me, then her, then me, and so on in a ridiculous treasure hunt that required ticks on a mental abacus to keep tally. In those times, records came to mean something very loaded, a material manifestation of deep personal anxiety and the warding off thereof. All along, the clerks and other patrons at stores were there for me, my version of the bartender-therapist.

Hunting for records is a crazy business. Anyone who has done it as a job will have extreme stories to tell—wacko people met along the way, needle in a haystack finds, bizarre stashes left behind when folks die, shelves of unopened copies, scams and cons and wheeler-dealer types. I once watched as a collector-dealer showed a full box of dead-stock singles to a musician who played on it four decades earlier, observed him freaking out at having never seen a copy, asked him to sign a couple, and then didn't have the generosity to give him one. An old woman who ran a record store in downtown Milwaukee in the '80s was certifiably out of her mind, down to the off-register lipstick and loose-fitting wig. Two steps from being in an institution, she oversaw a huge store filled with records and vintage pornography, disarticulated pages of which were strewn around the floor. Perusing the bins, if you looked down at your feet you were likely to see a spread-eagled woman staring up at you. After shopping there, I always felt like taking a shower.

Vast cultural differences are sometimes uncovered during the hunt. I used to shop at a store in a dicey neighborhood on the West Side of Chicago. It had a "rare room," with walls full of totally unsorted records, the few actually rare ones buried in tons of everyday contemporary R&B LPs, most of them moldy, warped, scratched beyond playability, or all three. The main stacks had about the same ratio of harder-to-find vinyl, so I confined my activities to that part of the shop, where one day I found a small pile of extremely fine old jazz and funk records in good shape. They were not priced—more on this in a second—so I took them to the counter, where the clerk told me it would be a few minutes. I returned after the allotted time, and she handed me the LPs, which now had prices written as large numbers in black sharpie directly on the covers. I cringed and put them all back. As I was exiting, she asked: "Don't you want any of those?" I told her that I'd wanted them without the permanent marker on them, and she said: "You don't play the covers!" A friend told me a related story about a collector he knew who went to India in search of 78s. He found some at a flea market, very roughly treated, but interesting. The woman at the stand said to wait, she had more, came back after a little while with a stack of very shiny ones. She and a friend had buffed them up with clarified butter.

Not that long ago I went to a store in Los Angeles run by someone who can only be called a staunch vinyl purist. After an hour's interrogation in the shop's entrance—I like vinyl, so I passed the entrance exam—I was allowed in and discovered a trove of unusual records, many of them unsorted and all of them unpriced. This should be the first red flag of record shopping. When things have no price tag, it gives one the feeling of something left undone, a task unfinished, but in fact it is often part of a proactive sales strategy based on self-selection. Rather than scour one's inventory, dividing up the desirables from the everyday and deciding what to charge for them, why not let the consumer do the work? When they come to the counter with their selections, you already know they want them, so you price accordingly. As a buyer, if you are at all sensitive to this sort of thing, the moment where you put unpriced records in front of the store owner you feel like a giant dolt—like saying, hey, these records here are very exciting to me, please sell them to me for a fair price. Not likely. Records with no price are treated as if they're that: priceless.

In this case, I searched the huge store, brought some finds to the front, and as anticipated he priced them very high. I chose two, the cheapest, just to be a sport, and declined on the rest. He was not happy. "You're buying *two records*?" he shouted. "Oh, that's right, you're from Chicago." I asked what that was supposed to mean, and he said that Chicagoans are window-shoppers and they waste his time. "Your prices are insane," I countered. "But if you had something I was really looking for, I'd pay for it." "What are you really looking for?" I had an answer ready: "Well, I don't carry a want-list with me, but . . . Harry Partch's 1954 debut, on his own pre–Gate 5 label. The so-called trust fund Partch." He smiled a wicked smile, raised his right arm, and without looking grabbed a record in the stacks above and behind him. It was like he was doing a magic trick. He slapped it gently in front of me. Excellent condition, signed and numbered. I just about fell over. I'd never once seen it before, and he had pulled it out of a hat on command. He knew he had me over a barrel. He put a gouging price on it, and still in disbelief I handed him my credit card.

Records can have a special burdensome quality. They're the classic collector's albatross, an object of affection that, when aggregated, weighs the owner down terribly, becoming a responsibility rather than an indulgence. And they're very heavy. One phenomenon that I've witnessed frequently enough to believe it's a full-blown syndrome is the collector who jettisons a complete collection. I have a friend who's done it several times. At some point, the weight is just too much, the whole thing has to go. Every time I've been privy to such a sale, the seller was buying right up to the end, sometimes acquiring and de-acquisitioning within the same week—hence, it's not really a matter of having lost interest, it's some other psychological process. I've felt the urge to purge from time to time, when the records have become obstructive or disorganized, when I have needed cash or wanted mobility. The last time I really sold anything I'd bought, though, was in high school, and I've always regretted it. I pledged that I wouldn't do it again, and now, if I ever do, I'm sure it will be the whole collection, for keeps.

There's a different kind of phenomenon, though, that I have experienced a couple of times, when people have given me something very special from their collections, sort of a token of appreciation from one collector to another. It has a loving character, this gesture. An artist friend gave me the entire collection of ten-inch jazz records his parents bought in the 1950s. During a studio visit, another artist gave me a pair of very rare Horace Silver Blue Note ten-inches. And then there's the friend of my parents who played trombone in the 1940s, running around with Charles Mingus and Mose Allison. His collection was focused on trombone jazz (anything else was deemed dispensable). In the 1950s a friend of his bought all the new Riverside and Blue Note LPs, promptly taped them, and gave the mint LPs to the trombonist. If they didn't have a trombone, he never listened to them again. These pristine castaways were shelved deep in a closet when he told me to go through them and take any that I wanted. Like I say, it has a loving character, something warm and feel-good, the prospect of giving records to someone who will really enjoy them.

I felt great taking those records, knowing that I wouldn't sell them and that they'd be put to good use in my collection. On another occasion, I felt less great acquiring in bulk. It was the fallout from a recent divorce, the ex-wife selling off a wonderful assembly of LPs, most of them reggae and traditional African music. "He was such an asshole," she told me, unbidden. "These remind me of him, and I can't get rid of them fast enough." I bought about 150 of them at fair market price, but the point wasn't the value of each record on its own, it was all the labor that went into finding and selecting the lot of them. I felt for their previous owner, put myself in his position, imagined him seeing all his attention, energy, and creativity being snapped up in one retaliatory sale, and, biting my lip, signed the check and hauled the records down to my car.

Maybe it sounds Episcopal of me to say, but records offer an opportunity for fellowship. Collectors may be part of this or that splintered-off group, collecting a particular and narrow niche, but the medium works as a kind of universalizing factor, vinyl serving as a common language that allows them to identify with one another even if they're hunting for very different music. I've met opera nuts with gigantic collections, basically of no interest to me, but the unfamiliar LPs are somehow fascinating anyway, their spines and catalog numbers and inner labels constituting an intricate signifying system the gist of which I can decipher. The opera collector and I are fellow freaks, united under the sign of the groove.

Still, listening can be a hermetic business. I've done it alone much of the time, whether auditioning for review—something best done in seclusion—or just spinning at home. The other side of the equation is the deejay collector, a listener whose experience is by and large done with and in the service of others. There's a special subculture built around the Selector, with unique disc jockey protocols and hierarchies, mores and taboos, initiation ceremonies and rites of passage. I like that atmosphere, the air of playful one-upsmanship that helps spark a great night sparring with someone in the booth, the epic sound-clash. But I think my favorite kind of communal vinyl experience is the listening session. Informally, people gather, maybe for a party, maybe with the express idea of spinning some discs. The results are open-ended and can be uncommonly exciting.

I think of one special evening that epitomizes the listening session for me. I had organized a concert in celebration of an exhibition at the Art Institute of Chicago by Christopher Wool, and everyone came over for dinner the night before—Wool, James Nares, whose film we screened, Richard Hell, who read from his memoir, and musicians Thurston Moore and Joe McPhee. After eating and drinking, I revved up the stereo with some favorite LPs of improvised music—the classic Po Torch session *Weavers* featuring drummer Paul Lovens, trombonist Günter Christmann, and bassist Maarten Altena, for instance—and the Detroit proto-punk band Death, who folks didn't seem to know, as well as the inconceivably rare *Brother to Brother*, a spoken-word record that contains an uncredited appearance by McPhee clucking like a chicken. What can I say? We were on a roll.

Thoroughly into it, a faction of us broke off and proceeded to the basement to peruse the records. I pawed my way into an unsorted row, past Merle Haggard and Holger Czukay, NRBQ and Jimmy Deuchar, and stopped as I hit *No New York*, the seminal No Wave compilation. "I was almost on that record," said Nares, whose filmmaking and art career were paralleled by his work as a noisy guitarist. "You were?" queried Moore, whose rock 'n' roll pilgrimage to New York in that period led him to stay there until a couple years ago, helping define the city's post–No Wave sound. "Yeah, but I quit the Contortions just before it was made," said Nares, adding: "Eno took that cover shot."

I held up the jacket, and we all marveled at its atmospheric, sickly green photograph. It's an image that I'd obsessed over as a teenager, as well as the lyrics, which were printed on the *inside* of the inner jacket, making reading them a pain in the ass. Appropriate, I'd always understood, for such abrasive music. But somehow I'd never known that Eno, who produced the record, made the album art. In the dim light of the basement, standing between an original Contortion and No Wave's starchild son, I felt a dream-like buzz come over me, the material history latent in this one resolutely uncommercial but commercially released album providing fertile ground for our imaginations, music revealed as what Beethoven once suggestively called "electrical soil." A social and cultural field made palpable, sprouts poking skyward, a little fellowship of freaks planted in the same patch of earth.

/////

Collectors come in different flavors. There are indiscriminate amassers, for instance, like Zero Freitas, the wealthy Brazilian obsessive who has bought vinyl in mass quantities since childhood, now purchasing them literally by the truckload. These are not collectors, really, but hoarders, and their activities are mildly offensive to actual collectors, as inexplicable as a person claiming to be a rock collector because they have a pebble driveway. Some folks just buy for value. Everyone loves a bargain, of course, but often these are people masquerading as collectors; their real identity is as pickers or dealers. (Difference is that pickers are looking for things that are already underpriced but can benefit from a context shift, like moving them from a junk shop to a boutique, while dealers are also looking to buy things that will go up in value and count on their reputation as highly sensitive experts or tastemakers to facilitate easy resale.) It's sometimes to the advantage of the dealer to pretend to be a collector. Cheaper prices can be commanded when the impression is that the item is earnestly prized and will find a loving home in this buyer's wonderful and welcoming collection. Always disappointing when that turns out to be a ruse, and the stroked object is thrown back onto the market at a vast markup. To recognize these innocent-acting resale-dealer-collectors, a twist on caveat emptor—let the *seller* beware.

Other collections announce participation in a community. Records bought at basement punk shows or from merch tables at jazz festivals or mix tapes procured at rap concerts, for instance, are as much totems of attendance as they are things to be sought and acquired. Their appeal is at once an immediate one and a nostalgic one. Gig ends, a fan approaches the stage, buys a single, perhaps chatting with the musician. This kind of collection is an especially intimate one—like an autograph book, the record object is there to suggest that, at least once, for a moment however brief, the autograph owner and the signatory were in close proximity. They were together in the same place and the same time. The John Hancock is there to demonstrate that closeness.

Some collectors are looking to have complete collections of items that are commonly known and collected. If done in a brute force way, this is just a show of power. Like sending a personal shopper to do the dirty work, it's got a slightly nasty-smelling, unearned quality. However, in the process of assembling a collection of this sort, what in the art world we know as trophy collections, a collector might get so absorbed that they become obsessive. This is a good sign that someone's becoming a freak.

The transition from collectorhood to freakery is an exciting one, often a steep slope. It can be alarming for the collector or their loved ones. The heart speeds up when you're around records. You may find that you develop clairvoyance. My wife swears that I can sense records energetically, like a douser. Once when we were in an unfamiliar neighborhood in Greece, I stopped and told her I knew there was a great record store nearby. She shook her head as we rounded the corner and I ducked into a shop where they had incredible discontinued jazz LPs, including a Fred Anderson title I'd never seen.

The true freak is a scholar. A grassroots researcher, hunting information as much as material objects. Or hunting information in order to find more material objects to desire. And seek. And find. Take a guy like Gayle Dean Wardlow, who in the 1960s canvassed black neighborhoods in the Mississippi Delta in search of the rarest blues records. Or John Tefteller, who sets up shop outside Milwaukee every year, taking a full-page ad in the newspaper inviting anyone with blues and related 78s to bring them; he pays top dollar—really, up to $40,000 for a rare Paramount—and is absolutely fair. And against all odds he has found needles in the haystack, a whole sewing kit's worth of them. Tefteller's greatest pleasure is to find something incredible, which unfailingly he then issues to the public in the form of an annual CD chronicling his year's worth of acquisitions. The scholar-collectors are anxious to share their booty; at core, they're altruists, engaging in the thrill of the hunt in order to feed the entire village. Mr. Tefteller is a freak. A freak's freak.

Walt Dunn seven-inch singles
(Repeto, mid-1960s)

A good chunk of the music initially is-sued on the independent label that Sun Ra and his business manager, Alton Abraham, started, El Saturn Records, has found its way onto reissues, includ-ing the singles by Yochannan the Muck Muck Man, a completely bizarre Christ-mas record by a group called the Quali-ties, and some mainstream blues by Lacy Gibson. After Ra left Chicago, Abraham continued releasing some non-Ra mate-rial as well as tending to the Arkestra. A few stray items of this sort have re-mained in the vaults, including Gibson's full-length LP and several singles, two of them released on the Saturn subsidiary Repeto.

These short-play slabs of vinyl are beguilingly anachronistic. If you found them without knowing anything about them, you could be forgiven for thinking they were from the '50s—sweet, syrupy songs with a doo-wop tinge and the kind of rough, amateurish, on-the-fly arrangements and perfor-mances that make them more attractive and durable than slicker, more cau-tious counterparts. The lead singer is Walt Dunn, a Chicagoan with a broad, dramatic delivery, backed by a couple of "ah, ah, ah"–ing male singers and jazz rhythm section. On "I'll Close My Heart," the B-side to the first of two singles (credited to Dunn and the Metros), a tenor saxophone repeats the melody verbatim, without variation, while on "Christina, Eugena, Marie" (note the worthy lyric: "Cecilia, Emilia, Leslie . . . which one will my love be?"), on the flip side, the able hornman—whoever he is—is given a longer leash, playing a nice little solo over the breezy, skewed-bossa rhythm, barely managed by the drummer.

The A-side of Dunn's second single, "When You're in Love This Way," has an instantly catchy opening, rolling drums under a little repeated piano figure, though the band can hardly keep things together, like a conga line that keeps bunching up. It's got an endearingly fumbling quality, as the tenor soars over the messy time. Two times there are sloppy hard edits that bring everything to a complete halt, chopping off ringing cymbals—unintentionally, it sounds extremely contemporary.

If I'm making these recordings sound ugly, well, they aren't exactly elegant or masterful. But they've got such soul and depth of feeling that the songs are, in their quest to be something that they can't exactly be, ultimately delightful. (More so, certainly, than the extremely strange Dimpna B. Clarin singles on Saturn. These were Schumann-esque art songs sung by a Filipino chanteuse in Tagalog and Visayan.)

There's another angle on these rare Repeto singles for us vinyl snoops: the pianist on them is Muhal Richard Abrams. His playing is interesting. He adds tart little harmonic ideas and manages the wayward rhythms with ingenuity. Particularly on "Christina, Eugena, Marie," Abrams counters the inane words with gritty, substantive playing. So, Abrams and AACM completists, if you've already got the Abrams LP with Sonny Stitt, then you'd better get combing those flea markets for these hilarious, eminently listenable Dunn singles.

[December 2006]

POSTSCRIPT 2016: *Sometimes the reissue process turns up intriguing new scholarship, or opportunities therefore. In this case, the presentation of these singles on the monumental fourteen-CD Sun Ra set* The Eternal Myth Revealed *(Transparency, 2011) has brought into question Abrams's presence on the sessions, leading to the speculation that the pianist is in fact Sun Ra. And the reason they sound like they're from the 1950s is that a newly discovered rehearsal tape for some of these songs suggests that they were recorded in 1956, not 1963, when Alton Abraham had established copyright on one of them. For much more on this and all things Saturn or Sun Ra, consult the Goliath website that Robert Campbell, Chris Trent, and Robert Pruter maintain at myweb .clemson.edu/~campber/sunra.html.*

Leonard Feather, *The Night Blooming Jazzmen*
(Mainstream, 1971)

Now, why would Kitty Doswell's name be a font size smaller than everyone else in the band? And whose record is this? Is that the band's name, or the title of the record? One could be forgiven for being confused about this LP, with its "Under the Direction of Leonard Feather" credit subbing for a bandleader's name. *The Night Blooming Jazzmen*—sounds like a pseudonym.

But it's not. It's Feather's all-star group, turning in a record consisting exclusively of his pieces, with strong work by trumpeter Blue Mitchell and guitarist Fred Robinson, both of whom recorded the following year with John Mayall's Jazz-Blues Fusion. Saxophonist Ernie Watts is featured across the record, most effectively on the Caribbean-tinged "Calypsoul" and in cahoots with Mitchell on "Funkville U.S.A." Saint Louis organist Charles Kynard plays on the date, though his name is omitted from the credits. That's weird because his photo appears and he was at the time a Mainstream artist.

"I Remember Bird," a tune that was already ten years old by the time of *The Night Blooming Jazzmen*, gets a spirited reading and injects a little more bop energy into the bluesy session. Drummer Paul Humphrey adds punch to the proceedings, raising them above the generic level they might otherwise have sunk to.

Considering the fact that he regularly wrote about people he worked with and was known to encourage musicians to record songs he'd copywritten (hey, a royalty is a royalty), Feather's career as a composer, arranger, and bandleader inevitably begged conflict of interest questions. To be fair, anyone who writes about music and is also a musician (or composer or arranger) has to deal with conflict of interest issues. But readers should be able to demand that writers have a clear disinterest in the work they review, fiscally speaking. Feather's many compositional credits included eight pieces on *The Night Blooming Jazzmen*. Of these, most are blues-based, including the meditative, twenty-four-bar "Nam M'Yoho Ren'Ge Kyo." The small-fonted Doswell sings "Evil Gal Blues," one of Feather's cash cows (sung, as the notes remind us, by Aretha Franklin and Joe Williams, among others).

No letters, please. *The Night Blooming Jazzmen* was reissued once on CD. But that was back toward the beginning of the era of discs, and if you're looking for this music, you're more likely to find it on LP than on the rare CD. And with a cover like this, you'd want every bit of that big twelve inches.

Guitarist Thurston Moore has a good Feather story that this record in particular brings to mind. Once long ago, he bought a Eugene Chadbourne LP at a flea market; inside was a letter from Chadbourne to Feather, introducing himself and suggesting that, although the record might be outside his focus, he might find it rewarding. Just imagine if Feather had responded by asking Chadbourne to record one of his songs!

[January 2007]

Eddie "Lockjaw" Davis, *Modern Jazz Expressions*
(King, 1954)

Talk about a great tenor sound; Eddie "Lockjaw" Davis's was tops. With a swooping phraseological practice and an Exacto-sharp tone, he was able to bridge the booting gruffness of R&B honkers and the more sophisticated harmonic palette of jazz stylists. That's a devastating mix when it's managed with care.

Browsing my collection, I recently noticed that without trying I'd amassed quite some acreage of Davis LPs. Most of them are Prestiges, the great ones with organist Shirley Scott and drummer Arthur Edgehill, including the dynamite Cookbook series. These classics were all available as OJC reissues, but I wonder how the new regime coordinating the Prestige vaults will handle the back catalog of Davis records. Some add other horns or bassist George Duvivier, and an astonishing batch of them pit Lockjaw and Johnny Griffin against one another in a duel to the best. I've got a beaut called *Goin' to the Meeting* with Horace Parlan on piano and Art Taylor on drums. *Lock, the Fox*, a later session for RCA, adds Les Spann's electric guitar to good effect on various standards, and a '70s release on the British Spotlite label, *Chewin' the Fat*, finds Davis with a French band with pianist Georges Arvanitas.

The record that has most singularly caught my attention is an old King side, back from when they sometimes manufactured LPs using shellac rather than vinyl. (Careful, it's like glass!) Davis had made an international name for himself with a solo on "Paradise Squat" in 1952, with Count Basie. Just after Lockjaw left Basie the following year to pursue a career as a leader, he recorded this amazingly stripped-down record. With a sometimes unhip Doc Bagby on organ—he's got none of the greasy goodness of Scott, but has his own churchy charms—and the background support of drummer Charlie Dice, the program is all Davis, short tracks designed perfectly to be played on jukeboxes, as was King Records' main objective.

There are recordings where Davis plays some nasty, screaming tenor, but on these tracks he's more in the Don Byas mode of redolence and style, serving ballads like "This Is Always" with a steaming side of passion. Dig the sweet little trills and hesitating delivery. It could be Ben Webster, but it's too direct, too firm and straightforward—a proposal rather than an insinuation.

A neat take of Dizzy Gillespie's "Dizzy Atmosphere" signals that this isn't just another soul-jazz date, and Davis's false-fingering and sometimes acidic delivery are counterbalanced by his large vocabulary. One of the most savory moments is a take of Billy Strayhorn's "Johnny Come Lately" on which Dice kicks it up a notch. Simply and directly recorded, without too much echo but with a soft drum sound and a front-forward horn, it's a tender and emotionally complex rendition.

[February 2007]

POSTSCRIPT 2016: *After more recent digging, I've discovered that* Modern Jazz Expressions *was available on CD in 1987, but lapsed quickly into out-of-printness.*

Archie Shepp, *Plays the Music of James Brown*

(Impulse!, never issued)

Cozy Eggleston, *Grand Slam*

(Co-Egg, circa 1969)

A few times lately I've had the good fortune to stumble on exciting record materials in the flat files of artists. For a record hound, an original record cover design is a nearly sacred object. It's something more than artwork. It has the mystique of having been turned into a mass-produced commodity, which somehow makes the original object itself seem impossible, fictional, unreal, and given entirely over to the duplication of industrially assembled productions. Seeing the actual painting, drawing, or layout of a familiar release is always a shock. It brings home how wonderfully tactile and material the good old twelve-inch format is—even employing a one-to-one design ratio, which is a decent amount of space for a visual artist.

Four months ago, in New York, I was leafing through the work of an artist who did covers for ABC. He also did films with Andy Warhol and Claes Oldenburg and was friendly with Willem de Kooning. But what damn near jumped out of the cabinet and into my hands was a fully designed mock-up for a record by Archie Shepp titled *Plays the Music of James Brown*.

Now here's one for you: in this column we tend to consider LPs that have never been made into CDs, but how about LPs that were never made at all? What a nice thought: late-'60s Shepp, so burly and swaggering and ridiculously potent, plucking some low-hanging fruit from the late, great JB's tree. Maybe it's an outgrowth of the stellar Shepp funk track "Mama Too Tight" from the Impulse! record of the same name, copping a little high school marching band vibe for good measure. Stunned, I examined the design, its lovely hand-painted letters (classic Impulse! font) spread across the acetate overlay and an abstracted close-up of the saxophonist on hardboard underneath. I'm still humming those tunes in my head, imagining Shepp's tenor soloing on "I Can't Stand Myself" or "Money Won't Change You."

A couple of months after this discovery, I happened upon another stash of designs, this time in Chicago, in the files of Ralph Arnold. A brilliant collage artist, painter, and printmaker, Arnold died in May 2006, and while helping organize his estate, I ran across a set of sketches for lettering and a few design ideas for a record that I immediately identified as Cozy Eggleston's rare '60s jazz-funk classic *Grand Slam*. The final cover image, which was not among these preliminary versions, was a clever Afro-Matisse baseball collage sporting a hilarious image of the hipster saxman, but the earlier postulations were equally playful and funny.

Eggleston himself is an underappreciated figure from Chicago, his warm tenor saxophone having made it onto a States 78 in 1952, only to wait more than fifteen years before recording again as a leader, on *Grand Slam*. An all-out soul blue flame, the self-produced, independently released record features boisterous originals, an of-its-time spin around "Joker's Wild," and a sweet take on "The Nearness of You." The LP fetches serious scratch on eBay these days. When I bought it I got lucky: there's a ninety-nine-cent sticker on the inner label.

[March 2007]

POSTSCRIPT 2016: *Byron Goto, the artist who designed the unused Shepp cover, which I've never seen again, made many other great packages, including ones for the Soft Machine, Albert Ayler, John Coltrane, the James Gang, George Russell, the Impressions, and Dick Hyman's Moog synth* LP.

Black Grass, *Black Grass*
(Shelter, 1973)

In the early '70s, Leon Russell had his own record label, which he launched with some friends. Shelter Records was designed to issue Russell's solo material and records with Asylum Choir, some of which are unjustly overlooked, some of which are cult classics, some of which are, well, justly overlooked. Shelter was eventually distributed by Capitol Records, which meant that the vinyl was floating around readily available, and the label was the launch pad for Tom Petty and the Heartbreakers and Dwight Twilley.

Shelter ran into trouble when its logo, an upside-down Superman "S," was discovered by DC Comics. In a move that probably wouldn't fly any more, they kept out of court by putting a black mask over the center of the offending "S."

Russell's band included a keyboardist and vocalist named Reverend Patrick Henderson, and in 1973 Shelter issued an LP by Henderson's own project,

Black Grass. That eponymous record, the only one by Black Grass, has never been reissued.

I don't know why this record is so unbelievably scarce. In years of searching, I've seen it only once, and I bought it based on the weirdness of the cover, which featured a surreal painting of blue feet, some liquid coming out of a jar, and other inexplicable goings-on. On the cover's back, the Reverend looks like he's spent a weekend partying with Funkadelic—crazed eyes, pimp clothes, and a foregrounded tambourine. How could this be bad? A gaggle of great-looking background singers clinched the deal, and I added *Black Grass* to my shopping basket. I went years without listening to it, maybe subliminally scared by the front cover, maybe just wanting to preserve the thrill for a later date.

As it turns out, it is a mixed record. The best parts shine, and the worst earn their place in the dustbin of history. As for the latter, the record's single, "Lock Stock and Barrel," is the most egregious, a tedious soul plodder. A version of "Burning Love" is so bad it's good. Elvis Presley turns in his grave whenever the groove hits the needle, but it's heartfelt and features an over-the-top '70s soul arrangement.

But there's plenty of high-energy action in the form of up-tempo gospel. The opening track, Shirley Ceaser's "Sweeping through the City," is a spirit-rouser produced by Russell that might remind one of James Cleveland, as might the traditional "Great Day." The parts of the record that I like most are the details, like the huge fuzz bass riff on "Come Across Your Bridge," which deserves to be sampled by some enterprising young hip-hopper, and some zany little synthesizer fills.

Much of the LP seems to have been made by someone who listened to the soundtrack to *Hair* a few too many times, with that '70s Broadway song-writer sound that afflicted many ambitious soulsters. But hot tunes like "Going Down to the River" more than make up for it, and the combination of its rarity, the outlandish freakishness of its cover, and the handful of indispensable tracks make it a primo piece for vinyl hounds to sniff out.

[May 2007]

Records are most often spoken of and written about, at least in the arena of "real time" music like jazz, as a document of an event, a stand-in for those who couldn't be there or a token for those who were. In this capacity, records have little of the special ambient sensibility of a gig, not only in terms of the environment (sights and smells of the venue, the shared quality of listening as a group), but in terms of the live nature of an event. The whole nature of performance and contingency, the great X-factor of improvised music, is utterly undocumentable. Records are a hapless substitute for the live experience.

Of course, we love records, but we don't love them the same way. In another respect, perhaps they can function differently vis-à-vis live performance, not as a replacement but as a fragment. At one time, records sold from the stage were an integral part of live music activity. Sun Ra famously had batches of his records printed up specially for given concerts, and he also hand-decorated them for the gigs. Punk rockers have been selling their wares from stage's edge, pre- or post-gig, for three decades now. It's an important part of the musical interaction, not only for disseminating the music but for sealing a bond between listener and performer. Right there, the venue where the live musical exchange has occurred becomes another site of transaction. Maybe they serve as a tip, a bonus, or a way of personally telling the player that his or her music meant something that night. Either way, the intimacy of buying and selling merchandise at gigs remains an important part of the musical process.

Case in point: a few months back, in Vasteras, Sweden, at the biannual festival that saxophonist Mats Gustafsson and producer Lennart Nilsson organize called Perspectives, I was captivated by a duet I'd never heard of before. Two Danish twenty-somethings took the little stage by storm, whipping the packed house into a frenzy. Yohs played baritone saxophone about as far from a jazz feel as you could get, blowing through various distortion boxes to achieve his reed instrument's striking version of garage-punk guitar. Incisive, pointed, loud, and infectious, Yoke's ferocious drumming met Yohs's ostinati head-on. The drummer then added more contemporary fills to their vintage '60s heavy sound. Reminiscent, in a distant way, of Gustafsson's own forays into the free jazz / garage nexus, Yoke & Yohs delighted me for their short, sweaty set.

As they snuffed out the last note, I ducked out to the record stand and was happy to see a Yoke & Yohs single, replete with four songs sporting titles like "The Wizard of the Dungeon" and "Satan's Dukes." A repugnantly beautiful cover features a disgusting deli platter, with various inedible concoctions—one includes Nutella with cocktail onions, hard-boiled eggs and lingonberries, all on dark bread. It's as volatile a mixture as the music, which I was pleased to encounter in the flesh. If I'd just heard the record, it might not have meant the same thing. But now it's a treasured little slab of vicious vinyl at the top of my playlist, a fragment of that jolt the two young Danes gave my system.

[July 2007]

The Bill Dixon Orchestra, *Intents and Purposes*
(RCA Victor, 1967)

Many of the Vinyl Freak entries concern neat-but-obscure records, sometimes justifiably unknown. There's another category of LP, admittedly shrinking, the out-of-print status of which represents nothing short of a cultural crime. Trumpeter Bill Dixon's 1967 masterpiece, *Intents and Purposes*, is such a record. Made when the most energetic of the free jazz records were being waxed, it announced another kind of creative music—a translucent, often quiet sound that drew on the power of a chamber aesthetic more than the notion of unbridled or unleashed emotionality. *Intents and Purposes* is regularly discussed in terms of its singularity and significance, but for almost thirty years it has been unavailable to the layperson and remains a difficult score even for the dedicated crate-digger.

Perhaps the most incongruous thing about the record appears on the front cover. Underneath the orchestra's name, a little motto appears: "The new sounds of the music of tomorrow." This tagline seems to echo the mottos of independent labels like Saturn and ESP, but it looks particularly strange right next to Nipper, the RCA dog, and the "Dynagroove" logo, which I associate with the wonderful Bluebird reissues that Victor released around the same time. RCA had no commitment to futuristic jazz music, but one wonders whether the indies had the majors a bit worried that they'd missed the boat. Perhaps improvised music was set to be the next rock 'n' roll? Would free jazz really cause a musical revolution, or at least a consumer revolution? You could feel them sweating.

Of course, RCA Victor had an active modern classical roster, and this might be mistaken for one of those records. Classical-style liner notes, without attribution, explain Dixon's credentials, where he studied composition (Hartnett Conservatory), with whom he studied privately (James Brokenshire, Carl Bowman), and that he is an accomplished visual artist. But the folks at RCA clearly marked this release to differentiate it from its classical records with "The Jazz Artistry of Bill Dixon" emblazoned on the back of the jacket.

The music is utterly unique. Two spare tracks, "Nightfall Pieces I" and "Nightfall Pieces II," feature Dixon's trumpet and flugelhorn (with George Marge on accompanying alto flute and Dixon overdubbed on both horns on "Nightfall Pieces I"). At the time he had such an intense and personal voice as to make it hard to compare him to anyone else. Textural and timbral, drawing on Anton Webern and Cootie Williams, Dixon's sound is the spiritual grandfather to all the "lowercase" or "low dynamic" improvisers of today. A slightly larger chamber ensemble, with Catherine Norris on cello, Bob Pozar on drums, Byard Lancaster on bass clarinet, and Jimmy Garrison on bass, performs "Voices."

The largest group adds bass trombonist Jimmy Cheatham, Marge on English horn, the alto saxophones of Lancaster and Robin Kenyatta, Garrison and Reggie Workman on bass, and Mark Levin on percussion. Dixon had been working with Cecil Taylor in 1966, playing on the landmark Conquistador LP on Blue Note, and that feel reverberates on this track, which extends the approach Dixon had initially recorded on his 1964 Savoy septet side. It's unclear why this music has never been issued on CD. It was reissued on LP in the '70s in France. But for some reason it has languished in the vaults, one of the richest and most compelling LPs to taunt and tempt listeners into a life of freakdom.

[September 2007]

POSTSCRIPT 2016: *Bill Dixon died in 2010. The following year,* Intents and Purposes *was reissued, lovingly remastered by International Phonograph. A small edition, the CD is now also a rarity.*

Orchestre Régional de Mopti, *Orchestre Régional de Mopti*
(Mali Music, 1970)

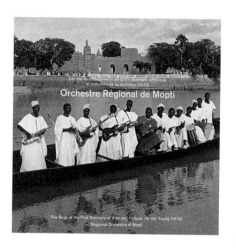

When I went to college, I took my nearly complete Smithsonian Folkways Explorer series. Listening to ethnographic recordings from Bali, Kenya, and Zimbabwe in my dorm room sealed my reputation as a geek, and it also presaged a stint studying ethnomusicology with the great scholar of music of Ghana and Mexico James Koetting, who died unexpectedly my junior year. His grad-level course on field recording methodology was way over my head, but it got me thinking about the ethical issues in the process of ethnographic documentation. To the point: Who chooses what to record, how it is recorded, how to release it, how to package and notate it, to whom it is credited, and, if it makes any money, who should be paid?

Studying with Jim also hopelessly turned up the heat on an already burning interest in ethno LPs, which I began to collect assiduously. Under his tutelage, I learned about the Folklyric Records Mexican recordings, which continue to astound, and the enormous legacy of Folkways recordings, which includes not only that Explorer series, but many earlier recordings from all over the world, some of them by pioneer ethnographers. Hugh Tracy's cassettes document African music in exhaustive and exhilarating detail. Over the years since Jim's passing, I have often pulled out a self-produced record of Afro-pop from Ghana that he lent me just before he died, thinking about how inspiring it was to a famished little freak.

Ethnographic field LPs remain one of the greatest untapped realms for vinyl hounds. Among the most fantastic acquisitions I've made in this realm was a complete collection of LPs, recorded under the series banner "Mali Music" (subtitled "Production du Minstere de L'Information"), by the German label Bärenreiter-Musicaphon. The series includes compilations of traditional music from the steppes and savannas of the African country, a sampler of ancient stringed instruments, full LPs dedicated to singers like Fanta Damba (singing epic songs of Mali), Fanta Sacko (accompanied by Foussenou Diabate on guitar), and the blind "old lion" of Malian singing, Bazoumana Sissoko, as well as albums by popular Malian groups like L'Orchestre National "A" de la Republique du Mali, Orchestre Regional de Segou, and Orchestre Regional de Sikasso. Starting in 1962, these regional groups competed against one another in national arts festivals. In 1970, the best of the competitors were recorded for the series.

When I first took this booty home to listen to it, I was most intrigued by the image that graced *Orchestre Régional de Mopti*: a full band of thirteen men, jet black against their bright white smocks, holding trumpets, a tenor saxophone, hand drums, a Fender bass, and two guitars futuristic enough to belong with the Ventures. Behind this lineup is a sand-colored building on the shore of a Malian waterway (the Mopti region is called the Malian Venice), and across the water stretches the long, thin boat that bears the load of this rocking armada. It is, perhaps, the baddest-ass cover in my collection. When I put the disc on, strangely, I recognized one of the tracks. It turns out that "Boro," with its hypnotic, repeated guitar figure and aching melody, was appropriated by Don Cherry and retitled, appropriately enough, "Mopti." The arrangement is almost exactly the same, down to the beautiful way the drums enter, opening up and propelling the piece forward. Of course, the Cherry version is essential listening, but so too is this version, which itself adopted a traditional tune for an electric update. The entire record is full of delights—funky, slinky and redolent of the burning sun.

[November 2007]

POSTSCRIPT 2016: Orchestre Régional de Mopti *was reissued without license as an LP on Mississippi Records in 2010. Meanwhile, ethnographic records have become increasingly desirable among rare-record enthusiasts.*

The Jihad, *Black & Beautiful . . . Soul & Madness*
(Jihad, circa 1968)

Many of the important rap antecedents currently languish out of print. To understand the evolution of hip-hop, particularly the more politically engaged variety, without thoroughly knowing the Last Poets is impossible. "White Man's Got a God Complex," "This Is Madness," and "Jones Coming Down" are essential 1960s pre-rap street poetry, the lyrical forebears to KRS-One and Dr. Dre and the musical grandparents of Clipse. *Blue Guerrilla* by Last Poet (Gylan) Kain is difficult to find, as is *Hustler's Convention* by Lightnin' Rod, made in 1974 and featuring Kool and the Gang as the backing band. These records come in and out of print in myriad forms, but they're not consistently available the way they should be.

One of the rarest and most incendiary of the foreshadowings of hard-core rap comes in the form of the third release on Jihad, the self-produced record label run by poet and playwright (and onetime *DownBeat* contributor) Amiri Baraka, at the time known as LeRoi Jones. Jihad first released drummer Sunny Murray's important, little-acknowledged LP as a leader, *Sunny's Time Now*, with Albert Ayler on saxophone and Don Cherry on pocket trumpet, and the strange, not particularly listenable LP of Sun Ra's music for the Jones play *A Black Mass*. The Murray record was reissued on a Japanese CD, now hard to locate, while *A Black Mass* was the first of what was reputed to be a series of CD issues from Jihad, including never-released treasures from the vaults such as a Pharoah Sanders / Ayler recording. Now impossible to find, *A Black Mass* seems to have been a false start in the Jihad revival.

Black & Beautiful . . . Soul & Madness features an uncredited band with a vocal ensemble that called itself the Jihad. Jones recites his poems with an emphatic delivery most definitely of its era. He combines by-all-means-necessary Afrocentrism with heavy Euro-tinged philosophical contemplation on tracks like "Form Is Emptyness" and "Madness," while the fist-pumping vibe imbues "Fight" and "Unity" with a righteous civil rights focus. Jones is such a compelling reader, with such superb timing and a rich vocal timbre, that the dated arrangements don't matter. It's delirious proto-rap, performed by one of the most profound and controversial figures in black American culture and released on his own label.

Black & Beautiful . . . Soul & Madness is closely related to the small-press poetry publications that circulate the most cutting-edge verbal art. If there's a more poorly tended to area of cultural production than underground records, those chapbooks may well take the cake. It is nearly impossible to find originals or reproductions of those amazing artifacts of vanguard intellectual life. At least the diligent vinyl freak stands half a chance of digging up a copy of Jihad's LP, though most of the time you'll find it with a plain black cover. It's particularly rare to find one with the stunning picture sleeve.

[January 2008]

POSTSCRIPT 2016: *Sonboy Records reissued this Jihad LP on CD in 2009, adding the full name of the band: Amiri Baraka & the Spirit House Movers; Sonboy also reissued the ultrarare Sun Ra soundtrack for Baraka's play* A Black Mass. *Baraka died in 2014.*

Milford Graves / Don Pullen, *Milford Graves & Don Pullen at Yale University*
(S.R.P., 1966)

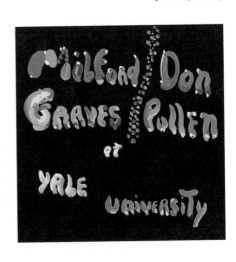

A live duet recording of drummer Milford Graves and pianist Don Pullen turned into one of the most prized LPs of American free jazz, best known as *NOMMO* but initially issued in a handmade cover under a different title. I asked Graves to put the self-produced record in some context, to explain some of the nuts and bolts of its creation and for some reflections on the astonishingly inventive music, now more than four decades old.

S.R.P. was your own label, right?

Yes. Self-Reliance Program, that's what it stands for. It was a political environment at the time—in the Far East, China specifically. I was educating myself as to what was happening in the rest of the world relative to the civil rights movement in this country. People didn't want to record the new jazz, so I said we can't always sit around waiting for someone to help us, we've got to help ourselves. I was asked to do a solo concert at Yale University, and I called Don Pullen, asked him to join me for a duo.

How much lag time was there between the live music and the vinyl?

It was immediate. We had agreed to split the money for the concert equally, but beforehand we decided to take the money and invest it into the LP instead. The person who was instrumental was the visual artist Jan Tilding, who was working at Sam Goody Records. John Tchicai introduced me to him. He worked in the business office of Sam Goody, and helped me figure out how to go about releasing it. Jan helped me order black blank covers. He said, "Just write on the covers yourself!" Don and I were at my house, got acrylic paint and the covers, and we made some abstract designs around our names—all because we couldn't afford to print the covers. We were sitting around a table, very casual. The one that you have, that's my hand.

Where did you get the records manufactured?

There was a Brooklyn place that printed the records. We got one thousand of them made. The person instrumental in getting the record distributed was Amiri Baraka. He gave it a five-star review in *DownBeat* with our postal address. Orders came in from all over the world.

Did you and Pullen play other duets after that?

Don and I did duets, mostly in Harlem. We would take records in a box and sell them ourselves. When we started selling them from the stage, we had proper covers produced for the record, and we retitled it NOMMO. We had a second volume, too, but that one never came out. As I listen now, I realize something about the feeling when you do this music. There was a different environment in the '60s. Because of the protest of the Vietnam War, the civil rights movement, people felt they needed change. Without being overly intellectual, that's what it seemed. Today it sometimes feels more academic, but empty. People seem to be playing outside themselves. At the time people didn't worry so much about conservatory training. We had an environmental conviction to express ourselves.

[May 2008]

POSTSCRIPT 2016: *I have been working with Milford Graves to reissue* NOMMO *on Corbett vs. Dempsey in a deluxe box with extra material. It may take a little while yet, as the tapes still need to be excavated and transferred, but in principle we have agreed to the project. Hopefully there are more Roy DeCarava photographs like the one on the cover of the second edition. Fingers crossed. And if we're lucky, we'll also reissue* Babi, *another sensationally rare Graves date, this time with a trio featuring saxophonists Hugh Glover and Arthur Doyle.*

Heikki Sarmanto Sextet, *Flowers in the Water*
(EMI / Columbia, 1969)

G.L. Unit, *Orangutang!*
(EMI / Odeon, 1970)

In the late '60s and early '70s, European major labels weren't opposed to experimenting with some pretty wild music. For instance, the British outposts of CBS and RCA issued LPs by groups led by drummer Tony Oxley featuring guitarist Derek Bailey and saxophonist Evan Parker. Together, these three musicians soon thereafter founded the artist-run label Incus to take the matters of release into their own hands. But the sizable batch of large-label free-music releases from the period includes Lol Coxhill's underacknowledged classic double LP *Ear of Beholder* on Ampex in 1971. In 1974, Italian RCA even went so far as to reissue a 1966 Giorgio Gaslini record, *Nuovi Sentimenti (New Feelings)*—quite a move with a record that probably sold a few hundred copies in its original release.

Major labels with Scandinavian branches were particularly busy slinging adventurous jazz. Finnish EMI/Columbia issued the fine LP of tunes by pianist Heikki Sarmanto's six-piece band, highlighting the warm, wonderful saxophone work of Juhani Aaltonen, already a star in Finland and recognized internationally. Brisk modal tracks like "Princess of Darkness" and "522" suggest the impact Miles Davis's modality had on the deep north, their compositions almost parroting *Kind of Blue* but their feel and soloing expressing something indigenously Nordic. The most engaging piece on the rare record is "CB?," a fourteen-minute slowish blues with a glorious alto solo by Aaltonen—beautifully developed, sculpted, unclichéd—that portends what people would hear later in the saxophonist's work with the great, late drummer Edward Vesala. Trumpeter Bertil Lovgren almost lives up to the liner notes' claim that he's "one of Europe's leading trumpets." Davis informs his style, but he's crisp and into the upper register. Bassist Teppo Hauta-Aho has gone on to play in excellent contexts with Cecil Taylor and John Tchicai, among others, and he clicks with drummer Matti Koskiala. While the leader has nothing singular to mention in his playing, he's accomplished and the record's a sweet find.

Flowers in the Water is not nearly as sweet, however, nor as unique and bonzo as G.L. Unit's *Orangutang!*, recorded in Stockholm for Swedish EMI/Odeon. Multireed player Gunnar Lindqvist is composer and nominal leader of the "unit," which swells from sixteen to twenty-three strong. Where it might easily be pegged as a free jazz freakout, *Orangutang!* is at the crossroads of all sorts of impulses in late '60s European music. In some respects—periodic outbursts of screaming, taped sounds of ocean waves or seagulls—it hearkens to Fluxus, happenings, and the "expanded arts" scenes that were as familiar to Swedes as was Davis. There is the influence of Albert Ayler—indeed, Bengt "Frippe" Nordstrom, who first recorded Ayler, plays alto and tenor here—and there are intimations of Sun Ra's approach to orchestral free play, which makes sense, given that Ra had commenced his first European tour in Stockholm earlier the same year *Orangutang!* was recorded.

Contemporary classical music, sound collage, and audio art all swirl in the completely unhinged mix, which includes an amazing cast drawn from all corners of the Swedish jazz world. For its rarity, uproarious cover, originality, and joy, it's an LP to watch out for on trips to Sweden.

[September 2008]

Ernie and Emilio Caceres, *Ernie & Emilio Caceres*
(Audiophile, 1969)

In 2003, a fetishistic little reissue was produced in a run of only five hundred copies of a 78-rpm ten-inch record on the Paris Jazz Corner imprint. Sporting artwork by R. Crumb, it presented music by the Brothers Caceres, Emilio and Ernie, recorded for Bluebird in the 1930s. Aside from catering to the splinter group of vinyl collectors dedicated to the antiquated format, it offered listeners a rare chance to hear these legendary but too-little-known Mex-Tex jazz musicians from San Antonio.

Baritone saxophonist and clarinetist Ernie was, of the two, far more famous. Starting in the late '30s, after he had toured extensively with the small band led by his violinist brother Emilio, he played in various higher-profile settings, including the bands of Bobby Hackett, Glenn Miller, Tommy Dorsey, Benny Goodman, and Woody Herman. From 1949, he led his own group in New York. Along with the sweet early swing, he recorded in a wild array of settings during his productive life, from dates with Eddie Condon and Sidney Bechet and intermittent television gigs with the Gary Moore Orchestra to a Metronome All Stars trumpet-heavy session with Miles Davis, Fats Navarro, and Dizzy Gillespie, as well as Charlie Parker. Meanwhile, family man Emilio opted to live and work close to home in Texas.

Ernie moved back to San Antonio in the mid-'60s. In 1969, two years before his death, he teamed up with Emilio once again for an LP of their old favorites, recording for the little Audiophile label, based in Mequon, Wisconsin. It's a wonderful prize for those who can track it down, exploding with color, warmth, and musicality—the wisdom born of experience—and rollicking, mischievous, filial joy. Emilio is terrific, with nimble fingers, a gorgeous, sensuous sound, and voluminous double-stops that recall his early love of Joe Venuti (as well as a little of Stephane Grappelli's sugar), but also betraying a sensibility that recalls his heritage in norteño music. It's been said that the brothers' sound, matching a big, unforced baritone sax with the violin, also has its affiliations with a Mexican aesthetic. This may be true, but the music is genuine swing, uncut and unambiguous.

With Cliff Gillette on piano, George Pryor on bass, Curly Williams on guitar, and Joe Cortez Jr. on drums, the group romps through pieces they'd recorded thirty years prior, like "Gig in G," updating it by switching Ernie from the original clarinet lead to a lurking, supporting role on bari, with Emilio kicking heavy booty on fiddle.

Harry Carney aside, there are too few chances to hear the big sax featured in a convincing way in swing, but one listen to Ernie flutter his way through "Poor Butterfly" and the possibilities become immediately clear. He's a quick-silver clarinetist, too, featured sassily on a brisk "I Found a New Baby," but his most distinctive mark might be on the baritone. Along with the rosin workouts, Emilio submits a luscious romantic ballad, "Estrellita," his brother joining for a joint moment of clarinet and violin.

There's nothing frumpy or out-of-date about this great record. It's a family testimonial (check it out, there's still an active Caceres musical line in jazz): two great musicians toward the end of the line giving a brilliant bear hug of a performance.

[November 2008]

Maarten Altena, *Papa Oewa*
(Claxon, 1981)

This month, our fair column considers the materiality of records. As the occasion of this reflection is a recent move, I am of course marveling over the weight of LPs—oh, my aching back!—but other aspects of their physical existence as well, such as their volume, their relative solidity and durabil-ity (schlepping them en masse, our movers calculated that one box bore at least one thousand pounds at the bottom of the stack in the truck), and the dizzying array of variations on the circle-in-a-square format. Surveying the rows of records before preparing for the move, I thought about the basic premise of the album, the way each spine represents roughly the same amount of time, like a proportional composition stretching from one end of the room to the other. Consider such a collection of records as a long multistylistic com-position, each eighth-inch swatch of color, text and design a marvel of con-cision that signifies about forty minutes of musical time. Taken together, a modest box of records contains about five days of continuous listening—in sheer endlessness, enough to make Bruckner envious. Despite its spatial economy, a bevy of records still has mass, true heft, and vinyl accumulates with terrifying ease.

Packing up the collection was, for the most part, a cakewalk—just a matter of throwing them into small-ish boxes. Records fit together so beautifully; they're made to be collected in bulk. But certain unconventional covers drew attention to themselves automatically through their unwillingness to be safely packed, in particular a few Dutch examples. In Holland, musicians and their designers seem bent on making a mockery of conventions of domestic portaging. I was especially fretful over the velvety purple veneer on the periphery of my mint copy of the Instant Composers Pool classic (never reissued) twofer "candy box" (ICP 007/008), a hodgepodge of different groupings from 1969 and 1970. Would it be crushed in transition? Or multireed player Willem Breuker's terrific *Baal Brecht Breuker*, on BVHAAST (1973), with its burlap second cover which makes it impossible to fit in a box with the other LPs. Breuker and pianist Leo Cuypers made one of the boldest odd-shaped covers, taking the normal LP square and turning it into an isosceles triangle with sides at a tangent to the vinyl's circle. Most of the copies I've seen have been bent to conform to the normal record shape. Mine is a bit ragged, but not folded.

The most subtle subversion of LP format is perhaps bassist Maarten Altena's solo outing *Papa Oewa*. First of all, it's a record worth having, and like the rest of the Claxon catalog, it remains exclusively on vinyl. Altena's significance before he turned to classical music can't be overlooked, and the aggressive, open, often hilarious records he made alone and with his great small and midsized groups should be sought out vigorously. On *Papa Oewa*, he's playing a lot of cello, some crackle-box and other odds and sods, as well as his gloriously gawky bass. Recall that Holland was very Fluxus-friendly, and the interest in little instruments and alternative packaging makes more sense. What's so confusing about the cover is that it seems, at first blush, to be perfectly usual. On closer inspection, however, it turns out not to be square, but just off-square, a parallelogram, with the top pitching ever so slightly to the right. Hence, when slid into a stack of records, its bottom right always pokes out, and the top left, if jammed in, gets damaged. In the end, I chose to move *Papa Oewa* by hand, like most of those Dutch weirdos.

[December 2008]

POSTSCRIPT 2016: *Almost all of the fine records on Claxton are still out of print, save for the Altena / Steve Lacy duets* High Low and Order, *which came out on hatART.*

The London Experimental Jazz Quartet, *Invisible Roots*
(Scratch, 1973)

When I was given a sealed copy of *Invisible Roots* by the London Experimental Jazz Quartet (LEJQ) a few years ago, my mind immediately filled with speculation about what could be on it. Maybe a lost Trevor Watts date, a session with Evan Parker or Howard Riley? Or could it be a late Tubby Hayes session, Phil Seamen on a free jazz bender, Barry Guy in a preimprovisational context? A quick check and the mystery deepened: I didn't know any of the players. I thought I'd heard of most of the major UK progressive jazz figures, but this features Eric Stach, a saxophonist and crew touting the flag of experimentalism. A reminder, then, that if there's a Paris, Texas, and a Berlin, Wisconsin, there's also a London, Ontario. I should have known better—that's from where my friend Ben Portis, who gave me the LP, hails.

Quick research revealed that the LEJQ was, in fact, the second-best-known free-music group from the mid-Canadian city, topped only by the great Nihilist Spasm Band, which had predated them by about a decade when Stach formed the band in 1971. The group lasted until the mid-'70s, toured Europe and the United States, and made the Canadian jazz circuit. They had a similar countercultural orientation to the NSB, and perhaps being away from the jazz centers kept them a bit fresh and unjaded. The music doesn't feel routine, although it is almost willfully without polish or guile.

Compiled on a breakbeat CD by Kon & Amir (*Off Track Vol. 1*) in 2007, "Destroy the Nihilist Picnic" is one of a few funky tracks, featuring heavy vamping piano and groovy bass. On the other end of the spectrum, several cuts sport the unmistakable influence of Sun Ra. The flute on "Jazz Widow Waltz" (with no treble time in sight) recalls Marshall Allen's early '60s Afrocentric modality. On "Edible Wallpaper," strumming on the strings under the lid of the piano is accompanied by Stach's overblown and slurred saxophone, distant flute, and sporadic percussion hits, each submitted to tape delay. "Ron Martin Special with Mustard" presses the joyous noisemaking further, without delay—you can easily imagine people playing it at a party as the weirdest thing they'd ever heard, but the squall's got a playful musicality as well as an appealing crudeness. The band suddenly leaps out of a listless meander in the middle of "My Dog's Tail Is Longer Than Yours" to sprint into an up-tempo swing, only to jump right back out of it with a lugubrious baritone sax and arco bass dialogue.

Reportedly improvised freely in the studio, the session is edgy and full of enthusiastic energy. It relies on modal jazz—the looping vamps and ostinati common to many '70s liberated jams—in large part, but the fact of being big free-form fish in a relatively little metropolitan pond rings through clearly. The sound is not revolutionary, despite some jagged shards here and there, but the record remains a great document of an obscure scene. A fan page established for LEJQ (ducktape.ca/bitsnbobs/lejq/index.html) suggests that Invisible Roots will be reissued soon, but this is a promise that's gone long enough unfulfilled that you should make sure and hunt up a copy of the rare vinyl, just in case the economic downturn further delays its resurrection.

[March 2009]

POSTSCRIPT 2016: Invisible Roots *was reissued on a Shout! Productions* CD *in 2012.*

Sunny Murray, *Big Chief*

(Pathé, 1969; reissued Eremite, 2008)

Solidarity Unit, Inc., *Red, Black and Green*

(self-produced, 1972; reissued Eremite, 2008)

The fate of independent production is now hanging in the same precarious balance as the major music industry, with major shifts in distribution and production potentially rearranging the entire organization. A signal of the upcoming shifts may be the decision this March by Chicago-based Touch & Go to jettison its distributed labels entirely. This will potentially spell the end of some of the key independent labels they have aided and abetted. In tough times things shift, and when the recession eventually releases its grip we may be faced with a different cultural landscape. Nonmainstream music, of which jazz and improvisation is part, will need to adapt to a new set of materials and conditions, including a new delivery system.

That system may be vinyl. Of all the object-based delivery systems for music, the record still seems to hold the strongest allegiance for its users. Two vinyl-only releases by Eremite are an excellent case in point: these are two of the rarest free jazz classics, both of them virtually impossible to find. I had only one of them, Sunny Murray's *Big Chief*, and I had to pay dearly for it. Solidarity Unit's *Red, Black and Green* was something that I'd only heard due to the kindness of Manny Maris from New York's Downtown Music Gallery, who had burned me a disc.

From one perspective, these would be perfect items for release on CD. Until now they have been available only on LP and have grown more rare as collectors buy up any available ones on the vintage vinyl market. But Eremite decided, against that logic, to issue them on vinyl only. It's perhaps a savvy move, amplifying rather than diminishing their fetish power. In a matter of months, when these two pressings (limited to six hundred copies each) are sold out, they'll probably be almost as valuable as the originals. Get them now or forever wonder what they sounded like.

The Murray LP is one of the drummer's best efforts. Working with a largely Parisian band, augmented by American bassist Alan Silva (here playing violin), and British musicians Kenneth Terroade (tenor sax) and Ronnie Beer (alto sax), it's an intensely raucous set of relatively short free jazz bursts. These include "This Nearly Was Mine" (which Murray had been performing with Cecil Taylor) and germinal tunes like "Hilarious Paris," familiar in a different version from Murray's self-titled ESP record. Poet H. LeRoy Bibbs gives a period recitation on "Straight Ahead." The sharp recording sounds great on this 180-gram pressing.

Red, Black and Green comes from a few years later and a whole world apart. Undertaken by drummer Charles "Bobo" Shaw, it is a seminal work of St. Louis's BAG (Black Artists Group), with key members Oliver Lake, Joseph Bowie, and Baikida Yaseen (later known as Baikida Carroll). Open, a tad funky, and venomously strong with room for drift, it was a tornado of a recording that should have been heard, though with its tiny private pressing it remained the domain of specialists alone. For a minute, on vinyl only, that's no longer the case.

[May 2009]

Dick Wetmore, *Dick Wetmore*
(Bethlehem, 1954)

The decision to purchase this '50s Bethlehem ten-inch—in great shape with a beautiful, high-contrast Burt Goldblatt photograph and cover design—was a no-brainer. But it took me a while to get around to listening to it. When I did, the sound sent me back to the cover for information. I'd heard these tunes before (some, at least), and they were fascinating, quite modernistic, not at all the trad fare I'd been expecting. One name in the notes set me straight, appearing boldly along with the musicians rather than buried in post-song-title parentheses: Bob Zieff, credited with compositions and arrangements.

Zieff is the adventurous and unsung hero to emerge from the Boston vanguard jazz bohemia. Though he's spent the period from the '60s forward teaching around the United States, Zieff is best known for the compositions and arrangements performed by Chet Baker in the mid-'50s, when the young composer had moved from Boston to New York. Indeed, with the exception of a session with Anthony Ortega, Zieff's discography is clustered around recordings, live and studio, made by Baker. Part of what makes the Zieff/Baker tracks so essential for their fans is the piano playing of Richard Twardzik. Twardzik was a visionary musician and composer, one of a few at the time who were taking the complexity of bebop harmony seriously in the context of early twentieth-century classical music. A prodigious student of Zieff's, Twardzik was supposed to be on this date, but the same thing that kept him from the recordings—heroin—is what killed him at the terribly premature age of twenty-four.

His replacement, Ray Santisi, plays nicely, perhaps without the ferocious austerity and insight that Twardzik brought to these pieces, but with a like-minded sense of restraint. Drummer Jimmy Zitano is deft and supportive, while Bill Nordstrom's bass alternates between swinging along with Zitano and engaging more contrapuntally with Wetmore, whose violin playing is lovely and playful, sometimes adding little bluesy flashes, sometimes pulling out the weirder aspects of the tunes with glisses and slurs. It's not every day you hear modern jazz performed by a violin-led quartet, but in this case, with the pronounced orientation toward new classical music, it makes perfect sense.

One of the joys of this music is that it so thoroughly synthesizes its components. Rather than jamming them together, as more ham-fisted third-stream music does, it takes ideas from classical and jazz and looks for commonalities, threading one through the other. At the opening of "Just Duo," one of the most beguiling pieces, Nordstrom (playing arco) and Wetmore commence as the title suggests, Bartok infusions breaking open into Wetmore's splendid solo over gently rocking rhythm. Zieff's compositions take unexpected turns as a matter of course, and they're often unusually structured. "Sad Walk" is a fave from Baker days, along with the slightly evil "Brash," which Swedish baritone saxophonist Lars Gullin recorded with Baker, and the deceptively sweet "Rondette." Only "Shiftful" never made the transition to the Baker book, perhaps due to the complexity of its form.

Wetmore died in 2007. Zieff is still alive, deserving more attention than he's gotten. (Read Jack Chambers's great essay on him, "Revenge of the Underground Composer," available online at langtech.dickinson.edu/Sirena/Issue2 /Chambers.pdf.) No doubt it's time to add another line to the abbreviated in-print column of Zieff recordings, but until then this will remain for freaks only.

[September 2009]

United Front, *Path with a Heart*
(RPM Records, 1980)

United Front is usually cited as one of the founding ensembles of the new Asian American jazz movement in the 1980s. The San Francisco quartet is best known for its work with drummer Anthony Brown, who joined in 1981, but they had already made this great record by then with Carl Hoffman in the percussion role. The rest of the band was as it remained, with bassist Mark Izu, saxophonist Lewis Jordan, and trumpeter George Sams. I was a freshman in college, working the graveyard shift at WBRU in Providence, Rhode Island, when my jazz buddies there hipped me to this wonderful, now woefully scarce item. It was in heavy rotation from midnight to 3:00 a.m. for a few seasons.

Twenty-eight years since I first heard it, *Path with a Heart* endures the test of time. Its working model is certainly the Art Ensemble of Chicago, replete with intrusions of "little instruments" played by the ensemble members. Hoffman's "Feel Free" starts with ratchet noises, arco bass, bicycle horns, and sparse altissimo horn squeaks and multiphonic honks, before Izu kicks into the buoyant groove underpinning the sweet and sour tune to his delightful "Don't Lose Your Soul," which includes an awkward time shift much like those on some

AEC classics. The more swing-based pieces have that tasty off/on-ness that I associate with Roscoe Mitchell and gang, as well as Fred Hopkins (whose playing Izu often recalls). No idea where he went, but Hoffman sounds perfectly at home here, breaking up a groove or bolstering it. Though they don't have household name recognition, Sams and Jordan are worthy figures, conversant in the Ornette Coleman–derived post-bop vocabulary, deep in the thick of the milieu of "new architecture" that the Midwest's AACM and Black Artists Group had so copiously spread around the globe starting in the late '60s. Sams's "March In Ostinato" starts the B-side with a very Anthony Braxton–ish composition, the hyperextended theme bounding off Hoffman's press rolls.

These fellows had their own thing, too, bringing in pan-Asian instruments and ideas. With its sheng and knobbed gongs, "Forgotten Spirits" has a gagaku element, which was certainly unusual at the time, anticipating the full-on Asian American jazz developments from Jon Jang, Glenn Horiuchi, and Fred Ho, signaled by the first Asian American Jazz Festival in San Francisco, which was held in 1981. RPM was an artist-run label organized by United Front; pianist Jang's LPs *Jang* (which featured the quartet) and *Are You Chinese or Charlie Chan* (which featured members of the group), as well as the foursome's *Ohm: Unit of Resistance*, were released on RPM in the years following *Path with a Heart*, which was the label's debut. RPM was defunct by the end of the '80s, and much of their activity shifted to Asian Improv Records. United Front also recorded for the German SAJ label, a sister to Free Music Productions. This release remains incredibly rare, so much so that a Google search barely yields anything. If that's the measure of things that are truly obscure nowadays, this album doesn't deserve to be so hidden from view.

[November 2009]

Joseph Scianni with David Izenzon, *Man Running*
(Savoy, 1965)

Talk about a disjunctive discography: pianist Joseph Scianni made a single record for Savoy in the mid-'60s (along with an unissued session with an enticing Don Cherry / Pharoah Sanders fivesome, love to hear that!), only to cease recording for more than thirty years. In the mid-'90s, he made a flurry of recordings for CIMP, in various groupings, but what happened in the intervening three decades is apparently undocumented.

Too bad, since the initial offering held such promise. Not a bad start that it featured the great bassist David Izenzon at the height of his powers. Izenzon of course both was a classical titan and worked with the Ornette Coleman trio (with Charles Moffett), and he could basically do whatever was called for. But his arco was something particularly special, and he brought new ideas from contemporary classical bass into the improvised music lexicon at an extremely high level. Here, in the exposed, stripped-down setting of piano-bass duets, you can hear exactly how powerful his musical intellect was.

Scianni sounds like he'd been listening to Lennie Tristano, though his fastest lines don't whip around with quite the vertiginous fervor of the master. His keen sense of polyphony is evident, with an extremely independent left hand. He's highly chromatic, never completely dealing with clusters and pure energy, always still aware of some sort of tonality, even if it's tentative and shifting. You could think of a much rougher, less elegant (partially because of a not-so-great piano), and less indulgent Keith Jarrett, extrapolating in a liberated way. Much of the soloing builds on little motifs, and indeed the compositions—all Scianni originals—are terse and motivic. The most exciting tracks are the swifter ones; when things slow down, they seem to lose impetus. But there's a very intriguing alternative version of jazz-classical hybrid represented here, one not based in Romantic classical music, but instead in a more contemporary classical scene. It's extremely unusual, like nothing else I can think of, and it's a terrible shame that it's never been reissued.

Izenzon's contribution is really the kicker. He's a sensitive duo partner, ducking and weaving with the pianist's lines and chords, sometimes buoying a section—including a sudden and unexpected blues segment—with supple walking that reminds me of Ronnie Boykins. But he's also able to move away from Scianni, sometimes quite far, as when he shifts to playing below the bridge, conjuring a wonderful set of sounds quite unorthodox in this period. When he kicks into a furious bowed line, like he does at the outset of side one, there's really nothing else that can touch it.

[January 2010]

The Residents, *The Beatles Play the Residents and the Residents Play the Beatles*
(seven-inch single, Ralph Records, 1977)

Among the weirdest record artifacts in my collection is the "registration card" that accompanied this wonderfully strange early seven-inch by the mysterious band the Residents. The single, released in 1977, was produced in a limited edition of five hundred, with a quite beautiful silkscreened cover featuring the Beatles' heads grafted onto naked bodies (female bottoms, male tops, I think). Each one came hand-numbered in pencil in an embossed seal stamp labeled "Official Limited Edition—Ralph Records." As if someone would be counterfeiting them.

The limited number—mine is number 89—is reiterated on the registration card, which is tucked inside a little flap in the interior of the gatefold cover. A text on the card reads: "This record is a limited edition and should be duly registered with the Cryptic Corporation by returning this form with name and address of owner. An annual report of current collector values of Ralph recordings will be made available to Ralph's friends."

I'll readily admit that I didn't register my copy, though I was tempted by the offer of continued updates. What a strange concept, playing on the fetishistic tendencies of collectors, gathering info on the five-hundred-odd (and I mean odd) folks who would buy such a single, sending them some sort of investment review. But this was the subversive '70s, when the idea of twisting the codes of commercialism was an important part of the cultural landscape. The Residents, whose early years in the '60s or early '70s are shrouded in secrecy, loved to tease American fan culture, in this case picking up on the cryptic cult that had grown up around the Beatles. There is, of course, a particularly rabid kind of fanaticism associated with the Fab Four, which flourishes among the "Paul Is Dead" crazies who have sought hidden signs and messages secreted in Beatles records. Couple this with the Beatles' own interest in backward recordings and tape music, and you have the nut of the Residents' nasty little homage.

On the A-side, "Beyond the Valley of a Day in the Life," the Beatles are credited with "covering" the Residents. It's not exactly true, but nicely screws up the who-did-what acknowledgment, since the track consists of snippets from Beatles songs (seventeen in total, plus one John Lennon solo song), arranged à la Residents into a paranoid, noisy, "Revolution No. 9"–style Fluxus sound piece, the center of which is a loop of Paul McCartney saying: "Please everybody, if we haven't done what we could have done we've tried." Back before sampling was a musical mainstay, this was still called audio collage. You can hear the blueprint for much of the subsequent Residents' music in their dismantling and reconfiguration of Beatles tunes. On the B-side, the Residents cover the Beatles' "Flying" with typical goofy, loping aplomb, adding a sneering recap of the McCartney quote and some mock-sinister cabaret music that sounds dopey but is actually quite brilliant, like much of the first part of the Residents' discography.

[March 2010]

John Carter / Bobby Bradford Quartet, *Flight for Four*
(1969, Flying Dutchman)

Self Determination Music
(1970, Flying Dutchman)

Having just written liner notes for the Mosaic Select release of the great early recordings that John Carter and Bobby Bradford made for the tiny independent Revelation Records in the late '60s, I've been deeply immersed in their two Flying Dutchman LPs. It remains one of the greatest disappointments that these two key records, bridging the freebop innovations of the Ornette Coleman foursomes of the early '60s with the architectural achievements of the Anthony Braxton quartets in the '70s, remain out of print. Emphasis on creative linearity is the lineage (as it were), and these Carter/Bradford groups should be every bit as much the watershed as those more widely heard artists.

Flight for Four was produced by Bob Thiele, whose work for Impulse! had already made him one of the most important producers of new jazz. The quartet features a very strong rhythm section, the same one that made the first Revelation LP, *Seeking*, with Tom Williamson on bass and Bruz Freeman on drums. Freeman, who was the brother of Chicago guitarist George Freeman and tenor saxophonist Von Freeman, is extremely resourceful and able to cover both the more swinging material and the open-ended areas. The leaders, both Texans who, like Coleman, had relocated to Los Angeles, are models of independent interdependence. Carter is best known as a clarinetist. Rightly so, as he revolutionized the instrument, bringing to it a totally fresh, different, nonsaxophonic attitude, but finding ways to push the licorice stick harder than other great innovators, like Jimmy Giuffre, had. Bradford continues to be one of the most wonderful trumpet players in creative music, and these are some of his first triumphs, essential listening.

On *Flight for Four*, however, Carter also plays alto and tenor saxophone, and it's a special treat to hear the latter, on which he excels. Makes you wonder what he'd have done if he had picked up that horn more often. Appropriately, *Self Determination Music* was produced by Carter and Bradford. The cover features an oil slick, no doubt a reference to the 1969 Santa Barbara oil spill (strangely familiar again forty-one years later!), but unlike some of the other Flying Dutchmen releases—notably Gil Scott-Heron, Angela David, or Pete Hammill's *Murder at Kent State University*—the political content is not overt but is infused in the ferociously committed playing.

These two classic records have languished for decades, out of print and difficult to find, apparently the casualty of a dispute over rights to the Flying Dutchman vaults. Sad that such important music could be lost to generations of listeners for such petty reasons.

[July 2010]

POSTSCRIPT 2016: *International Phonograph, the label run by Jonathan Horwich, put out a beautiful reissue of* Flight for Four *in 2013; Horwich had already repackaged the music he recorded with Carter and Bradford on his prior imprint, Revelation Records, on a Mosaic Select box set. The British label BGP issued* Self Determination Music *in 2015, not quite as spiffily.*

I get a shock every time I play this record. Not because of the music, which is terrific soul-jazz, but because of what's on the inner sleeve. Of course, this record was made back when simple white paper envelopes were designed to protect the LP, which made them the perfect place for an amateur artist-cum-record-collector to draw. When I pull out the LP, I'm treated to a cartoon-ish pencil drawing of an especially well-hung, smiling donkey. Apologies to Johnny Lytle, who, were he alive (he died in 1995 in his hometown and lifelong base of Springfield, Ohio), might take solace in the fact that the presence of such a drawing probably meant that this was a treasured, often reached for item. Lytle was a sensitive vibraphonist, adept at super-down-tempo ballads, like his radiant version of "Somewhere Over the Rainbow," full of sweet little bluesy fills, exultant swells and breathy hesitations. This was Lytle's debut, waxed for Jazzland with the leader's regular trio, Milt Harris's churchy organ and soft, perfectly supportive drumming by Albert "Tootie" Heath. Later outings on Jazzland were picked up and reissued by Riverside, as in the case of *Happy Ground, Moon Child* (with Ray Barretto on congas), and then Lytle went straight to Riverside, as on his two best-known sides, *Got That Feeling!* and *The Village Caller!* (all exclamations all the time!), though another one to look out for is the LP he made with Johnny Griffin on tenor, *Nice and Easy*.

There's loads of lounge sound here, the quietude saturated with groove on "Movin' Nicely" and a slightly overemotive version of "Autumn Leaves." The vibes/organ combo is a bit eccentric, but it works fine here, Harris and Lytle avoiding each other most of the time, now and then ganging up in tandem on the unsuspecting quiet passage. You can't fault Lytle and crew for laying it on thick—it is the heavy romantic crowd they're playing to, the stuff of wistful nights at the bar alone with the jukebox and the trusty barkeep. Nice, too, when they dig into a bit more funky stuff, like "Mister Strudel"—served like you like it: flaky, with sweet sugar frosting.

[September 2010]

POSTSCRIPT 2016: *Upon review, this column entry feels like a tease. The full story on the inner sleeve was that it came from the collection of a well-respected disc jockey in Chicago whose hobbies included naughty (and funny) pencil drawings, of which his wife did not approve. Looking for a place to draw that she wouldn't find, he settled on the blank inner sleeves of his fifteen thousand records. Buried as they were, the sketches were unlikely to fall into her hands, at least until I was buying* Blue Vibes *from her and pulled out the inner sleeve to check the condition. Be careful what you leave behind; it might surprise your loved ones!*

Orchid Spangiafora, *Flee Past's Ape Elf*
(Twin Tone, 1979)

Dateline: A midwestern college town, late 1970s. A budding high school music nerd, already lost to the world of vinyl freakery, who has recently moved from post-punk to jazz and improvised music, is trawling the incoming bin at his favorite record store. The cover catches his eye, and believing that you can tell a book by its cover at least 73 percent of the time, he digs out a little expendable income from lawn mowing and takes the plunge. The back cover successfully seals the deal, tweaking his love of Dadaism—a Hannah Höch–style collage, recontextualizing some bits of pop magazine faces. And, hey, it's got a palindrome for a title—a dumb-sounding, ungrammatical, meaningless one, which might be even better. But he's not sure exactly what kind of cool-ass cuts could be on this LP, given that it's on the Minneapolis-based Twin Tone label, which he knows for its great independent pop and rock records (later to include the Replacements and Soul Asylum), like those by the Suburbs and the killer *Big Hits of Mid-America Volume III* compilation, which had blown his mind just a few months earlier. Seems like a good bet, he thought, walking home expectantly.

Needle hits the groove: complete and utter confusion. Despite being adventurous and open-eared, he'd never yet heard musique concrète or Karlheinz Stockhausen or John Cage or concrete poetry or experimental tape music. About as close as he'd gotten to that was playing records backward on his parents belt-driven turntable, discovering that Electric Light Orchestra had placed a secret message on one of their songs. First track kicks off with short, looping, sometimes repeating bits of commercial TV and radio, focused on funny bits of text, all pastiched into an amusing subversion of the original words. "Numbers? I worked in banks," a man's voice repeats, until the last word is suddenly replaced with "church." Game show hosts, voices of authority, bursts of applause, no surrounding music to couch the word surgery, virtually nothing but voices, all strung together into a ruthlessly pulverizing audio collage.

And the next piece proves even more beguiling: a twenty-two-second study of a little laugh, sound of tape rolling over head, sensual and funny and gone. Totally gone. The title track becomes his favorite, with its goofy vocal noises and the repeated phrases "Normal? Foam, foam, foam" and "I like nudes." It's about the stupidest—and greatest—thing his wee teenage heart has ever heard. Indeed, one of the most ambitious pieces on the LP is titled, appropriately, "Mondo Stupid," and it proves to be the gateway drug to a life of experimental audio. It would be a couple of decades before he found out anything detailed about this enigmatic record, which came with virtually no information on it. Like the fact that it was made by Rob Carey with assistance from Byron Coley (the great music journalist and champion of things abrasive and weird). Now, with the benefit of the Internet, you can read the entire history of Orchid Spangiafora (orchidspangiafora.com/old/old/history .html), but to hear it you've got to put on your crate-digging fingers and rev up the old freak!

[January 2011]

POSTSCRIPT 2016: *In 2014, Feeding Tube Records reissued* Flee Past's Ape Elf *as a two-LP set. They used my column as liner notes. Sweet circle of life!*

Noah Howard, *Space Dimension*

(America, 1970)

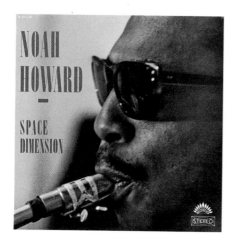

Earlier this year, seventy-four books once in the collection of Thomas Jefferson were discovered to belong to the library at Washington University in St. Louis. Collections, we know, are meant to be assembled, categorized, sorted, studied, loved, and maybe even, certainly in the case of a library, shared. But they are also places in which things hide. Trolling a collection, perhaps one's own collection, can involve a process of discovery, in some cases one with amazing surprises in the wings.

It's taken me a few weeks snuffling around in my memory banks to recall the circumstances of acquiring Noah Howard's *Space Dimension*, an LP that I'd completely lost in my own archives. It was a particularly fruitful jaunt to Milwaukee about twenty years ago, in a junk store that had somehow turned up a selection of unusual fusion and free jazz records. Strange now to think that at the time the Howard record was twenty years old. I've had it buried in my collection for just as long. It's twice as vintage. And, it turns out, exceptionally sought after.

Howard, who died at sixty-seven in 2010, was a fixture in the adventurous mid-1960s Village scene. His first two records were made for ESP; he was associated with Sun Ra, Albert Ayler, Archie Shepp, and most extensively, with tenor saxophonist Frank Wright. With Wright, pianist Bobby Few, drummer Muhammad Ali, and bassist Alan Silva, he became a regular face in the expatriate American free jazz scene in Paris in 1969. In this context, he and Wright recorded three closely related records, with basically the same bassless quartet, two released under Wright's name (*Uhuru Na Umoja*, also on America, and *Church Number Nine*, on Calumet) and the record in question under Howard's.

Where Wright is as voluble and gruff as can be, Howard is the perfect complement, a compact, focused sound. By 1969, he's left the freebop vestiges of his earliest LP for the eruptive, ecstatic world of Ayler, Sanders, and late Coltrane. On the title track, which ladles on an extra helping of echo—

putting some space into "Space Dimension"—Howard leaves earthly orbit by means of a hard, sustained split tone, aided by Wright on harmonica. Odd man out on the session is drummer Art Taylor, hard-bop vet with curiosity about these New Thingers. You can hear him rooting around pretty effectively for what to do in more open ionospheric material, but on the groovy "Viva Black" (titled "Ole Negro" on Howard's LP *The Black Ark*), he's at home with a little shuffle, and on the bouncy, childlike "Song for Thelma," he finds an appropriate place for some swing.

Pianist Few provides one of the hallmark features of these sessions, his pedal-down mass-of-sound giving it both a lugubrious quality and an unmistakable fingerprint. On "Church Number Nine," the one track that swaps in drummer Ali, the whole machine takes its rightful shape, Wright screaming bloody murder, Howard joining for the ridiculously perfect little R&B/gospel riff, a maniacal laugh and corkscrew multiphonic ending the track on an unhinged note. It's as if the LP was insanely happy to have been rediscovered in my collection.

[May 2011]

Baikida Carroll, *The Spoken Word*
(Hat Hut, 1979)

That's what happens when a record label waits so long to reissue a great LP—the music gets posted on YouTube. You can listen to all of the wonderful St. Louis trumpet player's late '70s solo record, rather nicely transferred from the gatefold double LP, on your laptop or PC. Nobody would argue that the fidelity is as good as the original (let's face it, MP3s just mash out the acoustics), but then again, thanks to one 13Samarkand, the beneficent soul who has taken the time to upload the vinyl, now anyone in reach of a computer can hear it. It definitely deserves a listen.

Carroll was part of the Black Artists Group, St. Louis's equivalent to Chicago's Association for the Advancement of Creative Musicians. He joined BAG in '68 and quickly became a central figure, alongside Julius Hemphill, Oliver Lake, Joseph Bowie, Charles "Bobo" Shaw, and Luther Thomas. He played on Hemphill's monumentally important debut, *Dogon A.D.*, and, following the lead of the Art Ensemble of Chicago, left the United States for a year, along with several colleagues, to play in Europe in the early '70s. While there, in '73, he led the collective's first record, *BAG in Paris*,

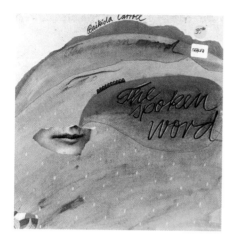

an incredibly rare slab of wax. I'd never heard it until I got the reissue, which finally came out last year; it confirms what a forceful and unique voice Carroll had on his instrument.

That's amply demonstrated on *The Spoken Word*. Solo trumpet records are rare enough, much more so thirty years ago. Carroll would have had Lester Bowie's broad, hilarious "Jazz Death" (from the 1968 Roscoe Mitchell LP *Congliptious*) to consider, a few Leo Smith outings, but for the most part solo wind was reserved for the reeds. *The Spoken Word* is less bodacious than Bowie, sparer, in places even quite aggressively experimental. On "The Spoken Word I," which starts with some quiet burbling mouth noises, Carroll goes on to use a tube extension to create a bleating saxophone sound. On the other hand, with a beautiful, radiant tone that most recalls Smith, Carroll approaches "Rites and Rituals" with a measured, phrase-by-phrase introspection, leaving odd spaces between his gorgeous lines. With crickets in the background, laying a pulse bed, Carroll plays gentle, sweet and sour melodies, adding Harmon mute, then bathing his soft calls in reverb. It's a very special record, extremely approachable, lovely and refreshing.

Hat Hut's early years included a great number of wonderful releases that have never been made officially available in digital form—numerous Joe McPhee LPs, a revelatory solo David S. Ware twofer, a Philip Wilson record with a youthful Olu Dara. It's certainly one of the most important archives of untapped vinyl, gaining in obscurity with each year, aching to be reissued. Until then, happy hunting!

[September 2011]

POSTSCRIPT 2016: *Along with multiple McPhee and Steve Lacy recordings, Corbett vs. Dempsey has bought the masters for* The Spoken Word *and Wilson's* Esoteric. *David Ware's* Birth of a Being *was reissued by Aum Fidelity.*

Randy Weston, *Blues*

(Trip, 1972; recorded circa 1964–1965)

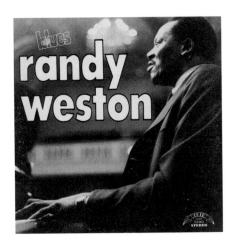

Sometimes a long-held question gets answered as soon as it's asked. On a recent panel discussion, saxophonist Geof Bradfield mentioned pianist Randy Weston's State Department–sponsored trip to Africa, wondering aloud whether there was any documentation (none of the rest of us on the panel knew) of the music he made with a small group in the '60s that included tenor saxophonist Clifford Jordan and drummer Edward Blackwell. Half an hour later, we were standing at the back of the room with Weston, who was telling us about tapes he has of the concerts, including one with a spectacular New Orleans–style solo by Blackwell. The reel-to-reels apparently need some conservation, probably nothing a crusading little tape freak couldn't handle.

Meanwhile, in lieu of that intriguing possibility, we can find another Weston session, from around the same period, a recording that managed to find its way briefly—and dubiously—onto vinyl. I say dubiously because it appeared on the Trip label, a budget outfit from New Jersey that seems to have specialized in bootleg or near-bootleg releases. I remember having had a Jimi Hendrix rarities LP on Trip as a kid; later, knowing a bit more about the complexities of licensing, I wondered how this could have come to pass. Anyway, along with whatever murky deals they made, Trip issued things on the cheapest-quality vinyl with cut-rate design and nonexistent, incomplete, or misleading documentation. On the plus side, they always made a point of releasing everything on eight-track tape, so you can't say they didn't have the choosy consumer in mind.

And they sometimes issued great music, like this Weston sextet material. Unlike the better-known Weston records from the period, notably *African Cookbook* (issued by the pianist on his own Bakton label in 1964, reissued in 1972 on Atlantic), this group didn't feature Booker Ervin on tenor, whose career as a leader had started to take off at the time. Other Weston regulars are there—Ray Copeland on trumpet, Vishnu Bill Wood (listed as Bill

Woods) on bass, Lenny McBrowne on drums, Big Black on congas—but the tenor seat is taken by an obscure fellow named Frank Haynes. I recall the name from some Grant Green records, on which he sounds really good, and Haynes made appearances on outings by drummer Dave Bailey, trumpeter Kenny Dorham, and pianist Les McCann, among others. He died not long after the Weston session, in his early thirties.

Blues features three Weston originals, all of them wonderful. On "Blues for Strayhorn," Haynes gets the spotlight, and it's enough to make one very sad he didn't live longer. Against magisterial, bittersweet chords, with a surprising uptick in the melody, Haynes is vulnerable and forthright, his soft touch and unsentimental tone evincing just the right Ellingtonian mood right up to a brilliant cadenza. The atmosphere is relaxed, informal, perhaps twenty people in the audience, plainly but nicely recorded, capturing the live feel. Weston is beautiful as always, filtering Monk back through Ellington, with big chords and ultrasensitive timing. Copeland is featured on "Sad Beauty Blues," a darker composition taken at the same slow tempo. The trumpeter is likewise wonderful, fluttering and parsing the harmonies like a surgeon.

The track "Afro Blues," properly known as "Afro Black," takes up the full eighteen minutes of the other side, McBrowne digging into the kind of snare parade that evokes Blackwell, a calypso atmosphere overcoming the sorrowful blues of side A, Weston contributing tersely Ellington-like piano, percussionist Big Black in a long solo, snugly pulling tight the two sides of the hyphen "African" and "American."

[November 2011]

Charles Bobo Shaw Human Arts Ensemble, *Çonceré Ntasiah*
(Universal Justice, 1978)

The late 1970s in New York was such a fertile, volatile moment. Tributaries from around the country—Chicago and St. Louis in particular—had helped feed the city's indigenous new jazz waterways, and all variety of mixing and blending were taking place. The loft scene was in high gear; acronyms like AACM and NMDS were on the tip of everyone's tongue; David Murray was making uncompromising music with a drummer named Stanley Crouch; the downtown improvised music world was in formation, the Knitting Factory still a decade away. Recall the unlikely combination of jazz and No Wave in Defunkt, or the fresh version of jazz-funk fusion ushered forth by Ornette Coleman's Prime Time and Ronald Shannon Jackson's Decoding Society. Lots of great music was made in the period, not all of it adequately remembered. Drummer Charles Bobo Shaw was one of the central St. Louis musicians associated with the Black Artists Group (BAG), which he helped found in the mid-1960s. A stint in Europe later in the decade put

him in touch with various international figures, and when he returned in the early '70s he was rapidly becoming one of the best-known drummers in creative music. With his mutable group the Human Arts Ensemble, leadership of which he shared with saxophonist Luther Thomas, Shaw issued some of the classic LPS of BAG music, including the incendiary *Red, Black, and Green* (with Solidarity Unit, reissued on LP a few years ago) and *Junk Trap* (Black Saint, 1978), as well as three essential records with Lester Bowie, produced by Michael Cuscuna and released on Muse, the final one a 1977 duet called *Bugle Boy Bop*.

A year later, Shaw took a version of the Human Arts Ensemble with BAG mainstays Julius Hemphill and Joseph Bowie into the studio to record *Çon-ceré Ntasiah*. Never since reissued, it's a great document of the period and a wonderful listen overall, with Hemphill's probing saxophone and Bowie riding ebullient roughshod trombone over various different grooves. Cellist Abdul Wadud, one of the most prominent players in the period, joins forces with guitarist Nyomo Mantuila and bassist Alex Blake, laying down and coloring the light, bossa-inflected "Jacki B Tee" (man, I miss that Wadud strut!) and the chugging rock boogie of "Steam Away Kool 500." On the kit, Shaw is a chameleon, able to move between these different feels with ease. As a dedicated fan of Hemphill's alto, I was almost disappointed to see him listed exclusively on soprano on this ridiculously rare record, but the fact is he sounds terrific, perfect complement to Bowie's big, brash bone. The title cut features an African vibe, Mantuila's nylon-string guitar acting as a kora, Wadud's quick glisses goosing Hemphill during his solo. Exciting sounds from a time when everything seemed possible and all roads converged in the Big Apple.

[January 2012]

Lee "Scratch" Perry, *Double-7*

(Black Heart, 1974)

About twenty years ago I hit a gold mine of reggae and African records in an otherwise crummy secondhand store. Among notable finds were some incredible Nigerian Afro-pop LPs, Prince Far I records I'd never seen, and a little slab of wax packed in a nearly blank white sleeve, with a hand-stamped title on front: *Double-7*, Scratch the Upsetter. A vintage Lee Perry side, holy smokes, I mused. With a giddy feeling in my stomach, I bought it and quickly brought it home to decant.

I was already familiar with an LP by the same name, released as part of a three-LP (later two-CD) set on the British Trojan label, titled *The Upsetter Compact Set*. Since then, Trojan has reissued *Double-7* as a stand-alone LP with the original UK cover, which sports a '70s photo of the great producer, clad in a knit cap and replete with headphones, singing in the studio. As a dedicated Perry-o-phile, I had studied the music on the record carefully; it's both devilishly soulful and represents one of his wacko masterpieces. With outstanding toasting by both U-Roy and I-Roy, as well as instrumental tracks featuring the Upsetters and some inimitable vocals by Scratch himself, it stands as one of the best of the early Black Ark–era recordings in Perry's hilariously extensive discography. Buying the record was foolproof—it's a classic.

What I had not expected was the fact that this version of *Double-7* would sound so different. Indeed, I had always noted that Trojan's Upsetters material had a slightly muffled quality, particularly when compared with similar or identical work released on Jamaican labels or licensed through other channels. I'd read about the nefarious deals that Perry had made with Trojan, selling them Bob Marley's early work and pocketing the cash. With the Upsetters material, I wondered if he might have provided the Brits with masters that were multigeneration dubs, maybe purposefully saving the spiffier versions for himself. I'd had a similar shock listening to *Blackboard Jungle Dub*, a spectacularly important LP from a year before *Double-7*, which had widespread release in the United States on Clocktower, but was issued from an inferior master; when a version taken from a cleaner master was released a few years ago, it was like dust being blown off a Rembrandt.

In the case of this *Double-7*, released on the US label Black Heart (some sort of Black Ark partnership), the bass is significantly enhanced, the separation and basic pressing quality far superior. This means a better picture of Perry's warped humor on "Cold Weather," which features the maestro speaking over a sinister backing, with a tape of running water overlaid on top. "Are you cold?" Scratch asks as the water runs out and needs to be rewound—while the song is running!—and started up again. Toward the end of the cut, Perry begins to pot the water track up and down, distinctly evoking the sound of a man relieving himself. On "Waa You Waa," one of the most incredible moments in the Scratch oeuvre, a soul song is treated to extreme manual manipulation, a potentiometer workout, the backing band audibly raised and lowered, like a hand is reaching into the music and reconfiguring it. It foreshadowed Public Enemy's "Terminator X to the Edge of Panic" by twenty-one years. "OK, OK, let's take it from here," Perry leads off "Kentucky Skank," the first song, and from there on *Double-7* is a revelation. The cherry on top, in this case, was discovering something I had missed when I bought the LP. On the reverse, the cover bears handwritten titles for all the songs, sketched out in Lee Perry's familiar script. Scratch scratch, in other words.

[February 2012]

POSTSCRIPT 2016: *To dive more deeply into the difficult to fathom sea of Lee, I recommend Jeremy Collingwood's* Kiss Me Neck: The Scratch Story in Words, Pictures, and Sounds *(Cherry Red Books, 2010), which goes the distance in untangling Perry's complicated discography. I have all the reissued versions, but I have still never heard a better sounding* Double-7 *than mine. This seems like a job for Pressure Sounds. Incidentally, I could positively ID Perry's handwriting because I have autographed copies of several LPs from when I spent time with him in Zurich in 1990. He signed them variously, one especially nice one: £$D (pounds, dollars, deutschmarks) Perry.*

Eddie Shu / Joe Roland / Wild Bill Davis,
New Stars—New Sounds

(Mercer Records, 1950)

Sometimes all it takes is a font. I recognized the sans serif design on this ten-inch as being early Prestige, but looking a bit closer found little evidence of the better-known label, just the intriguing Mercer appellation, which was at the time unknown to me. The text layout, the different font weights, the absence of images, even the little "non breakable—long playing micro groove," were all straight from the Prestige drawing board. The other puzzler was the presence of the *New Stars—New Sounds* title, which I remembered also being a Prestige speciality. There was a Lee Konitz / Stan Getz ten-inch called *New Sounds*, and a Lars Gullin one called *New Sounds from Sweden*, a Leo Parker one titled *New Sounds in Modern Music*, and a Sam Most record called *Introducing a New Star*—all Prestiges from the early '50s. Then again, there was a New Faces—New Sounds series on Blue Note, so it wasn't by any means a patented idea of the folks at Prestige.

On further investigation, it turns out that Mercer was the label run by Mercer Ellington and Leonard Feather, with financial support from Duke Ellington and Billy Strayhorn. A short-lived project, the label ran from 1950 to 1952, and it was relatively unsuccessful, falling in the nether zone between 78-rpm and 33⅓-rpm formats. Mercer released both, but couldn't seem to gain traction. In truth, listening to this strange little compilation of tracks, one could hardly imagine they thought they'd have a hit on their hands, but it is certainly an oddball, and a very enjoyable one. Three tracks feature the multi-instrumentalist (and part-time ventriloquist) Eddie Shu, together with a quintet featuring Denzil Best on drums and Barbara Carroll on piano, the latter sounding very solid. Shu switches between horns, playing alto sax, trumpet, and clarinet, but the emphasis is clearly on his bebop harmonica playing, which is remarkably happening, if also borderline kitsch.

Wielding his "real gone organ," Wild Bill Davis contributes two tracks, both sporting Papa Jo Jones on drums. On "Things Ain't What They Used to Be," Davis is joined by Duke Ellington (who was two-timing Columbia Records in the process), and together their interplay is perfectly in sync. Davis is still wed to a prehistoric sense of what the organ can do, but it's a great swing side nonetheless. The final three tracks are the hottest draw for me on this platter. Vibraphonist Joe Roland, who plays with the Shu band, leads a group billed as "his vibes and his boppin' strings." Truth in advertising, amigo. Starting with the Miles Davis classic "Half-Nelson," Roland and a string quartet (plus Joe Puma on guitar and Harold Granowsky on drums) wind through the hairpin turns and tricky changes. It is delightfully free of any third-stream pretensions, simply instigating the string players to kick up some dust and have some whip-crackin' fun. A sly line at the tail of "Dee Dee's Dance," a tune contributed by Denzil Best, ingeniously blends the various instruments' sonorities with a tart twist.

Back to the Prestige conundrum. In fact, there was a direct connection— Mercer was distributed by Prestige, and they may well have used the same designers and manufacturers. According to Feather, Prestige "invariably gave precedence to the selling of its own product," hence Mercer's demise. But not before they introduced these hot new stars and bracing new sounds.

[March 2012]

Cecil Taylor / Tony Oxley, *Ailanthus / Altissima*
(Triple Point Records, 2009)

In this month's column, I'm using a recent release as a way to talk about the crazy number of Cecil Taylor records that are digitally unavailable. Talk about a master whose music has been consistently well documented but poorly attended to as media have migrated, the pianist has essential records from various phases that are accessible only in their original format. To be fair, his is an impressive discography, and there are in fact quite a few great items in print, but consider the missing information from the 1960s and 1970s, culled from a casual perusal of my own collection. From the late '60s, a key time for Taylor as he began to introduce his solo concept to the jazz world, there is *Praxis* (Praxis double-LP, 1982), an Italian solo, and several volumes of *Nuits de la Fondation Maeght* (Shandar, 1969), an essential quartet recording with Jimmy Lyons on alto, Sam Rivers on tenor, and Andrew Cyrille on drums. From the '70s, there is the fearsome trio with Lyons and Cyrille, recorded at

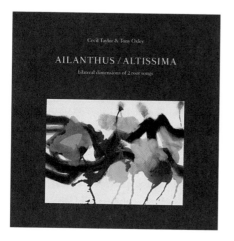

Antioch College, released as *Indent*, and *Spring of Two Blue-J's*, dedicated to Ben Webster, with a solo on one side and a quartet adding Sirone on bass (both of these released on Taylor's own Unit Core label in 1973, the year they were recorded). Other classic C.T. Unit records from the era, like *Dark to Themselves* (Enja) and *Live in the Black Forest* (MPS), were reissued on CD at the dawn of the digital era, but have lapsed from print and are now difficult to find. Plunge into the 1980s, and right away, the atomic *Fly! Fly! Fly! Fly! Fly!* (MPS, 1980) has never been revisited.

To these vinyl-only historical goodies, you can now add a newly issued double-LP duet by Taylor and British drummer Tony Oxley. It's as lovingly produced an item as one could hope to find, beautifully printed and pressed—reminiscent, in this, of Taylor's brilliant Japanese double-LP *Akisakila* (Trio, 1973), still worth hunting for even though it's been reissued—with an artfully designed booklet featuring facsimiles of Taylor's handwritten poetry and images of Oxley's paintings. The twosome has a long, deep partnership dating back to 1988 and existing for years as the Feel Trio with bassist William Parker. Here their dialogue is particularly direct and intimate, the percussionist often anticipating the pianist's next move or vice versa. Indeed, there's a yin-yang quality about the duo. Oxley has certain aspects of his playing that might be described as pianistic—lots of color, a vaguely melodic use of tuned metal, post-Elvin sense of deferred or subverted timekeeping; meanwhile, Taylor is of course a notoriously percussive pianist, his notion of the keyboard as a huge drum perhaps more apt as an octogenarian than it was when he was in his twenties. Clocking in at around eighty-two minutes, nicely recorded in 2008 at the Village Vanguard, *Ailanthus/Altissima* is subtitled "bilateral dimensions of 2 root songs," and if you follow the music carefully, you can hear how the song basis of Taylor's music is, indeed, at the root, spreading out in this case in (at least) two directions. As ferocious as his music is, you can often find sections to hum along with, little thematic segments that stick in the brain. There is plenty of aggressive free music here, but also these pensive moments of quiet and extreme tension, a Taylor specialty. A labor of love undertaken by producer/scholar Ben Young in celebration of the pianist's eightieth birthday, it should be treated as a necessary part of the well-stocked C.T. fan's library.

[May 2012]

POSTSCRIPT 2016: *I remain perplexed at the number of key Taylor recordings commercially unavailable to the consuming public. Imagine if Joyce's* Ulysses *or Pynchon's* Gravity's Rainbow *had been out of print for three decades. Taylor has turned eighty-seven years old and still makes occasional appearances, but is as ever unpredictable. I write this postscript on a plane returning to Chicago from New York, having just traveled to see him play a highly publicized concert at a tribute . . . to him. He didn't. Then again, I remember that he was slated to play at the benefit for Jimmy Lyons, his long-term saxophonist, as Lyons lay dying in the hospital. He didn't. Taylor's perverse streak is as wide as his music is rich and urgent; he is a true diva—erratic, demanding, insecure, powerful. If I had a chance to see him play again tomorrow, I would turn around and fly back to New York.*

Unidentified Kenyan Highlife Band, seven-inch test-pressing

(unidentified label, stamped 1969)

Coming above ground at the Port de Clingancourt, it's easy to get lost trying to find Les Puces de Saint-Ouen, the gigantic Parisian flea market. After wandering aimlessly a while a few weeks ago, Jim Dempsey and I suddenly found ourselves in an alleyway that opened onto a rabbit warren of booths, hundreds of vendors hawking everything under the sun, from tube socks and faux designer jeans to nineteenth-century taxidermy. Several hours of nosing around, making my way from one such labyrinth to another, and I finally found the area dedicated to books, photographs, and records.

The record booths were enticing enough on the face of things. Small cellules, open on one or both sides, with walls covered in rare LPS and singles, they each had their own soundtrack, a hint of the owner's orientation. One was rocking reggae, serious dub rumble shaking boxes of cheaper French pop seven-inches; another played vintage rock 'n' roll, with Chuck Berry at the helm and the requisite Beatles "butcher" album, *Yesterday and Today*, gracing the wall; yet another pumping out vintage Blue Note sounds, proving the Frenchman's penchant for great straight-ahead jazz. Inside, people made small piles of vinyl, bringing them to the vendor for a test spin, to be judged, valued, haggled over, and either bought or sent back to the racks.

I grazed the walls, sensing the vibe and wondering if I'd find anything of real interest. A few unfamiliar reggae singles almost tempted me, as did a couple of Saravah LPs I had only on CD, but the prices were a bit too dear and my desire to schlep them back across the pond weighed heavily in my mind's eye. Making my way to the back of the smallest booth, I found an area that looked intriguing titled "European Jazz." Ironically, the first real score was found here, but wasn't a European item at all; it was instead the debut LP by Karl Berger, recorded in 1966 for ESP, with Edward Blackwell on drums, Henry Grimes on bass, and Carlos Ward on alto saxophone. Somehow, this classic of American free jazz had eluded my attention; it was priced forty euros, but I needed to hear it. While the friendly clerk put it on the turntable, I kept looking, now in other sections. Noticing a freestanding box of African LPs, I recalled that we were in the land of postcolonial African music and got a quick jolt of anticipatory adrenaline. While Berger's vibes rang in the background, I pulled a stack of fascinating-looking West African LPs. Imagining that the Berger record had probably been reissued, I knew then I'd be turning my attention to the African offerings and asked the guy to replace it with *Ene Ba Sam* by Madam Ngowuka & the 1st Kongo Ogbo of Bolo.

This, too, wasn't cheap, at twenty-five euros. I started peppering my friend with questions about his African holdings, and he was happy to play a few great LPs, another Nigerian one of which went into the keep pile. I was ready to check out when he asked if I would be interested in African singles. Now, one thing to know about African vinyl—and I mean actual vinyl made and used in Africa—is that it's generally very hard to find in reasonable condition. In Africa, it would seem, they play the crap out of their records, they just don't mess around holding them by the edges and wiping them clean and fetishizing them. So when he pulled out a box that he told me was dead stock from a defunct store, I just about fell over. Multiple copies of unplayed seven-inches from the late '60s and early '70s, mostly East African, some featuring bands I knew (Les Bantous de la Capitale), but mostly by names

I'd never encountered. Then he pulled out a stash of test pressings sporting covers decorated in hand-stamped designs and little marginal notes on the otherwise blank inner label. I bought them all, forty-four mint African singles, fifteen of them test pressings. Back at home, I decided to test them using Shazam, the cell phone app that IDs songs. It nailed the picture sleeve singles, but failed to identify even one of the test pressings, all of which are fantastic highlife and Afro-pop tracks. Without question, one of the great finds in my freakish little life.

[slated for July 2012, never published, Vinyl Freak terminated]

POSTSCRIPT 2016: *White labels, handwritten matrix numbers, no names—this all required some detective work. They turn out to be from the Kundi label and its sister operation, Sibuor. The spectacular kentanzavinyl.com lists some of my stash, but others are unknown, possibly never released. None of it has ever been reissued.*

/ **Specialty of the House**

Writing the Vinyl Freak column for *DownBeat*, I stayed conscious of the magazine's primary audience: jazz listeners, students, and practitioners. Though I tried to keep the entries diverse, they often came home to jazz, which gave the overall group of essays a particular flavor. This was also sensible for me as pound-for-pound jazz constitutes the biggest part of my holdings. Mulling over the column, I've come to realize a few particulars about my collection, facets that make it special and areas that are weaker or more pedestrian. On the one hand, I could have devoted a whole twelve-year-long series of essays to reggae and its related genres, or composed a post-punk singles column that would have kept things interesting; on the other hand, while I have some great soul and funk LPs and quite a nice stash of scarce singles, this would have been sketchier and perhaps less compelling than it might have if it had come from a real tracker dedicated to that music. There are plenty of them. And their collections are sick with rarities. Likewise with country music, where my choices are more impulsive and unsystematic, even if I do have a pretty complete George Jones section, all the County collections of vintage hillbilly music, and a copy of Johnny Paycheck's *Bars, Booze, and Blondes*. Then there's African music, which requires a great deal of specificity of attention to be really rich; I've got lots of African records, many of them quite special, but I'm not any kind of completist. In the African arena, I have bought things when they passed in front of me more than I have sought them out. I've been an opportunist. Which has worked just fine, having been in the right place at the right time often enough.

But returning to Vinyl Freak made me want to concentrate for a moment on the zone of my holdings that reflect my scholarship, the parts that I spent years building, agonizing over, and trying to complete: free improvisation and creative music. I managed to slip some of these records into the column, an act I thought of as subversive fun. Flipping through the collection now, I am still stunned to discover how many important records, even after so many years, remain out of print and nearly inaccessible. The pioneering labels of European free improvisation, Incus, ICP, and FMP, for instance, all still have significant missing pieces, and numerous important documents of American creative music, genuinely canonic works, became unavailable much too long ago.

The whole business of keeping this music on the market is tricky. Challenging music is not, by any means, an easy thing to create and sell. Take a hypothetical self-produced record of free improvisation, issued in an edition of 500. One hundred of them are perhaps bought by people on a whim at a concert, many going into the homes of people who never listened to them; plenty of these are subsequently thrown away; another 150 are dispersed around the community of dedicated listeners, some of whom die or get disinterested; 50 more are consigned to record stores or distributors, forgotten, and deleted or destroyed; the final 100 copies sat in the musician's basement for twenty years before being ruined in a flood. This winnows the number of copies in active service to roughly 50. Which turns the hunt for them into real sport and the prospect of reissuing them into pure foolhardiness.

A couple of terms crop up frequently enough in the following to merit explanation: "self-produced," "private issue," and "artist run." There are areas of overlap between these, but in general the differences are that self-production implies that the musicians issued it themselves, perhaps on a label that was invented specifically for the one release, where something privately issued may not have been published by the musicians. The musician-run label is a third category that denotes a label that's more than a vanity project (which is what self-produced and private issue vinyl is often pejoratively called), but involves musicians having actually set up a legitimate label in order to make all the creative decisions on their own behalf. Incus, for instance, was run by Derek Bailey and Evan Parker (with Tony Oxley, who left early), ICP by Han Bennink and Misha Mengelberg (with Willem Breuker, who left early), and although FMP was the headbirth of Jost Gebers, a lapsed bassist, it was guided by musicians including Peter Brötzmann, Peter Kowald, and Alex Schlippenbach. These were all small labels that were musician-run, and in turn they looked back to the earliest rumblings of DIY record production, pioneered in the 1950s by Debut (Charles Mingus and Max Roach), El Saturn (Sun Ra and Alton Abraham), and Gate 5 (Harry Partch).

For some reason, more creative music records have been reissued than those of freely improvised music, but there are huge ellipses in both. Keeping this in mind, I have selected 113 LPs, a gallery of delights extracted from the most prized parts of the collection, several choice rarities of experimental music and sound poetry thrown in for good measure, each entry annotated briefly to enhance the reader's delectation.

Muhammad Ali / Duo Frank Wright, *Adieu Little Man* (Center of the World, 1974)

Pared from more usual expansive quartet context down to an explosive twosome, drummer Ali and saxophonist Wright (here also playing bass clarinet) may well have felt at the center of the world, as the label that documented their exploits at the American Center in Paris where this and much more of their music was performed, would have it. A tender double-exposed photo on the back by bassist Alan Silva depicts the duo superimposed on a swan pond—a pastoral scenario that doesn't quite signal the volatility of the music.

Art Ensemble of Chicago, *Among the People* (Praxis, 1980)

Live Italian recording of AEC from the period of *Urban Bushmen*, released on a Greek label that always seemed a bit shady—see also possibly unauthorized Praxis records of Sun Ra and Cecil Taylor—but had impeccable taste.

At Different Times (Group-Music Productions, 1970)

Heavy rarity, private issue, beautiful silkscreened cover with unusual feature of hand-stitched envelope flap interior. Dutch free jazz by saxophonist Peter van der Locht, trumpeter Boy Raaymakers, with American pianist Burton Greene and Parisian expat Noel McGhee.

Derek Bailey, *Notes* (Incus, 1985)

One of several outstanding records on the essential Incus label left untended. Solo guitar, always tightly wound and incisive, here exploring distant harmonics with an elegance that could almost be called lush.

Karl Berger & Company, *Tune In* (Milestone, 1969)

Crazy that this post-bop beaut has never been reissued, with Berger on vibes, Carlos Ward on saxophone, Dave Holland on bass, and Edward Blackwell on drums. Michael Cuscuna wrote the liner notes, saying that the LP was "exhilarating in its creativity, and just possibly prophetic."

The Blue Denim Deals, *"Armed Forces" Day* (Say Day-Bew, 1978)

Superheavy surreal musical theater from Tuscaloosa, Alabama, released in a numbered edition of three hundred, one of two records on the Say Day-Bew imprint. Personnel include guitarist Davey Williams and violinist La-Donna Smith (here playing everything but violin), imported from the big city, Birmingham.

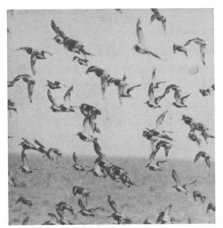

Lester Bowie, *Rope-a-Dope* (Muse, 1976)

The same Michael Cuscuna, who blossomed into one of the most important record producers in jazz, oversaw two sets of recordings under trumpeter Bowie's name, this one, with trios up to a sextet, very Art Ensemble oriented (Malachi Favors and Don Moyé in the lineups), and *Fast Last*, an incandescent LP of duets. These two records may be the most egregious absences from the digital domain on this list.

Polly Bradfield, *Solo Violin Improvisations* (Parachute, 1979)

Boxes of this brilliant fiddle outing, one of the best records of its kind, were reputedly discarded by Bradfield, having gone unsold for years. Knotty, intense, nuanced little sounds by an important early associate of John Zorn and Eugene Chadbourne. On Chadbourne's Parachute label.

Peter Brötzmann / Han Bennink, *Atsugi Concert* (Gua-Bungue, 1980)

Marvelous debossed silver cover, Brötz on front, Bennink on verso, from the duo period after pianist Fred van Hove left the fold, having grown frustrated at Bennink's volume.

***The Bugger All Stars* (Bead, 1981)**

Three key labels of European improvised music are still virtually untouched by reissuers—Claxon from Holland, Po Torch from Germany, and Bead from England. Sportingly clamorous microcosmic sound improvisation, with the great Phil Wachsmann on violin and madman Hugh Metcalfe (known to wear a gas mask for no discernible reason in performance) on guitar, the Bugger All Stars were a quartet that included Mike Hames covering both ends of the reed spectrum on alto sax and bass clarinet and Jim LeBaigue on drums. Metcalfe's artwork adorns the cover, paying homage to his frequent collaborations with concrete poet Bob Cobbing.

Dave Burrell, *High* (Douglas, 1965)

Pianist Burrell's debut, inexplicably rare and little known, featuring Sirone (then known as Norris Jones) on bass, Bobby Kapp or Sunny Murray on drums, and Pharoah Sanders on tambourine. The first side is devoted to a medley of melodies from *West Side Story*.

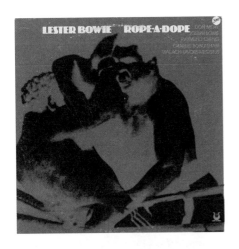

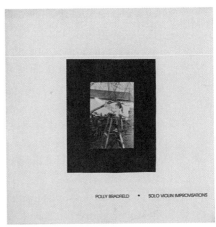

Günter Christmann, . .*off*. . . (Moers Music, 1979)

Speaking of potent little sounds, one side composed, one side improvised, culling trombone, compressed air bottle, bass, crackle box, mandolin, typewriter, found sounds, and transistor radio. Almost painfully intimate, charting the place where trombone ends and voice starts, Christmann's genius is all expert timing.

Günter Christmann / Paul Lovens / Maarten Altena, *Weavers* (Po Torch, 1980)

My favorite LP of free improvised music, as I've declared repeatedly. Perfect mix of interactivity and independence, made for Lovens's flawless label.

CCMC Volume 1 (Music Gallery Editions, 1976)

Great white northern classic, first outing from the band featuring artist and pianist Michael Snow (here playing trumpet), also including Nobuo Kubota and Bill Smith on saxophones, Larry Dubin on drums, and Casey Sokol on piano. They're identified in the notes as the Canadian Creative Music Collective, but Snow long maintained that the acronym was free-floating and could stand for many different names. All the early CCMC records, along with the Artist's Jazz Band LPs that predated them, need reissuing.

Eugene Chadbourne / Toshinori Kondo, *Possibilities of the Color Plastic*
(Bellows, 1979)

American guitar crazy meets Japanese trumpet nut in Knoxville, Tennessee. Hilarity and magic ensue, most of it apparently on the floor.

Community (Zyzzle, 1981)

British socialist improvised music par excellence, extending notions of democracy and egalitarianism to a huge group, with fragmentary components of traditional big-band music composed by saxophonist Will Menter. Amid the twenty-strong ensemble, some recognizable names: trombonist Alan Tomlinson, tuba player Melvyn Poore, guitarist Peter Cusack, French hornist Martin Mayes, percussionist Roy Ashbury, and cellist Georgina Born.

Cohelmec Ensemble, *Hippotigris Zebra Zebra* (Saravah, 1971)

Extra-uncommon LP from Pierre Barouh's label featuring French free jazz musicians (most of them otherwise unknown to me), including bassist François Mechali, whose work with Joe McPhee later in the decade, including the warm *Oleo*, was an influence on the evolution of my listening.

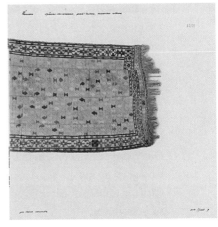

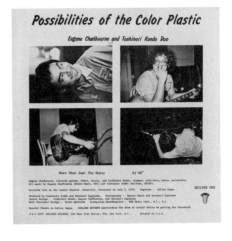

Jerome Cooper / Kalaparusha / Frank Lowe, *Positions 3 6 9* (Kharma, 1977)

Drummer Jerome Cooper (1946–2015) has been all but deleted from the story of creative music, unfairly so given his unique and refined approach. Obsessively repetitive and deeply into odd and additive time signatures, often combining kit and balafon, strongly influenced by Native American music, he appears here in solos, duets, and trios with two significant reed players whose different backgrounds converge in a bluesy honk. Also solo on a must-have LP *The Unpredictability of Predictability*, and a quintet record *Outer and Interactions*, both on About Time. Like many great jazz musicians who grew up in Chicago, Cooper studied with the legendary high school instructor Captain Walter Dyett, which perhaps helps explain his sensational self-discipline.

Tom Cora / David Moss, *Cargo Cult Revival* (Rift, 1983)

A personal favorite, monster acoustic noise music from the late, great cellist and the drummer/vocalizer. Later Cora would debate the value of music like this, which avoided most of the conventional devices like melodies and harmony and pulsed rhythm.

The Ed Curran Quartet, *Elysa* (Savoy, 1968)

Produced by trumpeter Bill Dixon when he was head of new jazz A&R for Savoy, one of a number of freer entries in the label's discography, fronted and featuring motivic tunes by saxophonist Curran, with drummer Robert Pozar, bassist Koyoshi Tokunaga, and Marc Levin on cornet. Curran dropped off the scene, but not before leaving this small treasure.

Lesli Dalaba, *Trumpet Songs & Dances* (Parachute, 1979)

One of the highlights of the less well-known downtown New York scene, Dalaba imbues spittle with phosphorescence and unveils a set of halting microscopic moves in solos and a duet each with Polly Bradfield and Wayne Horvitz (on bass instead of keyboards).

Diana David / Paul Gaudynski / Thomas Gaudynski, *Object Lessons* (a (R) t Noise, 1982)

Indigenous improvised music from Milwaukee featuring Diana D. and the Brothers G. Sprawling multi-instrumentalism, crunchy and pliant, compares fruitfully with Davey Williams and LaDonna Smith.

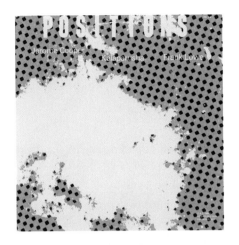

Hugh Davies, *Shozyg* (SAJ, 1982)

Lamented experimentalist, improvisor, and Stockhausenite who passed in 2005, here in concert playing bowed diaphragms and other Seussian doo-dads. Needless to say, a highly specialized procedure. On FMP's sister label, SAJ, named for drummer Sven-Ake Johansson.

The Dutch Jazz Scene (Radio Netherland, 1969)

The laudably diverse music of late '60s Holland, from Boy Edgar's Big Band (classic drummer John Engels matching sticks with a youthful Han Bennink), saxophonist Hans Dulfer's Heavy Soul Inc., and Nedly Elstak's three-some, to the Instant Composers Pool, documented twice, once led by Misha Mengelberg, once by Willem Breuker. This super-rare seven-LP box was produced by Radio Netherland for syndication to other stations.

Johnny Dyani / Okay Temiz / Mongezi Feza, *Music for Xaba* (Sonet, 1973)

South Africans Dyani (bass) and Feza (trumpet) with Turkish Temiz (drums), reminiscent of the best multicultural Don Cherry recordings of the era, some made for the same label. Subtitle: "Universal Folk Sounds Vol. 1."

Experiments in Disintegrating Language / Konkrete Canticle
(Arts Council of Great Britain, 1971)

I bought this British poetry LP for the second side—nutter Bob Cobbing collaborating with Paula Claire and Michael Chant as Konkrete Canticle—but the other side's not bad either.

Pierre Favre Quartett (Wergo, 1970)

Surprisingly released on a contemporary classical label, seminal early Euro free foursome matching the Swiss drummer with saxophonist Evan Parker, bassist Peter Kowald, and pianist Irene Schweizer. An important early Parker release, not so well known. My copy is the 1979 vinyl reissue.

Pierre Favre Trio, *Santana* (Pip, 1968)

Self-produced LP by the same group minus Parker, originally in hand-silkscreened cover, more commonly found as a vinyl reissue on FMP. Swiss-German cooperation, Kowald on the cusp of more distant geographic amblings.

EXPERIMENTS IN DISINTEGRATING LANGUAGE
KONKRETE CANTICLE

The Ferals, *Ruff* (Leo, 1987)

Nucleus of vocalist Phil Minton and percussionist Roger Turner, augmented by madcap trombonist Alan Tomlinson and Hugh Davies on electronics. One of the few LPs on Leo Feigen's label never to have been reissued. Also one of the best.

Alex Foster / John Lewis, *Transaxdrum* (Finite, 1977)

Lovely little self-produced LP of funky, modally oriented saxophone and drum duets featuring the future alto in the house band for *Saturday Night Live*.

Free Music Communion with LaDonna Smith and Davey Williams, *Ham Days* (Fremuco, 1981)

Linchpin on *Ham Days* is bassist Torsten Müller, here playing cello with his trio of Udo Bergner on prepared piano and Herbert Janssen on acoustic guitar, delightfully augmented by Americans Davey Williams on electric guitar and banjo and LaDonna Smith on violin. There's another Free Music Communion LP without Smith and Williams, also worthwhile, but this is the one to find. Plastic dinosaur meets chattering teeth in a dark alley.

Free Music & Orgel (Schwann / AMS Studio, 1969)

My dream of a band with Mats Gustafsson on saxophone and Chris Foreman on Hammond B-3 may not be fully sated with this gift from Mr. Gustafsson, but it sure is a kick in the head. The organ here is church organ, played versus a free jazz quartet with percussionist Pierre Courbois and Peter van der Locht (a bit of a mystery man who appears on three of the LPs in this list!), also featuring spoken word by writers, including Ingeborg Bachmann. Very unusual and hardly ever seen—thanks, Mats.

Free Improvisation (Deutsche Grammophon, 1974)

Took me fifteen years to find this puppy. Deutsche Grammophon, in a moment of open-mindedness, documents three examples of the robust freely improvised music being made in Europe, with the Brit trio Iskra 1903 (Derek Bailey, Paul Rutherford, and Barry Guy), the more classical New Phonic Art 1973 (featuring trombonist Vinko Globokar and clarinetist Michel Portal), and a more drone-oriented group called Wired (featuring sound engineer Conny Plank). One LP for each group.

Diamanda Galas, *Diamanda Galas* (Metalanguage, 1984)

Anyone following Ms. Galas who hasn't heard this is missing the pinnacle of her achievement—terrifying sidelong suites of multitracked vocal hysteria, some hushed, some screeched. On the label run by Larry Ochs of ROVA Saxophone Quartet—thank goodness he put this out.

Griot Galaxy, *Opus Krampus* (Sound Aspects, 1985)

Probably my favorite Detroit creative music LP. Jaribu Shahid on bass and Tani Tabbal on drums, with Anthony Holland and Faruq Z. Bey on reeds, the latter joining the rhythm team on readings. Recorded at the Nickelsdorf Konfrontationen, at the same truck stop town in Austria that was a flash point in the refugee crisis in 2015. In the Art Ensemble mode, but taken its own Motor City direction.

Barry Guy, *statements V–XI for double bass & violone* (Incus, 1977)

First solo outing by the technical brontosaurus of improvised bass; once planned for Unheard Music series, still out of print. Photo on the verso shows Guy playing two basses at once—literally, a double bass concert.

Erhard Hirt, *Zwischen den Pausen* (Uhlklang, 1983)

A really nice solo record by the German electric guitarist, featuring a befuddling cast of crackly, popping sounds. Love the title, which describes the music, as it were, occurring "between the pauses." Uhlklang is another FMP-related imprint.

The Jerry Hahn Quintet, *Ara-be-in* (Changes, 1967)

Despite standard-issue psychedelic San Francisco cover and silly title, this is a strong modally oriented jazz outing produced by Arhoolie Records head Chris Strachwitz, featuring violin and guitar as part of the Coltrane-influenced front line, Jack DeJohnette on drums.

Human Arts Ensemble, *Under the Sun* (Universal Justice, 1974)

Big St. Louis BAG-based group at this time under the leadership of saxophonist James Marshall, with guests from Chicago's AACM and a mysterious Bostonian collective called TSOCC, or The Society of the Creatively Concerned. Very early appearance on alto saxophonist and clarinetist by Marty Ehrlich. My copy is a second edition, but I've never seen a first edition.

Griot Galaxy: Opus Krampus

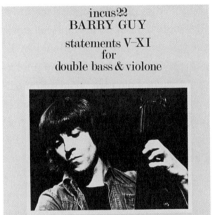

incus22
BARRY GUY

statements V–XI
for
double bass & violone

ERHARD HIRT

GITARRE SOLO

UK2

THE JERRY HAHN QUINTET

ARA BE-IN

STEREO

Under The Sun

Human Arts Ensemble, *Poem of Gratitude* (Universal Justice, 1972)

Another HAE outing led by James Marshall with his wife, Carol, this time as a quartet with Ajule Rutlin on percussion and the Funky Donkey himself, Luther Thomas, on reeds.

Idylle und Katastrophen (Po Torch, 1980)

Among the most monumentally significant LPs of improvised music with text. Sven-Ake Johansson's mutant Swedish-English-German is deliriously off center, countered by an all-star chamber ensemble assembled by pianist Alex Schlippenbach In the midst, the unbreakable Weavers trio of Christmann, Altena, and Lovens. Gorgeous cover drawn by Marina Kern.

Iowa Ear Music (Corn Pride, 1976)

Various artists based at the University of Iowa compiled music they'd recorded between 1967 and 1976, ranging from synthesizer, tape, and electronic music and experimental compositions to more jazz oriented and freely improvised tracks, some featuring brass players Candace Natvig and Jon English, the latter contributing a version of Ornette Coleman's "Lonely Woman" arranged for trombone and Moog. One side, labeled "sidechop," is listed as "documenting 18 formerly secret performances (panidiomatic improvisation)," while "sideflow" more cryptically presents "mandala lifesample." My high school–era guitar teacher, John Leake, is all over side one.

Guus Janssen Septet (Claxon, 1984)

I first heard pianist Janssen as a member of bassist/composer Maarten Altena's groups, and I saw him at the October Meeting in Amsterdam in 1991, which put him squarely in my pantheon. A brilliant, quizzical composer with a dry sense of humor, he's still making great music. This early chamber-like outing is only one of many records on Claxon available only to vinyl freaks, including label chief Altena's worthy output.

Joseph Jarman, *Sunbound* (AECO, 1978)

Putting an ideology of self-production into action, the Art Ensemble of Chicago had its own record label for a while, even at the same time that it was recording for ECM and Atlantic. A Jarman solo is the label's second effort, suitably homespun in packaging and recording. Memorable track title: "Movement for Piano Players on a Break at 1:30 A.M. Saturday Night in a Big City."

Leroy Jenkins and the Jazz Composer's Orchestra, *For Players Only* (JCOA, 1975)
One of several very important JCOA documents that have yet to be dug up, this would be a suitable first step with an incredible eighteen-piece lineup that includes Anthony Braxton, Charles Brackeen, Wadada Leo Smith, Joseph Bowie, Jerome Cooper, and Dave Holland. Not to mention that much of the Jenkins discography has lapsed from public availability.

Mauricio Kagel, *Acustica* (Deutsche Grammophon, 1972)
Composer Kagel's own words summarize *Acustica* perfectly: "the actual invention of the sound-sources: new instruments as self-evident supplement to currently existent sound-makers (together with experimental acoustical equipment, the manipulation of which presupposes a diverse musical faculty)." Double LP with gatefold book including images of twenty-seven of the instruments, including castanet keyboard, stones and pail of water, and gramophone record, knife (pickup), and paper cone (horn).

Toshinori Kondo / Paul Lovens, *The Last Supper* (Po Torch, 1981)
Another of the criminally neglected LPs on Po Torch, the trumpeter and drummer working together with surgical precision on a single piece stretching over two sides. Lovely cover painting by Herbert Bardenheuer.

***Peter Kowald Quintet* (FMP, 1972)**
Among Free Music Production's lost classics, brass-dominated quintet led by the German bassist, with elusive saxophonist Peter van der Locht. The cover is by twelve different nonmusicians, each conscripted by Kowald to contribute an image. Early versions had hand-colored elements and lacked the orange border; mine is a later pressing. Together with Rüdiger Carl Inc.'s *King Alcohol*, one of the most urgently underrecognized LPs in the FMP catalog.

Rolf & Joachim Kühn featuring the European Jazz-Avantgarde-Stars, *Monday Morning* (Hör Zu / Black Label, 1969)
Forays that the Kühn brothers made into free music never flipped my switch so much, but the band on this very scarce LP is too good to ignore, with the British band called the Trio (John Surman on baritone sax, Barre Phillips on bass, and Stu Martin on kit) augmented by Eje Thelin on trombone and second drummer Jacques Thollot. Dopey titles tell Rolf and Joachim's level of commitment: "Black Out," "Strangulation of a Monkey," "Dance of a Spaceman."

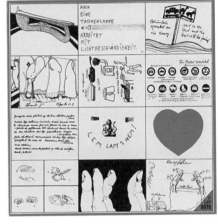

Steve Lacy, *Sortie* (GTA, 1966)

Extremely hard-to-find Lacy recordings from the transitional period between the trio with bassist Kent Carter and drummer Aldo Romano, which
recorded *Disposability*, perhaps Lacy's greatest early record, and the band he
would bring to Buenos Aires with trumpeter Enrico Rava. Lacy is often covered, but nobody tackles tunes from this LP like "Black Elk," "Fork New York,"
or "Living T. Blues."

Steve Lacy, *Points* (Le Chant du Monde, 1978)

There's a plethora of Lacy in the world, but certain LPs stand out, also for the
unfamiliarity of the program. Here the soprano saxophonist plays Ellington
as well as a suite of "point"-titled tunes performed by his group (Carter on
bass, Steve Potts on soprano, Oliver Johnson on drums) but without Irene
Aebi. The lineup appears on a gold sticker on the back cover, suggesting that
the label, mostly an ethnographic music outlet, forgot to list it.

Landelijk Vietnamkomitee, *Voor de Overwinning van de Vietnamese Revolutie* (LVK, circa 1970)

An explicitly political Dutch artifact, alternating proclamations and chamber-
folk arrangements of Vietnamese songs, featuring a few luminaries from the
improvised music world, such as trombonist Willem van Manen and clarinetist/
saxophonist Willem Breuker. I got my copy from Breuker on my only visit to
his house, during which he showed me the original cardboard punch cards
for *Lunchconcert for Three Barrelorgans* (1969), the third release on ICP.

Anne LeBaron / LaDonna Smith / Davey Williams, *Jewels* (trans museq, 1979)

Plenty left to excavate on Smith and Williams's own label, run out of their
Birmingham, Alabama, home base, including this trio with harpist extraor-
dinaire LeBaron. Williams's solo *Criminal Pursuits* and the brilliant Smith/
Williams duet *Direct Waves* are also ripe for rediscovery. On the Unheard
Music series, I reissued their quartet with Torsten Müller and Günter Christmann, *White Earth Streak*. The entire trans museq catalog is mandatory independent American music.

Le Forte Four, *Spin 'n Grin* (LAFMS, 1981)

Much of the vinyl associated with the Los Angeles Free Music Society, clustered around the Cal Arts community of twisted soundmakers, has remained in the dark, including this slab of giddy wack featuring recordings made from 1974 to 1978, as well as a 1963 recording of Le Forte Four members Joe and Rick Potts's grandfather telling a joke.

Peter Lerner Quintet, *Local Colour* (ESP, 1968)

Always fun to find a record on ESP that you've never heard, like this British free jazz led by pianist Lerner, with John Surman and Nisar Ahmad Khan on saxophones. The Carla Bley standard "Ictus" kicks it off. Good choice.

John Lindberg, *Haunt of the Unresolved* (Nato, 1983)

I'd totally lost track of this little diamond of a trio, released on the French Nato label, perhaps because of the ghastly cover. Lindberg is one of the most consistently great figures in creative music, here with Marty Ehrlich on clarinets and Hugh Ragin on trumpet and piccolo trumpet.

Frank Lowe, *Doctor Too-Much* (Kharma, 1977)

Oh yes, one of the real great unknown LPs, tenor saxophonist Lowe's sensationally gritty session with twin trumpets (Olu Dara and Wadada Leo Smith), Fred Williams on bass, and the monster Philip Wilson on drums. All the way wonderful, right down to the badass cover.

L.S.-F.M., *Adonis* (jnd, 1984)

Greek reed player Floris Floridis released a few lovelies with drummer Paul Lytton, bassist Hans Schneider, and tuba player Pinguin Moschner. I dig Floridis's hieroglyphic cover design.

Michael Lytle / George Cartwright, *Bright Bank Elewhale* (Corn Pride East, 1979)

Lytle studied electronic music at the University of Iowa, hence the Corn Pride connection. He was also an experienced clarinet improvisor, and together with saxophonist Cartwright made a few great records, including this more obscure one and two with a variable lineup they called Mutable Snaps It. A couple of tracks are available for streaming on a digital album titled *Early Duets*.

Paul Lytton / Paul Lovens, *Moinho da Asneira • À Cerca de Bela Vista à Graça*
(Po Torch, 1980)

A two-person Po Torch percussion summit, refined and ragged, energies meted out like a montage of miniature fireworks. The original bucketheads.

Radu Malfatti / Harry Miller, *Bracknell Breakdown* (Ogun, 1978)

Trombone and bass, from a time when Malfatti, now reserved beyond noise-makery, was still squeaking and belching in public. One of the great self-deprecating titles adorns side one: "The Audient Stood on Its Foot."

Christian Marclay, *Record without a Cover* (Recycled, 1985)

No way to reissue this digitally, given the concept that the inevitable scratches are a welcome part of the music. Mine also has a little yellow price sticker—five dollars—proudly stuck to the grooves in the same way Marclay uses stickers to prompt skips when he's playing turntables.

Marcel Duchamp Memorial Players, *MDMP*
(Marcel Duchamp Memorial Players, 1985)

Vintage experimental music from Chicago, featuring Mark Konewko on keyboards, James Gailloreto and Nettie McCortney on reeds, and John McCortney as engineer. DX7, gongs, log drums, and an instrument of their own devising called the "stroke rod." John was a close colleague of mine, recording countless improvised music projects at his AirWave Studios in the '90s, also helping unravel many mysteries in the Alton Abraham / Sun Ra tape archives.

Milk Teeth, *A Touch of the Sun* (Bead, 1975)

The very first Bead record is humbly magnificent, Peter Cusack's guitar and Simon Mayo's clarinets all splinters and scrap metal. An unsung watershed of British improvised music.

J.R. Monterose, *Is Alive in Amsterdam* (Heavy Soul Music, 1969)

One of the strongest tenor saxophonists of the '50s, Monterose is an important but often overlooked voice on his instrument. This rare LP, produced by fellow hornman Hans Dulfer, finds J.R. in dialogue with drummer Han Bennink on the first side, the second adding bass and more percussion (as if you need that with Bennink!).

MOINHO DA ASNEIRA · À CERCA DA BELA VISTA À GRAÇA
LYTTON & LOVENS

radu malfatti   harry miller   bracknell breakdown

Ogun

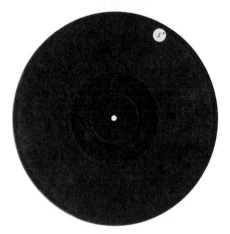

MDMP

MARCEL DUCHAMP MEMORIAL PLAYERS

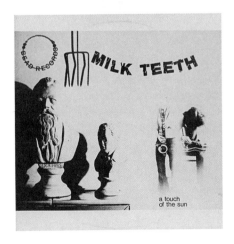

BEAD RECORDS

MILK TEETH

a touch
of the sun

JR
monterose
is
alive
in
amsterdam   paradiso
HSM 1502

Sunny Murray (Shandar, 1968)

With the uptick in interest in free jazz, it's a surprise that all the records of late '60s Americans in Paris have not resurfaced, but quite a few are still in the predigital dungeon. Drummer Murray's live recording with a French group is as woolly as you'd expect, the second side dominated by "The Stroller," a poem by Hart Leroy Bibbs, read dramatically by its author.

Bobby Naughton, *Nature's Consort* (Otic, 1969)

The profusion of activity in Connecticut during the 1970s was suggested by Wadada Leo Smith's Kabell records, presaged by this self-production by Smith collaborator Bobby Naughton, here playing piano and electric piano, with a scrumptious rhythm section of Mario Pavone on bass and Laurence Cook on percussion, and Mark Whitecage on winds. A particularly scrappy two-color silkscreen adorns the front, mimeographed page with credits pasted onto the reverse. Record as broadside.

Al Neil, *Boot and Fog* (Music Gallery Editions, 1980)

One of the oddest of my holdings, also a favorite, by the Vancouver pianist, writer, and artist. If Per Henrik Wallin was a Swedish Misha Mengelberg, Neil is a Canadian Per Henrik Wallin. Which is just to say he's a wonderfully casual post-Monk keyboardist, but add a pataphysical predisposition for nonsense utterance, sometimes served over prerecorded tape.

The New Acoustic Swing Duo, *In Japan 1984* (Jazz + Now, 1987)

Percussion mayhem from Han Bennink, tandem with saxophonist and erstwhile Instant Composers Pool founder Willem Breuker. Bennink, one of the greatest designers of LP covers, is in rare form. Hearty and hard to find.

Bengt Nordström, *Natural Music* (Bird Notes, 1968)

Meaningless (Blue Tower, 2003) is a CD comp of Swedish outsider saxophonist Bengt "Frippe" Nordström's group recordings from the '60s, but his self-produced LP, edition of one hundred, hasn't been reissued. He's best known for releasing (on the same label) the first Albert Ayler LP, which he recorded, unbidden. Frippe reused this cover for a dozen or so LPs made in minuscule editions, sometimes unique.

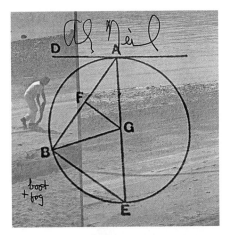

Charles K. Noyes, *The World and the Raw People* (Zoar, 1982)

In its day, one of my favorite American improvised music LPs. Featured collaborators include trumpeter Lesli Dalaba, saxophonist John Zorn, and guitarist Henry Kaiser. Great quotations on the back cover include this one from Anthony Wilden: "Language takes time, but for the child, crying says everything all at once."

Charles K. Noyes / Owen Maercks, *Free Mammals* (Visible, 1979)

I'm always a fan of the zoological cover. Here there are bats aplenty suggesting sonar, amply evidenced by small groups with drummer Noyes and guitarist Maercks, joined by Kaiser and Bay Area pianist Greg Goodman, an unsung hero.

***Oahspe* (Auricle, 1978)**

Collective trio of Ray Anderson (trombone), Mark Helias (bass), and Gerry Hemingway (drums), later known as BassDrumBone. First record, more evidence of the fertile New Haven scene.

Tony Oxley / Alan Davie, *The Tony Oxley Alan Davie Duo* (ADMW, 1975)

Davie is best known as one of the masters of Scottish contemporary painting, but he's also a multi-instrumentalist, rarely enough heard, here in a private issue long player with Brit drummer Oxley.

Evan Parker, *At the Finger Palace* (The Beak Doctor, 1980)

Perhaps the most important solo improvised reed record that's never been reissued, a monumental technical and creative achievement showcasing Parker's one-man/one-horn band, circular breathed and Gatling gun fingered. Released on pianist Greg Goodman's label.

Tom Phillips, *Words and Music* (Edition Hansjorg Mayer, 1975)

The artist whose ongoing project *A Humament* has intervened in and overpainted pages from a Victorian novel, some of which are read here, along with excerpts from Phillips's opera *Irma*, performed by pianist John Tilbury. Tiny art-house edition of important British poetry and music.

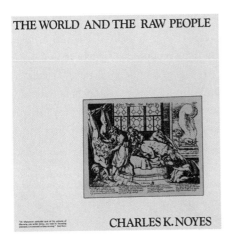

THE WORLD AND THE RAW PEOPLE

CHARLES K. NOYES

FREE MAMMALS

CHARLES K. NOYES
AND
OWEN MAERCKS

WITH
HENRY KAISER
AND
GREG GOODMAN

VISIBLE VS6791

OAHSPE

ray   mark   gerry
anderson   helias   hemingway

AURICLE RECORDS   AUR-2

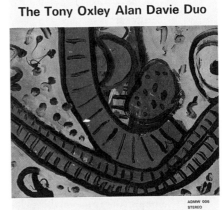

The Tony Oxley Alan Davie Duo

ADMW 006
STEREO

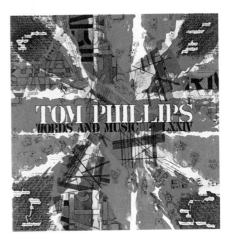

TOM PHILLIPS
WORDS AND MUSIC LXXIV

Picnic (Data, 1985)

Self-titled Dutch monster, with marvelous songs by cellist Tristan Honsinger, featuring trumpeter Toshinori Kondo (who recorded songfully several times with Honsinger, all worth seeking), late tenor Sean Bergin, singer Tiziana Simona, bassist Jean-Jacques Avenel, and drummer Michael Vatcher. I've said it before, but "Restless" has my favorite snare sound captured on vinyl. By the time you read this, Corbett vs. Dempsey will have reissued it.

Planet Oeuf (Xopf, 1985)

Swiss electroacoustic improvised music with invited guest Phil Wachsmann on fiddle. A microcosm squirming and jostling with life, hence the appropriate name: Planet Egg.

Les Oubliés de Jazz Ensemble, *"That" Nigger Music!* (Touché, 1973)

Really seriously hard-core Los Angeles free jazz, as offensive as possible, conceived and conducted by drummer Smiley Winters, with fellow Angeleans Sonny Simmons on saxophones and Barbara Donald on trumpet. I bet bassist Ray Drummond doesn't list this on his cv!

Cleve Pozar, *Solo Percussion* (CSP, 1974)

Enigmatic percussionist who played on two early Bob James records and Bill Dixon's seminal *Intents & Purposes*, then went on to fabricate a whole universe of music of his own, recording this outsider masterpiece for drum kit, marimba, vibraphone, self-made percussion, and loops on an Echoplex. Entirely unique concept, something close in feel to Harry Partch but incorporating jazz, Latin, and even rock elements.

Pygmy Unit, *Signals from Earth* (no label, 1974)

Massively rare private issue LP by a San Francisco group of multi-instrumentalist Darrell De Vore and percussionist Terry Wilson, with various others, including, on side two, tenor saxophonist Jim Pepper. Echoed-out horns and synthesizer wash over more abrasive textures, an overall vibe that would perhaps have been called "trippy" or "spacey." One side is labeled "Traditional," the other "Primitive"—with the more unusual sounds coming on the latter. Magnificent down-home package, with tipped-on cover drawing and a pamphlet with notes and more drawings. I found mine at the selectively stocked Stranded record shop in Oakland.

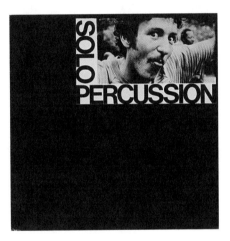

Tom Raworth, *Little Trace Remains of Emmett Miller* (Stream, 1969)

Raworth is paramount among poets who read their own work, precisely because he lets the language do its own thing, leaving out inflection and reciting at a blistering pace that evinces the words' inherent rhythm-a-ning. A very rare early LP.

The Recedents, *Barbecue Strut* (Nato, 1986)

Named because they all had waning hairlines, the Recedents were Lol Coxhill (sweet brilliant nut, RIP) on saxes and voice, Roger Turner on percussives, and Mike Cooper on guitar. Many of the best records on the French label Nato have yet to be reissued. A nice place to start if you've never heard free improvisation and you appreciate wry humor.

Dewey Redman, *Look for the Black Star* (Black Lion, 1975)

You didn't have to look further than this record to find the black star that was Dewey Redman. Celebratory live recording from San Francisco in 1966, a sense of wild abandon within rather straightforward formal limits, with Redman vocalizing onto, into, and around his tenor saxophone. Donald Raphael Garrett is on bass (and clarinet), circa his stint with Coltrane.

Hans Reichel, *Wichlinghauser Blues* (FMP, 1973)

The German guitarist and instrument maker, who died in 2011, age sixty-two, early in his extraordinary career, thoroughly exploring an eleven-string/three-pickup instrument of his own design. For its onomatopoeia, a favorite title for me, as ex-guitarist: "Krampfhandlungen."

Ernst Reijseger, *Taiming* (Hummeloord, 1980)

Dutch cellist solo program of shorties, some mining folkish tunes, some scrape 'n' blurt. One track duet with Alan "Gunga" Purves, the Scottish drummer, and side B featuring Reijseger, saxophonist/clarinetist Michael Moore, and drummer Han Bennink. First recording of the group that would later become the Clusone Trio.

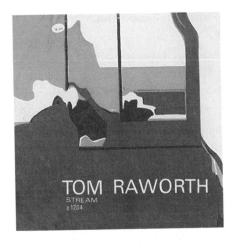

The Revolutionary Ensemble, *The People's Republic* (A&M, 1975)

Absolutely mandatory music from the '70s, from a moment that a handful of producers—John Snyder and Ed Michel in this case—were sneaking very outré recordings onto major labels. The Revolutionary Ensemble discography is mostly an LP game—many, including *The Psyche*, released in the same year on their own RE imprint, are very hard to find, but *The People's Republic* is relatively easy. Leroy Jenkins (violin), Sirone (bass), and Jerome Cooper (drums)—the whole band has passed away. Suitable memorial would be the reissue of this masterwork.

Bernt Rosengren med flera, *Improvisationer* (SJR, 1969)

Swedish jazz in the Don Cherry era on the cusp of opening even wider, Rosengren and frequent partner Tommy Koverhult on tenor saxes, playing Monk and Miles on the first side, transitioning to a suite of originals and Ornette tunes, then flip to find two Turkish melodies by trumpeter Maffy Falay, who joins the leader.

Dieter Roth / Gerhard Rühm / Oswald Wiener, *3. Berliner Dichter Workshop*
(Edition Hansjorg Mayer, 1973)

The great artist and adventurous soundmaker in collaboration with two artist friends. Tip of the iceberg in terms of collectable Roth records, including almost unlistenable box sets featuring the all-stars of Viennese Actionism. I have most of them, but my copy of this one is the more generic (edition of one thousand), not one of the one hundred that came signed and numbered with an original graphic by the threesome.

U.S. Steel Cello Ensemble, *Rutman: Sounds of Nothing*
(Art Supermarket, 1976)

Oh, how I love this record. Robert Rutman fabricated steel instruments in Cambridge, Massachusetts, including a single-string stainless steel cello and bow chimes, which is a curved six-foot piece of stainless with rods attached to a crossbar, played with a bow. Rich, dirty drones are the order of the day, with Indian singer Kalpana Mazumder joining for a garage raga. Private issue (blank inner labels). Only ever seen the copy I own. Nice feature: the LP is extracted from the *bottom* of the cover.

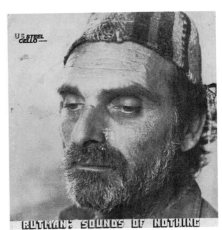

Mario Schiano & Tommaso Vittorini, *Swimming Pool Orchestra*
(Dischi Della Quercia, 1980)

The Italian free music scene was inspired by the eclecticism, theatricality, and humor of the Dutch improvisors, so records by saxophonist Mario Schiano (1933–2008) are all multifarious and entertaining. With multi-instrumentalist Vittorini, he plays a wild and wooly mix, including "Gee Baby Ain't I Good to You" and quotes from "My Funny Valentine" and "Just Friends," but includes weird songs like "Globe Me or Glub Me" and a piece for magnetic tape and voice that features legendary Italian actor Trottolino. Many of Schiano's up-roarious records (this was his nineteenth LP) are out-of-print collector's items.

Jamil Shabaka / Alex Cline, *Duo Infinity* (Aten, 1977)

Not a household name, even in free music households, saxophonist Shabaka made this beautiful record with fellow Californian Cline, spectral hues from the percussionist on dedications to Eric Dolphy and Sun Ra. Cover image by the drummer, printed by master printmaker Jacob Samuel.

Sirone, *Artistry* (OTC, 1978)

Such a lost treasure, the bassist's recording with James Newton on flute, Muneer Bernard Fennell on cello, and Don Moyé on drums. Cool cover with tipped-on corrugated cardboard frame, liner notes by Stanley Crouch, before the opening bell in New York's jazz wars had been sounded.

Michael Snow, *Musics for Piano, Whistling, Microphone and Tape Recorder*
(Chatham Square, 1975)

Renowned Canadian artist and musician Snow's work always attends to the medium at hand—if he makes a film, it's meant to be seen as such, same with videos, holograms, and, when he made LPs they need to be vinyl. This incredible double-record set is covered front to back and interior with text, Snow's liner notes, which start with his name the size of a headline and pro-ceed to diminish until on the back cover they're tiny. No way to translate this perfectly designed object into a CD or digital download, not to mention the music, which is extreme and rigorous and suitably structural to have come from one of the progenitors of structural film.

STEREO LP 1008/10
CHATHAM SQUARE

MICHAEL SNOW
MUSICS FOR PIANO, WHISTLING
MICROPHONE AND TAPE RECORDER

My first consideration in writing the text which you are now, I presume, reading ("presume": I guess that this text will still be here to read later even if you aren't reading it now) was to write something which when printed would cover all four faces of this album. Of several ideas for a design for this album cover or jacket this seemed at the time to be the best. Remains to be seen. Ruminations gradually clarified to this stage: I would write something that would fulfill several requirements, the basic one being that it function as a "design" or "image" that would be both decorative and "plastic". Another requirement that might better be approached now as an intention or ambition was the image

Sogenanntes Linksradikales Blasorchester, *Mit Gelben Birnen*
(Trikont Unsere Stimme, 1980)

Borrowing and updating sensibility from Kurt Weill and Hans Eisler, the "so-called left-wing radical brass orchestra" features young comrades Heiner Goebbels and Alfred Harth in marches and political tunes from Bach to Sun Ra, the latter a clear inspiration. Came packaged with a full-fledged newspaper tucked in the cover as credits—very authentic agitprop accoutrement.

Synthesis, *Sentiments* (RA, 1979)

A vanity production by drummer Rahsaan, who is otherwise completely unknown, here assembling an incredible band with Arthur Blythe and David Murray on saxes and Olu Dara on trumpet. Easily overlooked, but a fiery and fulfilling slab of vinyl.

Cecil Taylor Unit, *Spring of Two Blue-J's* (Unit Core, 1974)

One of the few records to appear on the pianist's short-lived label—half solo, the other quartet with Jimmy Lyons, Sirone, and Andrew Cyrille, dedicated to then recently deceased Ben Webster. Back cover contains a long poem by C.T. in his own handwriting.

Clifford Thornton / The Jazz Composer's Orchestra, *The Gardens of Harlem*
(JCOA, 1975)

Another figure whose thin discography distorts his real significance, Thornton was invited to lead the JCOA in his major suite delving into African and black Latin musics. Gorgeous, majestic, intricate, with cameos by Dewey Redman, Carla Bley, Wadada Leo Smith, and Pat Patrick.

Clifford Thornton, *The Panther and the Lash* (America, 1970)

Very different session featuring an aggressive French quartet engaged in a radical Afrocentric vibe. Though much of the America free jazz catalog was reissued, this one remains a highly sought after LP. Thornton is required listening for any Joe McPhee fan.

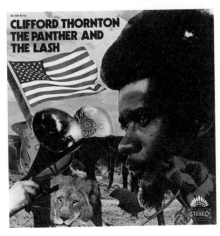

Toshi Tsuchitori, *First Solo / Drumythm* (DYM, 1978)

Warm polyrhythmic outing from Milford Graves acolyte Tsuchitori, recorded in Paris, beautiful drawings and collage cover by the drummer, extraordinarily rare. From the back cover: "This concert was one hour half, I've been play continuously in this time, sound was flowing, energy was flowing, but I have to cut this stream because of limitation for this record."

Text Sound Compositions 5 (Fylkingen, 1969)

One of a series of super sound poetry collections issued by the Swedish audio art institution Fylkingen, this one featuring Bob Cobbing (a fave of mine, you'll have noticed), along with the extraordinary Ilmar Laaban, important concrete poet Bengt Emil Johnsson, early computer poet Christer Hennix Lille, Czech tape collage artist Ladislav Novák, and Flemish nonsense poet Gust Gils.

Luther Thomas, *11th Street Fire Suite* (Creative Consciousness, 1978)

A pair of St. Louis Black Artist Group (BAG) musicians transplanted to New York, recording blues-inflected skronk for alto saxophone (Thomas) and flute (Luther C. Petty). I intend to reissue this one on Corbett vs. Dempsey; Luther gave me the master tape years ago for just that purpose, at the time that I reissued his free-soul throw-down *Funky Donkey*.

David Toop / Paul Burwell, *Wounds* (Quartz, 1979)

Two of the kingpins of '70s British improvised music, playing all sorts of instruments, mostly spread out on the floor of the London Musicians Collective. Some say you have to be there to enjoy this kind of music. Bosh. I am forever in awe of records like this, defying any and all market logic, fiercely declaring their independence. It's a rare LP that has this kind of ramshackle integrity.

François Tusques, *Intercommunal Music* (Shandar, 1971)

Politically charged music from Paris, three years after the student uprising, featuring "les forces progressistes" on side A and "les forces Réactionnaires" on side B. Pianist Tusques was an important bridge to New Thing jazz, on this date bringing together drummer Sunny Murray, bassist Alan Silva, trumpeter Alan Shorter (who recorded only a few times), and saxophonist Steve Potts.

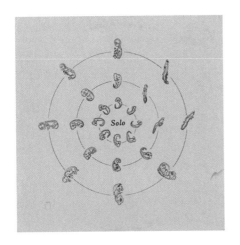

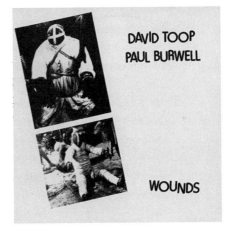

Roger Turner, *The Blur Between* (CAW, 1981)

Wizard-like minimal percussion by Turner, a rare solo from the Brit whose duets with singer Phil Minton are among the top improvised music records of the '80s. CAW also put out a nice trio with Turner, trumpeter Toshinori Kondo, and guitarist John Russell.

Charles Tyler Ensemble, *Voyage from Jericho* (Ak-Ba, 1975)

Saxophonist Tyler was a mainstay when I first started listening to creative music in the late '70s, but most of his music has fallen out of print, and you know the saying—out of print, out of mind. Heartfelt, rough-hewn compositions by the leader, with Sun Ra bassist Ronnie Boykins, trumpeter Earl Cross, drummer Steve Reid, and Arthur Blythe guesting on alto on two cuts. Self-produced.

James Blood, *Tales of Captain Black* (Artist House, 1978)

I'll freely admit that I bought this because it looked like a Funkadelic record. The comic cover art by Shelby McPherson places James Blood (Ulmer) in a superhero role, swooping in to rescue the bodacious damsel from a wicked city populated by sleazy go-go dancers and British guitarists. Released on Ornette Coleman's label, it contains one of the pinnacle programs of harmolodic music, with members of OC's Prime Time—Jaamaladeen Tacuma on slippery electric bass, Denardo Coleman on irregular beats, Coleman on soaring alto, Blood on slashing hollow-body guitar. Inconceivable that it's never been digitized.

Edward Vesala Trio, *Nana* (Blue Master, 1970)

Finnish drummer Vesala's meeting with saxophonist Juhanni Aaltonen and bassist Arild Andersen, long sought by me after hearing it at saxophonist Lars-Goran Uhlander's place in Saxnäs, Sweden, finally in the collection (with a dupe, just to be safe!), great pre-ECM Scandinavian jazz not unlike the early Jan Garbarek masterworks. Tried hard to reissue this once, worked with Vesala, who died midstream in 1999. Pursued posthumous release to no avail. Would still love to. Delicious cover.

Vienna Jazz Avantgarde (WM Produktion, 1971)

You'd expect the free music that comes from the land of Actionism to be pretty excruciating, and you'd be right. Not that they're extreme the way that Herman Nitsch, Günter Brus, and Otto Mühl were, but they're quite *off*. This roundup features two bands: the Masters of Unorthodox Jazz (for real, that's their name) and the Reform Art Unit. I've also got the latter's *Darjeeling*, which invites sitarist Ram Chandra to join the ensemble, but I'm still seeking the Masters' *Overground*, which sports an Arnulf Rainer drawing on the cover. Speaking of cover images, dig Franz Ringel's totally fucked portrait.

Phil Wachsmann, *Writing in Water* (Bead, 1985)

Radiant, unaccompanied improvisations by British violinist Wachsmann, son of a famous ethnomusicologist, bringer of gentle electronics and woody resonance. Another more-than-worthy Bead.

Marzette Watts, *Marzette and Company* (ESP, 1966)

Much-discussed free jazz LP from the heart of the New York scene. For me, "Backdrop for Urban Revolution," which takes up all of the first side, is as pivotal as most other ESP discs, Clifford Thornton's trombone and Byard Lancaster's and Watts's reeds elbowing their way through a dense wall of noise perpetrated by bassist Juney Booth, vibraphonist Karl Berger, drummer J. C. Moses, and guitarist Sonny Sharrock. Yes, the lineup is just that martial. Don't stop looking till you find it.

Lawrence Weiner, 7 (Yvon Lambert, 1972)

Conceptual artist Weiner's outstanding, mega-scarce LP of text recitations, repetitive and revelatory. On side A Weiner describes the seven notes of a scale ("A middle C sharpened carried done again perhaps not in the sequence stated"), while Pierre-Yves Artaud follows the instruction. Side B features a translation into French.

James Zitro, *Zitro* (ESP, 1967)

A nice off-the-beaten-track ESP LP, noteworthy as an excuse to talk about unheralded tenor saxophonist Bert Wilson, whose record *Now* on Arhoolie I'm still trying to track down. Wilson is a figure we should know more about, based on his outstanding performance on *Zitro* and another Arhoolie record, the Smiley Winters twofer *Smiley Etc.*

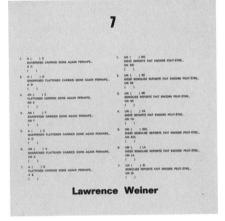

Anything Can Happen Day: Sun Ra, Alton Abraham, and the Taming of the Freak

By the time I stumbled to the phone, the machine had already picked up. "Rise and shine, sweetheart," crowed a chirpy electronic voice. "Day's getting old!" I interrupted the message, the receiver's hovering proximity to the transmitter instigating a brief convulsion of feedback, before switching the answering machine to "off" and murmuring hello to Vic. "It's now or never," he said. Still dazed, dopey from painkillers, I forced out a question: "OK, wow, that's kind of a big surprise, so what's the plan?" Vic seemed to have been awake for hours and mainlining caffeine. He spoke with flickering intensity: "Today is anything can happen day. Be ready to go in twenty minutes. I'll pick you up at your place." I registered assent. Vic punctuated the call's end with: "We ride!"

It was just after sunrise on a warmish September morning. I was decked out in Chinese silk pajama bottoms. Pulling them out by the elastic band in front, I examined the gauze pad, which had seeped a little with blood and pus in the night. Slipping into a T-shirt and tennis shoes, I splashed cold water on my face, kissed my sleeping wife, grabbed the vial of drugs, and set out for points south, the far South Side of the city that hugs the contour of the lake, into a neighborhood I'd never seen, the home of a man I'd known a little, about a stash of historically invaluable stuff he and I had once discussed. He'd been dead for more than a year.

Three months earlier, on a griddle-hot July afternoon, I'd been sitting in my un-air-conditioned home office, tooling around on e-mail, which then took what now seems an unacceptably long time to load. Among the new messages that oozed its way onscreen was one interestingly headed: "Emergency!!! Sun Ra's Home in Peril!!!!" It had been forwarded twice, once from

Mike Watt, bassist of fIREHOSE and the Minutemen, and then from an acquaintance of mine who knew about my abiding interest in Ra. The e-mail's source had been shed in the process of forwarding, but its contents gave a few details: Sun Ra's home in Chicago was being vacated and all his possessions were being thrown into the trash; could anybody help?; if so please write back to Mike. Somewhere in the message, the sender mentioned a film festival and her own name, which was Heather.

It wasn't Ra's house. I knew that because he'd left his Chicago apartment in 1961. But the hidden meaning of Heather's message was clear to me. Alton Abraham, Ra's first major supporter and his manager in the '50s and '60s, continuing piecemeal for decades after, had died nine months earlier. It was Alton's place. I remembered having thought to myself at the time I heard of his death about the mountain of materials he'd told me about—instruments, writings, tapes, documents. I had suggested finding a place to safeguard and archive these precious objects, and he agreed, charging me with finding the right institution. I'd made inquiries, tried to interest the few folks I knew who worked in those sorts of places, but got nowhere. Funny to think from this vantage, but a houseful of Sun Ra ephemera was not, in 2000, considered culturally significant enough to merit the cost of being stored.

Alton's death gave me first pause to think about the fate of these things. After consideration, I decided that there were plenty of people to attend to them, someone certainly would, if nobody else then Abraham's loyal sidekick, James Bryant. So I let it drop. These months later, sweating onto my keyboard, once again I had the same thought: surely there's somebody working on this already, at least from the thousand people who must have gotten the Watt S.O.S. My fingers assumed position to delete the e-mail. But just before I let them follow through, I was seized with doubt. What if nobody's on it? What then? Where will all that shit land? I reopened the message, jotted down the name Heather, and dialed the office of the Chicago International Film Festival.

A few moments later, I was speaking with Heather. She'd only sent the e-mail to her friend Mike half an hour earlier, and I was the first one to contact her, so she was flustered and a little wary. I briefly introduced myself, told her that I'd written about Ra, had spent some time with him on several occasions. She asked if I was free that night, said that she was busy with work. I said yes. "Meet us at the California Clipper," she said.

"Us?" I said.

"Yeah, there's three of us. Can you be there around eight?" We agreed and hung up. I thought for a minute about the insane speed of today's information superhighway, some idea like that, long since made quaint by the hyperbolic curve that technology's speed has followed in these intervening years. Amused, not thinking too much of it, I went about my day.

The California Clipper was dark and empty. A brown bar-back with ornamental detail occupied one side of the space, and a small stage with red velvet curtains sat unused in a corner. I arrived first. After a short wait at the front of the tavern, the door swung open and three young women stepped in. One introduced herself as Heather. The others gave their names, and we wound around to a rear booth, the three of them setting up on one side, me on the other, like a tribunal. I had not noticed the banker's box carried by one of the women, but after a slightly more involved round of introductions, Heather pulled something from inside the cardboard container at her feet and said: "What can you tell us about *this*?"

It was a shallow wooden block with a swath of metal affixed to one side. A print plate. I felt its weight in my hands, spelled out the words backward, controlled my excitement, and said: "This is what they used to print the record cover for *Other Planes of There*, which came out in the mid-1960s." I put it down. "I know you think this comes from Sun Ra's house, but it doesn't. If you look, you'll find some of what you have has the name Alton Abraham on it." The three women looked incredulously at one another; one reached into the box and put an envelope on the table.

Heather said: "How'd you know?" I examined the envelope, which was addressed to Abraham, the return address: Sun Ra in New York City.

"I knew Alton. He passed away a while back. They must have sold his house." They pulled more items from the box, and I identified them and gave a little lecture on each one, puffed up with the thrill of the moment. A note from Ra to Alton discussing possible record covers. The original drawing for the cover of *Discipline 27-II*. Assorted sketches with Ra and the Arkestra spelled out on them. A couple of record covers with space themes. I remembered the last meeting I'd had with Abraham, at Valois, the diner in Hyde Park with the greatest motto: "See Your Food." We had chummed around talking nonsense as if we'd been buddies—his voice so deep and cavernous it seemed to come from somewhere inside his large frame rather than his throat. I sensed a longing for camaraderie that might not be so alien to the predisposed loner.

"This is so incredible. You don't know how outrageously important this stuff is," I said, returning to the print block. "It took me five years of hunting just to find a finished copy of this record with an offset cover, and then I had to pay two hundred dollars for it, it's that rare. And here we are looking at the printmaking device that they used to hand-make the initial pressing in Alton's makeshift basement facility." I straightened up. "The history of DIY music production, the lost early logbook of the most important jazz big-band leader since the 1960s, one of the great visionary artists of all time. This is the root of it all!" The box emptied, we sat looking at its contents as a delayed round of drinks finally arrived.

"A friend of mine is a picker," said Heather. "He knows everything going on demolition-wise on the South and West Sides, and when something's being torn down or emptied out, they know where to find him. He got a call to salvage this place, but there wasn't anything valuable in his eyes, no modernist furniture or cool old fixtures, so he declined. Knowing that I liked spacey stuff and weird kitschy images from the '50s, he bought a handful of things from them and gave me my pick of the litter. I saw it and flipped out because I knew it was Sun Ra and I knew we had to save it."

Heather sipped her drink, and one of the other women spoke. "We sent out the e-mail, and here you are, as if we had called you. Or sent up smoke signals."

"What do you intend to do with it?" I asked.

"None of us has the expertise or inclination to do much of anything with it. That's why we went looking for the right person. Seems like you're the right person."

"I would be honored. The main thing would be to keep the bulk of it together. Break it up, and each part doesn't mean as much. I'll pledge to do right by it, whatever that ends up meaning." I leaned back, contemplating the most outrageous single acquisition that I would ever make with an unwarranted sense of circumspection. I still had no idea where this would go. I was pleased that I had not hit delete.

Heather selected a single object from the pile and said: "I want to keep one thing. Nothing too important, but a souvenir to remember this."

Sensing the end of the inquisition, the third woman moved to my side of the booth and proposed a toast: "To Sun Ra, wherever he now resides."

A few days later, I was in Vic Biancalana's backyard. Mats Gustafsson, the Swedish saxophonist, friend, and fellow record fiend, was in town for a gig, and he accompanied me on the visit. After hellos, during which we learned a little more about our host's work, including his greatest prize, which was vintage stained glass and historical terra-cotta, we retired to Vic's garage, where he storehoused and assessed his scavengings.

I liked Vic at once. Shortish and solid in stature, he was coarse, tough, and charming and spoke with an unrelenting Chicago accent: a working-class Italian American guy who panned the grounds of the city's once-opulent-now-destitute neighborhoods as their edifices were crumbling. He had a gentle smile cocked to one side, the genial hustler, and he spoke of things he would sell and ones he might keep for himself based on his wife's predilections. "She's the boss," he said, tongue only partly in cheek. From the lilting way he talked about his job, I got a feeling from him that Vic and I were of the same school of thought about material culture. We were both zealots of stuff.

Momentarily distracted by a pile of seven-inch records—Vic offhandedly told us we could have any of them we wanted—we surrounded a big olive-colored chest. "This is what I got," he said, pulling open the top and revealing a small container full of Ra paraphernalia on a par with but more bountiful than the Clipper unveiling. Mats and I rifled through the things, holding back gasps and shrieks as we uncovered more print blocks, El Saturn Records press releases from the '50s, and a business card for the Cosmic Rays, one of the vocal groups that Ra coached.

"Heather mentioned that you turned down a full-on salvage," I said. "What are the chances of you reconnecting? You think the house has already been emptied?"

"I drove by the other day, and it's as was," said Vic. "I don't know if she got someone else working on it, but I can try to find out. Might not be easy, though. One thing them asking you, another you asking them."

"How much for everything in this box?" I asked. We settled on a price; I cut him a check and loaded it into my car. Vic said he'd work on being in touch with the woman who was selling the house.

"It's been sitting there empty for a year, so we may have a little time. But if it's already sold, maybe they need to be out. We'll know soon enough."

Six months earlier, on the racquetball court with my cousin Tim, I had noticed a bulge in my shorts. Ignoring it for as long as possible, I had the hernia diagnosed and fretted about it endlessly, as only a good Eastern European boy can, ultimately by pretending it didn't exist. By the time of my initial meeting with Vic, the little inguinal bugger had become a pest. Weeks passed. I imagined that Vic would call and soon we'd be on a big haul, which gave me a great excuse to put it off. Every few days, I'd check in, and he would tell me he was working on it. I drove to his house a few times to look at other scores, some cool Prairie School chairs, a set of terra-cotta lions he'd extracted from the top of a building. The latter he was forced to give up by an alderman who threatened to shut him down if he didn't put them on her front lawn overnight. The island of misfit toys or the mafia of reclamation—sometimes it was hard to tell them apart.

Wondering about the potential contents of the house, I called an East Coast record producer I knew who had dealt with Alton. He said he hadn't heard anything about Alton's place being cleared out. "Anyway, it's nothing, I'm sure," he said.

"Nothing? You don't even want to check to make sure that important historical material isn't being trashed?"

"Let me make a few calls," he said. A week later, I called again. "I checked and it's nothing, it's *shit*. Nothing but forty years of junk, no tapes, nothing significant. Shit shit shit. Nothing but shit, you hear?"

I let his weird rant die out. "Yep, I hear you loud and clear." I knew four things for certain: (1) it definitely wasn't shit, there was something important at Alton's, maybe lost tapes; (2) it was of great historical significance; (3) he was after it; (4) I could never trust that guy again.

However, after six weeks of effective procrastination, I admitted to myself that the likelihood of salvaging the house was dimming and that I should schedule my surgery. Vic said he'd been in touch and they were "considering his offer," the specifics of which he would not divulge. But still time dragged on, and I steadied myself to go under the knife.

My father-in-law was the one person I knew who was experienced in the hernia surgery department, and his advice was not to worry, that he'd been up and at 'em later the same day. This seemed far-fetched to me, but it gave me courage as I was prepped and shaved and drugged. "Let's give him a really fun trip," I remember one anesthesiologist saying to another as the spike hit my arm. "Count backward from one hundred." I didn't make it to ninety-seven.

Experiences vary wildly, I learned, and I could barely stand up by the second morning. The second night my penis turned purple and I made a panicky call to the nurse, who said it was normal, happens all the time. "If there's even a *remote* chance of this happening," I grumbled unhappily into the receiver, "then you *must tell the patient about it*! It's terrifying. I thought it was going to fall off."

On the third morning, slightly better, upright at least, I stood on my front porch waiting for Vic. His pickup rolled alongside the curb, and I hobbled over and climbed in.

"Morning!" he said, handing me the joint he'd been toking. I shook my head, jiggling the plastic pill bottle at him.

"I'm high enough already," I said.

"Yeah, nice getup," he said, regarding my PJs quizzically. "What happened to you?"

"Hole in my GI. They had to patch it up."

"Should you be lifting?"

"Definitely not. You think you can handle it, let me play supervisor?"

"With my crew, no problem. You're the boss."

"I thought your wife was the boss."

"You see her here?" He flashed me a wolfy grin.

We made our way to the Kennedy Expressway, which was still clear just as the sun was snapping to attention. At the city, we off-ramped onto the Dan Ryan—Dangerous Dan, I always heard it called—populated by barely held-together 1970s American cars with no suspension going the speed of low-flying jets and changing lanes at random intervals. I glanced at Vic's hands on the steering wheel. Harsh and sandpapery, clenched vices, they were the hands I'd learned to associate with heavy duty junkers. Nothing to mess with. Unconsciously, I rubbed mine together and thought of their baby softness, which signaled privilege and life choice; the tips of my left fingers were calloused and stiff from guitar, a bit of my hands empathizing with Vic's.

At Forty-Seventh Street, we exited the highway and headed east. Looping around, Vic stopped for a few minutes at Valois, the very same diner, and grabbed us breakfast and coffee to go. Back up on Forty-Seventh we pulled up to King Drive, which used to be called Drexel Boulevard, and stopped at a light. From all sides of the intersection, men descended on the truck. "Hey, Vic, what's the score?" said one. Another leaned in on my open window. "Thanks for that dresser. I picked it up from the alley the other day, good as new. What people throw out, it's crazy."

"Glad to hear," said Vic.

"Whatcha got today?"

"I need five guys ready to go until the job's done," said Vic. "Down on South Euclid. Here's the address." He passed a slip of paper with the number. "Oh, and we need a truck."

"No problem, boss," and the men dispersed.

"Lots of bosses," I said, as Vic turned and drove south and then east.

"The real boss is always the one with the purse strings," he said. "These guys like it when I come around because I pay better than anyone else. So I can count on them. Most of the pickers on the south side pay thirty dollars for a day of work. I pay one hundred dollars. But they have to come to do their share, otherwise I use someone else. The guy I was talking to sometimes works like a foreman."

After about ten minutes, we pulled up to a small midcentury house in a suburban enclave, a well-kept neighborhood with pockets of disused and abandoned property. He parked the truck out front. Five men, one of them the foreman, sat on the front porch, a fifteen-foot moving van parked in the driveway.

"What took you so long?" said one of them, flicking the butt of a cigarette onto the street.

Vic left me and made contact with the owner, who turned out to be Alton's ex-wife. She and some friends were already hauling garbage bags to the front of the driveway. "It's clothes," she told Vic. "We'll be working alongside you for the morning." While they negotiated and hammered out the finances of the day—I'd already figured out that Vic would get it going and coming, being paid by her for the salvage and by me for the stuff—I went down into the basement in back, where I was greeted by an elderly man. I introduced myself, and he told me he was Alton's ex-father-in-law.

"I remember when Alton brought Sonny around. He and his band would come to this house wearing all sorts of funny hats and capes. The neighbors were pretty wigged out." He paused, a portentous gatekeeper, and I thought about finding a glass of water to wash down a booster pill, my groin beginning to throb. "You figure this stuff's worth anything?"

"Yes, I expect it is," I said. "But I'm more interested in its meaning than its value. I think Sun Ra was brilliant. He should be as well known as Duke Ellington and Count Basie. And Alton was essential in helping push him out there. There's a lot of the story that hasn't been told."

"Sonny was about my age," he said, pushing himself from the folding chair he was sitting in to his feet. "Strange gentleman. OK, well, good luck with all that." He left, screen door banging after him.

Alone, I surveyed the room. A basement: tools, lawnmower, hose, and gloves, interspersed with piles of record covers, stacked face-up. *Omniverse in Blue. We Travel the Spaceways. Holiday for Soul Dance.* I picked up the top one on a stack, which was empty. Another, same, the back cover never tipped on, baring raw cardboard. I picked up a third one, and it had an LP inside. I checked, and the short stack of maybe thirty beneath it was full of records.

On a nearby workbench, there were tapes, reel-to-reel boxes covered with elaborate writing, some unspooling onto the floor. I made my way to a room toward the front of the house, the inside of which was a post-Katrina-like mess. Laying on top of one mound of papers was a larger rectangle of cardboard, a chunk taken out of the bottom corner, on which was a familiar image of a topless space woman arching backward over a moonscape. Weird, I thought, that someone would make so perfect a copy of the cover image of the second edition of *Jazz in Silhouette*. As luck would have it, an empty cover of the record was sitting on a shelf alongside several more. I held it next to the drawing, the comparison yielding to the fact that they were exactly the same; this was the original drawing for the cover. At that point, I knew we couldn't take anything for granted, no matter how disposable it looked.

Moving farther along into the rearmost room where the furnace was located, I noticed what looked like a kid's tent, an out-of-place piece of interior architecture. Four triangles of cardboard had been adjoined at the sides with tape, making a pyramid that peaked at the ceiling. There was just enough space along the bottom edge to crawl underneath, as if into a teepee. Inside were throw pillows and notebooks, some signed Bryant, some Abraham, and the remnants of similar lined sheets that had been burned. Candle drippings covered the floor. It was clearly a ritual spot. Pages in the books contained elaborate wish lists addressed: "Dear Creator, please grant me . . ." They were immodest. Cars, boats, fancy houses, and zillions of dollars were divined in these books, along with world peace, the eradication of hunger, and the power of flight.

"Oh, yeah, I forgot to tell you about this." Vic's voice startled me. "Crazy, isn't it? I wonder what they were up to."

"What's the story upstairs?"

"We're all set. There's one room over here," he walked me to a small padlocked interior space, "that they don't want us to take. Everything else is fair game."

I looked at the room. Tapes and stacks of posters and record covers filled it. Weeks later that room would be the source of nagging questions. Why that particular stuff and not the things they left out? What great wonders were in that room? Where did they go? Where are they now? In the heat of the moment I had no time for such speculation and simply plowed ahead.

"Cool, off limits, got it. Let's go."

I outlined my excavation priorities for Vic so he could pass them along to the guys. Tapes, sheet music, writings, drawings and record cover designs, instruments, Ra-related papers, PR material, relevant books. If we came across anything else that seemed possibly worthwhile . . . into the truck. We could sort it out later.

Box by box, we began moving things upstairs and onto the porch. I knew I shouldn't antagonize my wound, but I schlepped along with the others, stopping more frequently, but calculating that without my help we would never finish. There were surprises—the bottom layer of things in the front basement room had been through a flood, so it was moldy and rotten. We left it. One box of records, totally full, was crawling with bugs. It too was a casualty. Otherwise, up things went. Two 35-mm film canisters sat in a basement office, bearing a strip of white tape on the top: *Space Is the Place*. I took them to the front door and dropped them off, to be brought to the truck. A few minutes later Vic pulled me aside and said they didn't want us to take the film. "Fine, whatever they say, but let them know that we're not going to dig things out for them to choose between. They had months to sort."

Upstairs, we were working on different rooms, all of which were filled with variously fascinating material. At a certain point, midday, I noticed another crew seemed to be working with us. Sussing out their chief, I took a break. "Hi, I'm John," I said. "Who are you?"

"Name's Will," he said.

"What are you doing here?"

"I'm taking things away," he said. "I have a shop and I'll resell them."

I looked around at his guys, wondering what they thought about working with others doing the same thing and getting paid three times as much. "Who hired you?" I said.

"Vic invited me. Said there was too much for him, that I could have some."

"Well, I'm the one paying for all this stuff, so sorry to say, but please pack up this last load and head out."

A cheap golden sphinx statuette observed us from a bookcase, flanked by little copper pyramids.

"Hey, man. What's the deal with a white boy coming down here and taking all this important booty?" His voice changed, his inflection hardened. "You're raiding Tut's tomb, my friend, like those anthropologists. Raiding Tut's tomb!"

"What are you planning to do with the things you take? Putting them in a museum? Gonna drag 'em up to Du Sable and make good on your cultural patrimony?"

"Shut up, thief! This is my culture, I'll sell the shit out of it if I want to."

Vic interposed himself, and Will backed down, taking a bag of hats and hailing his men. "Not cool, Victor," he called over his shoulder.

"Why'd you call him?" I asked.

"Look, there's extra, so I thought I'd give him a taste."

"Triple dipping. So you wanted to be paid *three* ways!"

"You got a problem with getting paid?"

Over nine hours we uncovered a full truck's worth, topping off in the back of Vic's 4 by 4. A seeming piece of trash turned out to contain, when opened, what was labeled "El Saturn Treasure Map," laying out the global ambitions of Abraham and Bryant and, by association, Ra and the Arkestra. The world, according to this 1959 Ouiji board cartography, would soon be theirs. Notebooks and ledgers were all half full, abandoned at some unexceptional date; the full parts were fascinating, intimations of a business plan that included establishing a Cosmic Research Center and the acquisition of a limousine with proceeds from their million-selling singles. As a statement of purpose, it was so earnest and naive that one couldn't help but be smitten.

Alton had told me about their secret society, Thmei Research, and the dictionary of occult terms that they'd been working on for years. This item magically appeared, the list of participants with Ra's original name, Herman Poole Blount, charted in the colophon. Nearby were various Thmei artifacts: stationery, books, some documents. A few things didn't surface that afternoon, including any of Sun Ra's writings—the broadsides he'd allegedly written and distributed in the early years—and Ra's name-change document that Abraham had shown me in our first encounter, as he put it, "to prove I am who I say I am." About a year later, a cache of sixty or so of the broadsides turned up in one of the boxes; the Cook County government document escaped our efforts.

Vic's crew worked hard. Most of them were younger than me, in their thirties; friendly and quiet, they kept to their labor. One guy was much older. Maybe seventy-five, he was the most diligent of the men, hauling twice as much as the others; shirtless, he had the physique of a bodybuilder, chiseled and taut, with a frizzy beard and hair frosted bright white against his dark skin. He looked like someone had collaged an old man's head onto a twenty-five-year-old triathlete's body. The few times he spoke, it was through a nearly toothless mouth. In my mind, he conjured the biblical figure Ezekiel.

The foreman left all decisions to Vic, but he helped organize the trips up and down, making sure nobody went into the proscribed room, encouraging occasional breaks, managing the procurement of lunch. I took a break and sat on the cement steps out front. The surreal aura of the afternoon was setting in, and I reflected on what we were doing. From my perspective, this was an archive on a par with that of the most important literary figure or artist in American history, but a mysterious and very disorganized one—imagine if Ernest Hemingway's agent had been a hoarder, or if Willem de Kooning had been the head of a Masonic society whose papers were discovered . . . in a blast zone.

The day resonated more personally, too. My relationship with Alton, our conversations about the stuff, even the specific objects—this had an air of unreality, a dream quality that was egged on by the painkillers and the way they subtly broke registration between what might happen and what was actually happening. As if through a veil, Alton's bass voice on the other end of the line: "Mr. Corbett, have you heard? The Germans bought a tape for one million dollars."

"Huh? What tape? What Germans?"

"I don't know exactly, but I have it from a reliable source."

"Whoever sold it must be a business genius; you could never recoup that much."

"Shows that the Germans are crazy for Sun Ra."

"Crazy would be the word."

I flashed to conversations with Ra himself, including one on his deathbed, his way of gliding between everyday reality and some unfamiliar kind of existence—another plane of there—in the span of a few words. We'd found the entire chain of production for the iconic cover of *Art Forms of Dimensions Tomorrow*, from Ra's own preliminary sketches, evolving over the course of several graph-paper pages in a notebook, through his refinements on onionskin paper and the addition of color, to the final ink drawing, the matching print plate, and finally test prints of the cover, which sports a flamboyantly curvaceous, cartoony outlay of his name with a jagged abstract drawing nested atop its central letters. The fact that all this might have gone into a landfill (where were the Germans now?), how tenuous all the connections were, the delete key, the rejected salvage, the fact that I was perhaps the only person Alton had told about the dictionary we'd just saved for posterity, the sheer amount of material that we were amassing and what the hell we would do with it. When I stopped to think about it, it was almost too much to fathom.

Work resumed, I snapped out of it and hauled and packed for the rest of the day. In a bundle of papers we found the original color separations, all hand-painted on velum, for *Sun Ra Visits Planet Earth* and *Super-Sonic Jazz*. I made stacks of books, quickly selecting ones that dealt with music, mysticism, race, astronomy, astrology, history, and philosophy, sometimes flicking through them to try to identify Ra's permutation-filled marginalia. Manuals for obsolete typewriters, common medical books, how-to guides for home improvement—these were left. A copy of *Sex and the Single Girl* seemed relevant in its incongruousness. Some of the more unusual medical materials, including a selection of obscure machines, we took. Alton was one of the first African American X-ray technicians in Illinois, the fact of which is particularly interesting in light of his fascination with the occult and enlightenment: creating secret societies and making the unseen visible.

"Corbett, come down here!" Vic's voice resounded as the workday came near its finale. In the basement, there was a freestanding safe. "Should we crack it?" he asked, sensing the answer.

"I guess so," I said. A crowbar was procured, and all the workers gathered around, some pitching in, some watching while Vic and the foreman pried the ancient thing open like a squared-off giant clam. Seven of us crowded the unfinished room, empty but for a few books and stray pieces of timber, a broken accordion backed against a wall. With a clank, the safe's door came loose to reveal an empty shelf. Vic was panting, sweating profusely. A little cloud of dust rose from beneath the black metal box.

With one slow but smooth movement, the oldest worker reached down and strapped on the accordion. "Hey, there," he said, tipping his grizzled head at my pajama bottoms and wheezing a few choked notes on the instrument. "You got the pants, now do the dance!"

Basking in the absurdity of the moment—where was I and what was I doing?—I did a wan little jig. But my crotch was shot, and I was beginning to fret over the next move. "I think we're done here," I said. "Vic, can we get to a phone?"

While the men finished packing and closing the truck, we drove to a pay phone, and I called home. My wife, Terri, had already been dealing with months of buildup to this, high anxiety and excitement and near obsession. She was the one who had at a much earlier point cautioned me against bankrupting myself—and, by proxy, her—with record shopping. But when she heard the tone in my voice, she knew it was serious.

"How much money do you have, in total?" I asked. She guessed, and I asked her to bring a check of hers, one of mine, and to get on the phone to find us a storage facility, preferably near where we lived, for a lot of stuff.

"What size storage?" she said.

"I don't know, exactly. It's a 15-foot truck and the back of Vic's pickup. Maybe 120 square feet?"

"Jeez," she said.

We swung back down to the house just as the gate closed on the moving van. Vic produced a beaten-up combination lock, passed out cash to everyone, and asked the foreman to meet us in a half hour at a Shell station on Cottage Grove. I thanked the guys as they one by one disappeared. Vic locked the front door and we pulled away, my head swimming.

Terri met us at the Foster-Ravenswood Storage, where she had procured two storage spaces, a big one, twelve by twelve feet, and another five by four. Ready for the day to be finished, we emptied the van first, sent the foreman on his way, then offloaded Vic's truck, the last of the items filling the bigger room to the grate that ceilinged it. Terri told me she had the checks, but together we didn't quite have enough money. I asked Vic if we could have a day or two. "I know where you live," he smirked.

That night I was tormented. My brain raced with the events of the day, images and words swirling together with perspiration and dust, a microburst of impressions. In the dark, we watched the Summer Olympics, swimmers and divers and runners doing their thing, breaking records or falling short. I had a fever. Changing my dressing was agony. And slowly a sinking feeling came over me. "Damn Sam," I said to my patient, comforting spouse. "We missed important things, I can feel it."

I phoned Vic and asked him to get us into the space again. He paused. It was very unlikely, he said, but if he could it would cost more. I told him fine, whatever it took. I slept restlessly, dream and drug and tension and elation mingling unhealthily.

Next morning, Vic told me we'd gotten the green light; we would have a few more hours in the house the next afternoon. After that, the new owners would take possession, and we'd be finished for real.

My rule of thumb, with repeat visits, if you've combed a collection or a store, is that they're generally unneeded. Intuition, sharp eyes, and the right frame of mind: one pass will suffice. You gather things in a state of autopilot, and like they say of car accidents, time extends to a point that you recognize the important things with near-flawless accuracy. Second-guess, go back for another survey, and you'll find the dregs, rarely anything that you would have chosen given all the time in the world.

That principle proved to be untrue in the case of the Alton Abraham archive. Vic and I once again drove southward, stopping for an early lunch at a soul food spot in a freestanding house. My recovery much advanced, narcotics downgraded to Tylenol, this time I wore pants—loose fitting, but slacks all the same. Vic knew half the restaurant's clients, animatedly greeting and being greeted, a table of two cops exchanging small talk with the celebrity picker. The waitress called him "Sugar" and gave us extra collards with our fried chicken, which, slathered in gravy, was divine.

At Alton's I immediately knew I had made the right call. A whole new room on the main floor seemed to have sprouted overnight, and inside there were more piles of posters and album cover materials. An air-conditioner box contained an Ampex reel-to-reel machine, possibly the one that Tommy "Bugs" Hunter had used to introduce on-the-fly tape-delay echo into Arkestra recordings, anticipating dub reggae by a decade. The forbidden room downstairs had been cleaned out, and the basement was basically empty. I took a roll of metallic filament from the workbench thinking it might be wire recordings; it turned out to be wire for fixing fences.

A huge walk-in wardrobe, which had been full of clothes two days earlier, was vacant except for a single black suit, hat, and white shoes—a tailor's apparition of Alton, which oversaw the final purge. Seeing the clothesless room, I realized one thing that I'd neglected to include in my priority list: costumes. As the story goes, Alton bought the Arkestra's first uniforms—anything but uniform—from a defunct opera company. I imagined the wigs and tricorner hats that Will may have taken, now for sale at a local junk store, the draping, sparkled, spangled garments hand embroidered by Ra, his beloved Buck Rogers caps with red flashing lights. No time for regrets, I thought, regretful nonetheless.

In the mounds of abandoned papers, which would have gone to the street along with everything else, I discovered the original documents for Ra's deal with ABC Impulse!, contracts which famously included the language that he and Alton crafted to cover extraterrestrial territories. Everywhere I looked, I discovered more tidbits. A scrap of Western Union receipt for a couple of dollars from Abraham to Ra, dated 1962. A little stack of unused tickets for a concert at Budland in 1956, sequentially numbered. The house fallen hollow and quiet, afternoon sun drew long and darkness settled on the day.

"Last call, Mr. Corbett." Vic's voice from the top of the stairs. "If you don't come up now, I'm leaving you here!"

I was on my hands and knees on the basement floor, pulling things from an overstuffed plastic garbage bag that sat alone in the middle of the room, readied for the curb. From the very bottom, I extracted a manila folder, inside of which were the original 1957 musician contracts for *Jazz in Silhouette*, the Arkestra's first LP on El Saturn, countersigned by all the players. John Gilmore and Pat Patrick's cursive handwriting looked alive in the underlined blank spaces. Tossing the folder on the small pile I'd erected, I took it all upstairs, joined Vic at his truck, and pulled the door locked behind me.

The next four years of my life were dedicated to the Abraham archive and research therein. It was an incredibly concentrated time, in parts frantic and a bit frightening for me. Far as I can tell, I came close to falling all the way down a well of compulsion. I could talk about little else. All conversation, no matter how it started, twined its way back to Sun Ra. I'm sure it was very boring, but I thought it was utterly captivating. I visited what we referred to as the "lock-up" almost daily, brought things home to examine them more carefully, began the daunting task of sorting and cataloging, bought a working quarter-inch tape player and sampled tapes into the late hours, establishing a notebook which I decorated with "Sun Ra Archive—Tapes," in homage to Alton's enthusiastic annotations.

Retrospectively, Terri entertained a supernatural view of events: from the beyond, she figured, Ra and Abraham discussed the destiny of all the stuff, wracking their brains for someone who would be lunatic enough to shepherd and account for it all. "*Remember that one guy? He's a total maniac,*" she'd say. "That was their conversation, just before you got the message. That e-mail didn't come from Mike Watt, it came from Sonny and Alton."

The piles still settling, Terri and I established a circle of advisers, people whose opinions, judgment, and ethics we trusted. We were judicious with whom and how much we divulged, in part out of a well-founded fear that Ra fanatics would hound us. The first week, distant acquaintances of Heather's e-mailed me, telling me they'd seen Ra in the '70s and just loved him. "All we want is a souvenir, something to feel closer to him." Hamza Walker, our old friend and a curator at the Renaissance Society, visited the lock-up at a preliminary point, taking photos and discussing a possible show. I'd already imagined an extensive exhibition. Hamza floated it by Susanne Ghez, the Ren's director; she was unconvinced that it made sense for the institution, which exclusively showed work by living artists. At a music conference at Wesleyan, I told trombonist and scholar George Lewis about the archive; he was enthusiastic and supportive, and he urged me to start writing about it. Rachel Weiss, head of arts administration at the School of the Art Institute of Chicago, and Anthony Elms, independent curator and publisher of WhiteWalls, both made trips to the lock-up in the first months, and they helped us think about the future of the materials. Jazz journalist Kevin Whitehead assisted as we began to collate the disparate material, segregating things into labeled boxes. Independently, I told music writers Lloyd Sachs and Peter Margasak about it; they both sat listening to the story, jaws slackened.

Stimulated by the notion of an exhibition, we contacted the Smart Museum, on the campus of the University of Chicago. Curators Stephanie Smith and Richard Born visited our apartment, looking through some of the prize pieces; ultimately, they decided not to do the show because it would all be coming from a single set of owners, a move frowned upon curatorially. Anthony and I discussed the notion of a show at the Hyde Park Art Center (HPAC). A proposal was tendered, and HPAC agreed, contingent on Elms joining the curatorial team, which would consist of me, Terri, and him. Around that time, we discovered Sun Ra's incredible early writings, a sensationally robust group of them, typewritten by Ra, some carbon-copied, others in manuscript form complete with his penciled marginalia. Anthony suggested producing a facsimile edition, which was published a few years later, just before the HPAC exhibition.

As much as I felt the free fall of fascination, I was simultaneously experiencing an identity crisis. On one hand, the material was rich and generative; as George foresaw, I was intent on digging in and initiating some literature on it, in hopes of others jumping in. But the vinyl freak side of my personality was experiencing its own libidinal glee: "Holy crap, I own all of this!" I fussed over which of the cover designs we would frame and hang at home, and fantasized over what incredible material might be hiding on the reels. Years of stalking record stores in search of any El Saturns, excitement over the occasional ABC Impulse! acquisition, also the rare ones nabbed from friends, ex-freaks who were selling their collections, including *Strange Strings* and the elusive *When Angels Speak of Love*. But what would happen to a freak if all his freakish desires were answered, more than he could imagine? Those past triumphs seemed trivial, mundane. This was the mother lode. I had been to the promised land. Be careful what you wish for . . . it might just crush you.

Terri, ever wiser than I, discussed these unfamiliar feelings with me. "You know, there's such thing as too much happiness. It's not good for you to be too excited all the time." This thought had never occurred to me, raised in a conventional pleasure-seeking household. "Happiness and excitement can be attachments." I recognized a Buddhist line of thought. "It seems to me that with all these things, you've gotten everything you could ever want, and now you're becoming too attached to them. We don't really *own* anything. You can't take it with you."

About three years into this phase, an acquaintance named Jim Dempsey called me about introducing a series of Sun Ra films at the theater he managed. I invited him to the lock-up, and we devised a small show of photographs in the lobby during a month of screenings, the first public light seen by the archive. Terri, Anthony, and I readied the stuff for the book and the show. Then, after about four years, I had completely exhausted myself and had to step away. By that time, Rachel had asked me to serve as chair of Exhibition Studies, a program in Arts Admin, and Jim and I, inspired by the fun of the film center's Sun Ra Sundays, had convinced ourselves that we should open an art gallery. My hands full, I had plenty of reason to back off the archive a bit.

Something changed inside me over the next two years. I found the notion of going record hunting slightly absurd—what could ever top the two days in the Alton house? And Terri's words rang true: we didn't own any of it, we were stewards, keepers, hyperspecialized salvagers. We continued paying to store everything, though we were living more or less hand to mouth. Inventorying and caring for everything was beginning to seem like a burden, more than a joy, although there was still something spine-tinglingly unreal about it. Sorting stuff meant tossing inessentials—candy wrappers, mouse poop, newspapers from 1982, an inoperative Luger pistol, Alton's gun license, some live bullets, anything personal of his that we found. Even weeding out we were only able to trim away the smaller of the two spaces. The large one remained full to bursting, big aluminum door roaring open every time I visited, the oversweet odor of unburnt incense from another locker wafting together with other normal storage facility smells of mildew, offgassing mattresses, and decaying cardboard.

When *Pathways to Unknown Worlds: Sun Ra, El Saturn & Chicago's Afro-Futurist Underground, 1954–68* opened at HPAC in October 2006, Terri and I had a plan. In one of the interviews about the show with a local paper, I dropped a hint that we were looking for an institutional home for the archive. We were inspired, as well, by a phone correspondence that turned into a friendship with Adam Abraham, Alton's son, who called HPAC a few weeks before the exhibition opened, having scouted it online. Adam's response to hearing the saga: he was disappointed he couldn't have been there to help save all his dad's material, life had intervened, but he was pleased and thankful that we had, particularly that we were keeping it intact, and he was excited about the prospect of it finding a proper permanent residence.

Not long after the night of the reception, which was packed with visitors, we were contacted by Deborah Gillaspie, head of the Chicago Jazz Archives in Special Collections at the University of Chicago's Regenstein Library. The three of us met for dinner, and Deborah asked us what we thought of the Alton material going to U. of C. Handshakes over dessert. Like that, we had a new place for the stuff, fulfilling our dream of it staying on the South Side, in a facility with ample resources, accessible to the general public and to scholars as well. Our negotiations over the following year included a few stipulations. They could have anything they wanted, but anything they left was ours to do with as we wanted. In perpetuity, we could use any of the materials that we could obtain rights for, and if anyone else was going to use it, they had to ask permission through us. The tapes would go to another archive; Special Collections did not have proper facilities to manage sound recordings. And we had been working on traveling the HPAC show, so we needed to be sure we could carry through on that.

My friend Lou Mallozzi was founder and director of the Experimental Sound Studio (ESS), where I often did remastering in preparation for releases on the Unheard Music series. I'd worked on some of the Ra tapes there, too, though the ever-jovial John McCortney at AirWave Studios had given me such a ridiculous rate for transferring that he and I digitized about fifty of the four hundred tapes, breathlessly waiting to hear what would come next as the tape randomly changed speed and format. A few tapes into it, we figured out that they would sometimes hide things at the out tail of a reel, a two-minute song camouflaged like a snake rolled up in a garden hose.

Over espresso at our favorite bakery one afternoon, I proposed to Lou that the world needed a sound-specific archive designed to save some of the imperiled tapes that were being orphaned as their caretakers died, lost interest, or were otherwise disinvested. As an example, I suggested the El Saturn tapes, which hadn't gone to the University of Chicago. After months of consideration, he agreed and inaugurated the Creative Audio Archive (CAA); the Abraham tapes and Michael Zerang's Links Hall archive constituted a hearty first two batches.

Pathways traveled to the Institute of Contemporary Art, Philadelphia, in 2010, where it received a glowing full-page *New York Times* review. Anthony published a couple more books: a catalog of the show and a compendium of the symposium that we'd organized in Chicago, the latter containing more unpublished images from the archive. A few years hence, direct quotations from the Ra broadsides cropped up in several visual artists' work. In 2013, the Studio Museum in Harlem featured Ra as a source of Afro-Futurism in *The Shadows Took Shape*, and it is now less uncommon to hear him discussed among artists as a major inspiration, perhaps due in some part to the dissemination of the Alton materials. The audio archive, dutifully and lovingly transferred to listenable digital format by a small cadre of engineers including Todd Carter, has been inventoried complete on the CAA website. Appointments are made to come listen to any of it, and through a commission program at ESS, young musicians and sound artists have put the previously unknown recordings into active service.

Meanwhile, a weight had been lifted from me. Not only in terms of the Alton material, also the vinyl urgency, a habit that had been transformed into something more reasonable, a trickle not a torrent. Nine months after salvaging the house, Vic called to say another picker had sold him some Sun Ra books that he'd found by the side of the road, things that had been discarded before we got there. I bought them from him, six copies of *Extensions Out: The Immeasurable Equation Vol. 2*, Ra's second book of collected poetry. It was a title that I'd never seen, an extreme rarity. We gave the library a couple of them, kept the others, along with plenty of multiples and posters, ones that they only wanted in a few copies for their collection. Much of the Alton-Ra book collection was deemed too moldy for the Regenstein, and we hung onto it. The artist Cauleen Smith later used the books for an installation.

Though we still had lots of Ra ephemera, a couple of years after we gave everything to the two institutions, I experienced a bout of what could only be called donor's remorse.

"Why didn't I just keep *one* of the original record cover designs?" I whined to myself.

It wasn't a month later that I was looking through my flat files, inventorying record covers that the library had left us. Shuffling though sheets of silver foil prints, I noticed one that didn't look exactly like the others, its image applied directly onto the blank silver record cover. I looked closely. It was drawn, not printed. Sun Ra's original mock-up for *Other Planes of There*. One final wish granted with a wink to a freak from out there in those other planes. Wherever Sun Ra and Alton Abraham now reside.

Le Sun-Ra and His Arkistra, "Saturn"
(Saturn seven-inch, 1956)

Tom Prehn Quartet, *Axiom*
(Sonet, 1963, not issued at the time)

In a ritual that has been played out many times, Mats Gustafsson arrives at our home, opens his overweight suitcase, and retrieves a box or bag of records. We have been exchanging vinyl for two decades, engaging in an endless potlatch that is both brotherly competition and absolute altruism. Mats has given me some of the most valuable and obscure items in my collection, many of them Swedish; other important gifts included a whole batch of LPs, all but impossible to find in the United States, by Japanese free jazz musicians including Masayuki Takayanagi, Yosuke Yamashita, and Akira Sakata, a full-fledged revolution of my mind. In turn, I have introduced Mr. G. to some of our homegrown American goodies, including the Leo's Five LP with a fresh Hamiet Bluiett and the zanily scarce single by Andrew Hill on Ping Records, which we happened upon once while shopping together.

Gustafsson has honed the art of the trade, establishing a regular column on his Discoholic's Corner website where he posts entries that he's willing to exchange for other vinyl of equal desirability. My sense of it is that he has established a unique little barter economy, a network of friends and strangers who participate in redistributing their duplicates and in the process turn one another on to lesser-known recordings. Having spent many years negotiating with record dealers, it's so refreshing to see something rooted in pure enthusiasm rather than profit motive.

On this occasion, Mats extracts a slim box, recognizably seven inches square, within which is contained a single prize: the first record by Sun Ra. It is unspeakably uncommon. Mats tells me there are four known copies. I first encountered one on eBay several years ago, but was too slow to buy it before it was taken down and sold privately. Until then, I'd thought it didn't really exist. But the sleuth Swede managed to drum up one, then a second of them, minor miracle, and now he's ready to swap.

I know immediately what he's after. The bastard wants one of my babies. Made by the Danish label Sonet as a pair of test pressings in 1963 for the pianist Tom Prehn and his quartet, *Axiom* was not issued at the time. The musicians rejected the vinyl as too noisy and then almost immediately felt that the music was out of date, so the projected release, which had a completely designed, printed, and finished cover, was nixed from the schedule and relegated to the players' closets. I had issued a later Prehn record on CD in 2000, and planned to follow up with *Axiom*, but again circumstances held it up, and it was not until 2015 that I managed to do so, having used the two LPS, given to me by Prehn, for the purposes of mastering. Mats once wrote a piece for *Stop Smiling* magazine titled "Five Records I Am Going to Steal from John Corbett's Collection." Naturally, it included *Axiom*. As soon as news was out that I'd reissued it, I had a premonition that Gustafsson would make a play for one of the copies.

I had to debate this transaction. Owning one of the Ra singles would be very meaningful to me. It's the debut Saturn. I've worked so extensively on Ra's legacy, writing and reissuing and salvaging, that this extraordinary five minutes of vinyl is exceptionally potent and tempting. It's in perfect shape.

The gold label sports an early variant of the band's name: Arkistra, rather than Arkestra. On a tape in the Ra archives that Terri and I gave to the Creative Audio Archive, recorded live at Budland probably in 1957, you can hear Alton Abraham's voice, after the group finishes a blazing version of "Saturn," saying: "That's our new single!"

On the other hand, if I make the trade I will lose one of my favorite punch lines. Asked by someone I'm giving a tour which of my records is the rarest in my collection, I was able to boast: *This LP was made in an edition of two; I have both of them.* That this is ridiculous is obvious, and that's what I've always liked about it. Beyond hubris, beyond the fetish, here's a record nobody knows about, music that is utterly unheard, and I've completely cornered the market.

No longer. Now I have shared the market with Mats. It is a glorious night. My friend and I toast each other with a cup of late tea, sealing the deal, each fondling our new record, comparing other recent finds—virtually all of them his, as he's a real hound—and setting off for the turntable, to listen to these and other vinyl records into the early morning hours.

Records are my measure of all things.

All things, that is, shorter than three feet. At greater length than a yard, I have other points of reference—my outstretched arm span (six feet), the height of our ceilings at home (nine feet), the largest dimension a painting can have and still fit through the door of our gallery (eighty-one inches). I'm fortunate that my foot is exactly a foot long, so I can walk off even longer distances toe-to-toe. But for approximating smaller spans, my most reliable gauge is vinyl.

I've been handling records for so long that they are ingrained in my muscle memory, palpable even in their absence: their density, their textures, their form, and especially their size. I don't actually need the record in hand to make the measurement; I can conjure it in my mind and map the distance by means of an innate sense. It's uncannily convenient that the LP, the most applicable of these surrogate tape measures, is in diameter the same length as a ruler: twelve inches. The album's standard size is so indelibly etched in my brain that it's the quickest calculation of space I can make.

If I am conjuring something that's twenty inches, I think of two albums and subtract a bit. For lengths shorter than a foot, I bump down to a seven-inch and adjust from there. Ten-inch records are too much in the middle and tend to confuse the matter. Say I have a filing cabinet that's eighteen inches wide and want to know whether it will fit in a particular place in the room. I measure the space by means of records—if an LP plus a single, minus an inch, would fit there, so would the cabinet.

I have relied on vinyl for much more. As puzzle, challenge, fetish, obsession, projection, screen, mask, bludgeon, toy, script, aphrodisiac, narcotic. As sand to bury the head; as a swift kick in the rump or chilling wake-up call. As a vehicle for traveling the globe and exploring distant cultures, all the while staying in one place. As a cipher, a private language of in-jokes only accessible to special friends; as a maypole for more public communities, a calling card or banner proclaiming membership. As tool for avoiding responsibility, green light for overspending, open invitation to waste precious time.

I have felt my way through life using records. Some crate diggers have coal miner's helmet lamps for early morning explorations, crawling around in a predawn flea market, foraging for rare music by the light of their foreheads. For me, the records themselves have served the role of illuminating the path.

I should also mention, I have chalked up two hernias by now. My sense of weight may not be quite as refined as my feel for lengths. But anyway, whatever help the records have been in getting me around, literally and figuratively, they have been less of an aid when it comes to their heft. My first trip to Europe I carted around bags of vinyl, accumulating more everywhere I went, through two months of Eurail and ferryboat passage to Greece and back, by journey's end having gathered more than one hundred LPs, which I refused to check and instead carried onboard.

The things we do. So records are like any other lover. They bring out the best in you, making you a superior citizen, lighting your way, serving as life's benchmark. And they make you into a moronic bore humping massive boxes from one place to the next. We are these two archetypes, we vinyl freaks, for better and for worse.

Acknowledgments

On behalf of my obsession, I dutifully thank my codependents and enablers, as well as those who have given me pause and made interventions.

Along the way, my primary record-hound buddies have been Scooter Johns, Phil Kirk, Doug Cannon, Tom Fry, Ben Portis, and Mats Gustafsson. A host of other accomplices and inspirations include John Corrigan, Russell Fine, Sue Cook, Jim Macnie, Robert Smith, Hope Carr, Sasha Frere-Jones, Jim O'Rourke, Warren Po, Thurston Moore, Al Ruppersberg, Tom Cvikota, David Grubbs, Scott Nielsen, Christopher Williams, Josiah McElheny, Christopher Wool, David Hollander, and Albert Oehlen.

A range of record store folks fed my habit, including Mike Wall, Hunt Blair, Bruno Johnson, Rick Wojcik, Harald Hult, Steve Wascovich, Bob Koester, Josh Berman, and the guys at BJ's, Discount Records, and the Record Collector in Iowa City.

I thank my parents, James and Joyce Corbett, for providing me with early vinyl to shake, rattle, and roll, and for turning a blind eye toward my record store hobbyhorse. My siblings, Jack and Jennifer, shared my excitement and posed impertinent questions about Echo and the Bunnymen to the deejay at the roller rink. To Uncle Tim for comic relief; to Auntie Jayne for the loan of her precious Seatrain LP; to Tim Fitzgerald for keeping music the first priority. To my grandmother, Rose Corbett, for driving me to Wax Trax and waiting outside in her pale yellow Cadillac.

DownBeat was generous to offer me the space to compose the Vinyl Freak column, and I thank my editors there, especially Jason Koransky, who agreed to the concept in the first place, and Frank Alkyer, who gave the green light to republishing the essays in this book. All of the Vinyl Freak columns reprinted here were first published in *DownBeat* magazine, except for the last one, which was commissioned and never published, and the one composed post-facto in 2016. There are too many people to thank for the assembly of the book, but a few essentials are Tom Van Eynde, Nicole Sachs, Sam Grossinger, and Michael Jackson. I consider myself uniquely endowed for this project with an editor who is also a record collector, and I thank Ken Wissoker for his light touch with the tone arm.

For the cover image, I posthumously thank Mauricio Kagel (and Benjamin Buchlow, who published it in *Interfunktionen 5* in 1970). For the rights to reproduce it, I am grateful to Mr. Kagel's daughter, Pamela Kagel.

Always first in my book, so to speak, my better half, Terri Kapsalis, who did not leave me despite the piles. Thanks god we have a basement now.

And finally, for a wild ride, gratitude to Vic Biancalana, no doubt scavenging in the afterlife.